The Disputa highlights the centrality of the Eucharist in salvation history. In the center are God the Father, Christ, the Holy Spirit and, in a crystal monstrance on the altar, the Blessed Sacrament. Beside Christ in heaven are Our Lady, John the Baptist, the Evangelists, saints, martyrs and patriarchs. On earth are the Fathers of the Church who have illuminated the doctrine of the Eucharist—on the right Sts. Ambrose, Augustine and Thomas Aquinas; on the left, Sts. Jerome and Gregory the Great. The angelic figure in the lower left is drawing the world's attention to the Sacrament of the Altar.

The Disputation of the Eucharist/Raphael

EUCHARIST
God Among Us

ESSAYS AND IMAGES
OF THE
EUCHARIST IN SACRED HISTORY

Joan Carter McHugh

825 S. Waukegan Rd., PMB 200, Lake Forest, Illinois 60045

Staff for this Book

Executive Editor
Tom McHugh

Editor & Research Assistant
Anne Richards Tschanz

Copy Editing & Layout
Daniel Gallio

Production & Cover Design
Peter Ptak

Theological Consultants
Fr. Patrick Greenough, OFM CONV.
Guardian of Marytown, Libertyville, IL

Fr. Lawrence Hennessey, PH.D
Dean of the Ecclesiastical Faculty,
University of St. Mary of the Lake, Mundelein, IL

Fr. William McCarthy, MSA, STB, MT
Director, My Father's Retreat House, Moodus, CT

Sr. Bernadette Sheldon, CSJ
Co-Director, My Father's Retreat House, Moodus, CT

Nihil Obstat
Reverend Charles R. Meyer
Censor Deputatus
September 9, 1999

Imprimatur
Most Reverend Raymond E. Goedert, MA, STL, JCL
Vicar General
Archdiocese of Chicago
September 9, 1999

The *Nihil Obstat* and *Imprimatur* are official declarations that a book
is free of doctrinal and moral error. No implication is contained
therein that those who have granted the *Nihil Obstat* and *Imprimatur*
agree with the content, opinions or statements expressed.

ISBN 1-892835-04-5
Library of Congress Catalog Card Number 99 096778

Printed in the United States of America

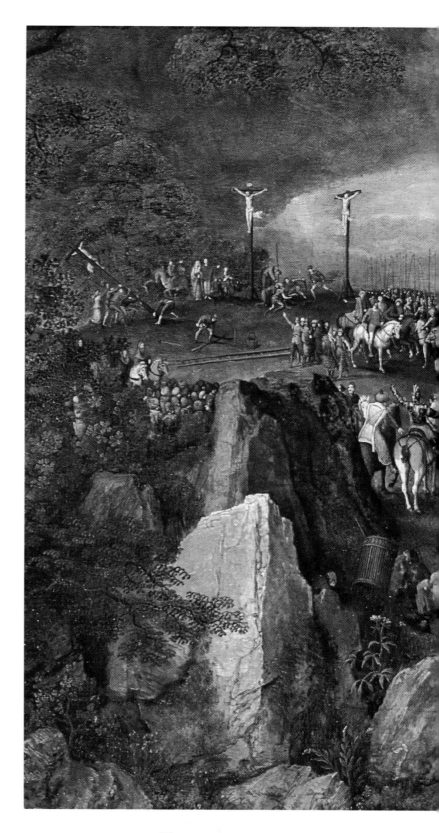

825 S. Waukegan Road, PMB 200
Lake Forest, IL 60045
847-735-0556 • 847-735-0911 Fax
Witnessm@aol.com

The Crucifixion/Lucas van Valkenborch

Calvary is the reservoir of all the graces and blessings and mercies that God has destined for all people. The Mass and the Eucharist are the channel through which those graces flow upon our age. "We adore You, Oh Christ and we praise You because by Your holy Cross, You have redeemed the world."

Other Books by Joan Carter McHugh

Leaping in Faith
Stories of Answered Prayers

Feast of Faith
Confessions of a Eucharistic Pilgrim

My Daily Eucharist I

My Daily Eucharist II

To Tommy, Katie, Danny and Rich

—my precious children.

Christ Blesses a Little Child/Carl Bloch

CONTENTS

Christ of St. John of the Cross/Salvador Dali

The Defenders of the Eucharist/Peter Paul Rubens

FOREWORD

ood books are like landmarks along life's spiritual path which often point us toward a new understanding of ourselves, our world and our God. *Eucharist, God Among Us* is just such a book. It comes in a timely way to enrich our celebration of the Great Jubilee Year 2000 which our Holy Father, Pope John Paul II, describes as being "intensely Eucharistic."

It is with immense joy that we celebrate the anniversary of the birth of our Lord and Savior, Jesus Christ, "The Word became flesh and made his dwelling among us" (Jn 1:14). We, like the disciples at Emmaus, are filled with wonder and thanksgiving for His continuing presence among us, which we recognize in the Breaking of the Bread. We express our thanks to God for the gift of His Son through the celebration of the Eucharist, where Christ is really present and where we are truly united to Him sacramentally.

Joan McHugh's book treats the theology of the Eucharist in salvation history in a scholarly, easily readable style. She presents a clear and compelling *apologia* for appreciating and understanding the Eucharist as the covenant of God's love through which He betroths Himself to His faithful in a union of everlasting love. Using Scripture, Church Tradition and teaching, the Church Fathers and the witness of the saints, up to and including today's prophets, *Eucharist, God Among Us* features the primacy of the Eucharist in God's plan of redemption. The artistic support lent by the Great Masters animates the text, enabling readers to personally relate to the teaching.

Eucharist, God Among Us invites the faithful—clergy and laity alike—to renew and celebrate their faith in Jesus Christ, "the living Bread come down from heaven." It will be difficult for anyone reading this book *not* to believe in His promise that "Whoever loves me will keep my word, and my Father will love him, and we will come to him and make our dwelling with him" (Jn 14:23). This beautiful book strengthens our belief that, when we go to Mass and Communion, we are receiving the Body, Blood, Soul and Divinity of Our Lord Jesus Christ.

It is my hope that this book will find its way into many homes and hearts, where it will shed new light and the warmth of Christ's love on a Sacred Mystery at the core of our faith—the Eucharist. May you welcome our Eucharistic Lord into your life as all the great prophets and saints in this book have done, finding in Him a Spouse Who loves and nourishes His Bride, the Church, with His bountiful unconditional love in the Eucharist.

Francis Cardinal George

Francis Cardinal George, OMI
Archbishop of Chicago

ACKNOWLEDGMENTS

Eucharist, God Among Us is the result of the work of many people. First, I would like to acknowledge my immense gratitude to the staff who put their heart and soul, not to mention time, into this effort. Each person contributed unique gifts and talents, which, when put together, resulted in a unified glorious whole. Without them, this book would not exist.

Joined to them are friends far and wide whose love for the Eucharist and this project has moved them to help in so many ways. The Lord sent them to accompany us at different stages along the journey, offering support however it was needed. We are so grateful for their contributions.

Velma Murphy generously offered her help in the office, her prayers, and discernment in the selection of the art; Cheri Klock volunteered "to do anything" for the book, which included reading the New Testament section; Judy Kozak helped with her excellent typing; Fr. Paul Cioffi, SJ, of Georgetown University, who teaches Eucharist at the North American College in Rome, was one of the first to encourage me and give me feedback on this project; Fr. Augustine Grady, SJ, of Fordham University, offered his expert opinion on the Early Church art; Kathy Reinbold contributed her design expertise; Marge Lukacs gave valuable suggestions on the art selection and layout; Holy Cross Fr. John Jenkins, CSC, critiqued the chapter on St. Thomas Aquinas; Fr. Steve McKinley, OFM CONV., Pastor of Holy Family Parish in Peoria, IL, gave insightful comments on sections of the manuscript; Fr. Gerald Ruane, PH.D, Director of the the Sacred Heart Institute in West Caldwell, NJ, read the manuscript and offered encouragement and important editorial suggestions; Passionist Fr. Howard Ralenkotter, CP, ordained sixty-one years, offered his prayers; Benedictine Fr. Leonard Ackerman, OSB, ordained sixty years, also offered prayers; Richard McHugh, my son and a recent graduate of the Literature-Writing Program at Columbia University, edited—and greatly improved—the Sacrament section of the manuscript; Bro. Juniper Kriss, OFM CONV., and his staff of resident volunteers helped to prepare Marytown's chapel to be photographed; Fr. Robert Melnick, OFM CONV., Associate Pastor of St. Anthony of Padua in Rockford, IL, tracked down the image of St. Francis of Assisi; Felicia Reilly, administrative assistant to Fr. John T. Render, CP, Director of the Passionist Research Center, Chicago, suggested the use of the painting "In His Image" for the chapter "One Body in Christ"; Jim and Cathy McCarthy helped locate the painting of "In His Image"; Fr. Peter Pappas of Sts. Peter and Paul Greek Orthodox Church in Glenview, IL, assisted us in locating the icon of St. Ignatius of Antioch; Kit O'Brien did an excellent job of proofreading; and I want to especially thank Herman Peterson, Mary Ann Ulz, Marian Johnson and Julie Trichta of the Feehan Memorial Library of St. Mary of the Lake Seminary, Mundelein, IL, for their patient and generous assistance.

PREFACE

Early on the morning of January 28, 1998, I was inspired to write this book. Three weeks prior I had driven up to Holy Hill Monastery in Wisconsin for five days of rest and prayer. My goal was to discern the next project I would undertake for Witness Ministries—an apostolate my husband, Tom, and I formed to promote devotion to the Real Presence of Christ in the Eucharist. While a blizzard raged outside and the January wind whistled through cracks in the doors and windows, I felt safe and warm nestled close to the tabernacle in a small chapel in an ancient wing of the monastery. I was grateful for precious time just to be in God's presence. I prayed for direction. The solitude and prayer did much to calm my racing mind and after five days I returned home—rested—but without an answer.

A week later I awakened at 5 AM with scenes of the video we had made on *The Real Presence* playing in my imagination. It portrayed the Biblical story of the Eucharist using great works of art and, judging from its continued popularity, filled a gap in peoples' understanding of the Eucharist in the history of salvation. WHY NOT TURN THE VIDEO INTO A BOOK? The idea jolted me out of my sleep. I could tell by my husband's reaction that it was a good idea. At Mass that morning I learned it was the Feast of St. Thomas Aquinas, *the* theologian in the Church whose life was centered in his love of our Eucharistic Lord. It dawned on me that this idea might be an answer to my prayer—through the intercession of Thomas Aquinas!

Vision of St. Thomas Aquinas/Sassetta

The project was daunting. The video had presented only the highlights of Eucharistic revelation; the book would require *much* additional research. Then there was the matter of locating the art. I had no idea how one could possibly find all the art necessary for a book of this nature. The enormity of the task was so discouraging as to make me give up before I started. Then I made a phone call to an art museum in Boston, inquiring how to obtain copyright permission for the use of one of their paintings. It was a Botticelli Madonna which did not ultimately make it into the book, but, in hindsight, I have a feeling that Our Lady was guiding this adventure. Over the phone a young man answered my questions, patiently informing me about the availability of art. After speaking to him I was ready to begin work.

I divided my time between Scripture and art research. It was a joyful quest, leading me first to dig deep into Biblical history to uncover the principal people and events in the development of Eucharistic revelation. When I approached a subject, such as the Exodus, I found myself immersed in Scripture, hungry to understand the story. This became a pattern. My teachers were recognized Biblical scholars and the books I accumulated developed into old friends who shared their treasured secrets with me—and now with you!

My husband and I combed the art section of used book stores and were blessed to "discover" not one, but two, special artists whose paintings you will find in this book. We first came across a turn-of-the-century book, *The Life of Our Lord, Jesus Christ,* illustrated by James Tissot. A popular French artist who painted provocative social scenes at the end of the nineteenth century, Tissot experienced a "divine revelation" while sketching in a church and spent the next ten years in the Holy Land tracing the footsteps of Christ. Tissot eventually gained international renown for his illustrations of the entire Old and New Testaments. We are privileged to use many of his images to illustrate *Eucharist, God Among Us.*

We also found a book illustrating the religious paintings of Carl Bloch, a Dane, who painted around the same time as Tissot. His historical paintings of the life of Jesus are known and valued all over the world. They, along with Tissot's images, add a special warmth and vitality to this work. And this, of course, is not to mention all the other Great Masters included in these pages.

Sometimes "a picture is worth a thousand words." I pray that the written text will come to life through the images, helping you personally to absorb God's love for you, His beloved chosen people!

Joan Carter McHugh
August 6, 1999
Feast of the Transfiguration

INTRODUCTION

This book is written proof that God uses the least among us and the smallest efforts performed out of love for Him to multiply our work far beyond our wildest dreams. Having said "yes" to the Holy Spirit's urging to write *Eucharist, God Among Us,* I was faced with a formidable task, considering I had no degree in theology and only a surface knowledge of the Old Testament. What I had going for me was a deep desire to share my faith in the Real Presence of Christ in the Eucharist. This was born from knowledge of the prefigurements of the Eucharist in the Old Testament, and was strengthened by a study of the Gospels, Sacred Tradition and Church teaching, the writings of the Church Fathers and the witness of the saints. All of these fed my desire to share the truth I had gleaned from my spiritual journey thus far: that the Eucharist is the axis on which the wheel of divine revelation turns—that it is God, through His incarnate Son, Jesus Christ, the Lord of the cosmos, the Lord of history, "the beginning and the end" (Rev 21:6)—who saves and sustains His people through the love He gives to them in *Person* in the Eucharist.

That is the essence of this work. I hope you will learn as much by reading this book as I have discovered in researching it. What I thought was my "plan" when I started was like a small acorn which grew into a huge oak. God's love is so much more than we envision! When we invite Him into our lives He fills our emptiness with the fullness of His love—as He did at the Wedding Feast of Cana—which overflows as choice wine. It is significant that Jesus began His public life with a miracle of transformation. His whole mission was to convert sinners into saints, to turn darkness into light, sorrow into joy, and to make death the gateway to new life. The imagery of a wedding feast shows the spousal relationship that God intends to have with us, a relationship in which He, the Bridegroom, takes us, His beloved people, for His bride, in a union which is more intimate than the marriage between a husband and wife. "I will espouse you to me forever" (Hos 2:21), He said through His prophet, Hosea. God wants to recreate us in His love—so that we can share in His own divine life.

Salvation history is like a colorful mosaic in which the Old and New Testament stories fuse into a portrait of God's outstretched arms beckoning us to receive His love. It is the story of God's love for you and me, God's "Delight" (Is 62:4), His beloved people to whom He reveals His *Presence.* From the dawn of life in the Book of Genesis to its close in the Book of Revelation, God, Who is a Trinity of Persons, Father, Son and Holy Spirit, accompanies us through every minute, hour, day, month, year and generation up to and including this present moment, leading us to Himself. It is a search which begins in the heart of God, says Pope John Paul II, and culminates in the Incarnation of the Word.

From the opening pages of Genesis, Christ is identified as the seed of a woman (Mary) who would crush the serpent of evil in human hearts (cf. Gn 3:15). While the world awaited the coming of the Messiah, God lavished blessings on His chosen people: life, fertility, animals, water, light and the earth itself, a paradise of plenty. He spoke through the prophets and revealed Himself through covenants. He also manifested His Presence through signs and rituals—such as the manna in the desert, the bread and wine offering of Melchizedek, the sacrifice of Isaac, the deliverance of the Israelites from Egypt, the Passover lamb and the *Shekinah* presence (the pillar of fire and the cloud over the Tabernacle). All of these prefigured a more personal and intimate revelation of God Who would come to us through His own Son, Jesus Christ.

God pledges His love through covenants, sacred promises through which He bestows divine blessings on His children, asking only that they accept His love by giving Him their allegiance. "If you hearken to my voice and keep my covenant, you shall be my special possession, dearer to me than all other people, though all the earth is mine. You shall be to me a kingdom of priests, a holy nation" (Ex 19:5, 6). Our first parents failed to accept God's love and were led astray by Satan, who deceived them. By alienating themselves through sin, they were cut off from the benefits of the covenant. Generation after generation of people broke God's covenants and set in motion the curses resulting from sin—alienation and death.

Jesus Christ came into the world to break the curses stemming from our sins and broken covenants, by taking the curses upon Himself through His death on a cross. God sent His Son to lead us back to the path of truth and light and love, and away from the path of darkness and evil. By sacrificing His life, Jesus overcame evil and freed us from the debt of our sin. By rising from the dead He showed us the way to eternal life, proving that death no longer had power over Him.

On the night before He died, Jesus shared the Passover with His disciples. It was the most important feast for the Israelites because they celebrated the memory of the great Exodus in which God freed them from their enslavement by the Egyptians and led them to the Promised Land. It was a sacrificial feast in which the Jews roasted a lamb and ate unleavened bread and other foods which commemorated events connected with their deliverance. *Pesach* is the Jewish root from which the word Passover is derived, and means "to pass over." It recalls the action of the destroying angel who "passed over" the Jewish homes when he killed the firstborn of the Egyptians. (This is what ultimately led Pharaoh to free the Israelites.)

The Passover is one of the strongest links between the Old and New Testaments. At the Passover meal which Jesus shared with His disciples, Jesus changed the bread and wine into His Body and Blood. Proclaimed by John the Baptist as "the Lamb of God, who takes away the sin of the world" (Jn 1:29), Jesus offered *Himself* at the Last Supper as the new and eternal Paschal Lamb, the supreme victim who would shed His blood for the salvation of the world. When He instituted the Eucharist, Jesus transformed the *Pesach* into the *Pasch,* a new Christian rite in which Christ's faithful would celebrate their deliverance from sin and death. At the Paschal dinner of the Last Supper, Jesus established a New Covenant in His Blood, through which His faithful would now be personally united to Him in the Eucharist. In the Old Testament, God asked the Israelites to memorialize His saving action with a feast to keep the memory of their deliverance alive for all future generations. In the New Testament, Jesus asked His apostles to perpetuate the memorial of His sacrifice, saying, "Do this in memory of me" (Lk 22:19). Through the Liturgy of the Eucharist all generations of believers can share in the sacrifice of the Cross, which is commemorated sacramentally.

In the New Testament we, therefore, refer to the heart of the Christian liturgy as "the Paschal Mystery." Jesus is the new Moses leading His people in a new exodus through His suffering, death and resurrection. For two thousand years the Church has preserved these Sacred Mysteries passed on through the apostles and St. Paul to the Fathers of the Church, to the saints—and to us, the People of God alive today. We continue to celebrate the Paschal Mystery—the dying and rising of Christ—in the Liturgy of the Eucharist where we unite our crosses to the Cross of our Savior. United to the Flesh and Blood of Christ, we rise with Him to new life and victory over suffering and evil. United to Christ as branches to a vine, we draw life from the spiritual sap of God's love which flows from His Spirit into ours at the Eucharist.

The Church Fathers taught the catechumens that the Eucharist is like a nuptial banquet. When the Body of Christ is placed on the lips of the baptized who have been purified from their sins, they said it is truly a kiss given by Christ to the soul, an expression of a marital union between Christ and His beloved. The Lord referred to Himself as a bridegroom (cf. Mk 2:19). We, as Church, are the Bride of Christ, intimately united to Christ, our Bridegroom, in the Holy Eucharist.

In Andrei Rublev's icon of the Holy Trinity, the Father, Son and Holy Spirit are seated around an altar on which rests a gold chalice. The chalice contains a small blood-red lamb's body symbolizing the sacrificial death of Christ, the Lamb of God. The Father extends His hand above the chalice in a gesture of blessing, inviting us to communion in Jesus. Through the Eucharist we enter into the heart of Christ and, through Him, into the heart of the Trinity. In them we are made one with all people. This is the Messianic Banquet, our sharing in the liturgy of heaven. Pope John Paul II says that heaven is a living, personal relationship with the Holy Trinity. It is our meeting with the Father which takes place in the risen Christ through the communion of the Holy Spirit.

The Holy Trinity/Andrei Rublev

Jesus Christ came into the world to bring us God's *Presence* and to show us where to find Him. God knows that, if we find Him, we find *life*. He is the one, after all, who gave us our hunger and, then, Who gave us a way to satisfy it— through Himself in the Holy Eucharist. Mother Teresa of Calcutta once said that in this great United States where we have "everything," people are starving to death because of a lack of love. Our hunger for love is not being satisfied. Could it be that we are looking for love in all the wrong places, or rather *not looking* where Jesus told us we could find it? We are no different from the people who lived in the time of Christ. They wanted the bread Jesus provided to fill their hunger, but they didn't want to acknowledge *Him* as their food. They wanted the benefit of His covenant blessings, but they wanted to set their own terms.

The answer to our alienation, I believe, is to follow the spiritual path God provided us in Jesus, who leads us to light, love, truth, reconciliation, peace, joy, and an abundance of life—all of which are to be found in Him—in the Eucharist. It is a foretaste of heaven on earth.

THE OLD TESTAMENT

The Eucharist Prefigured

Fire from Heaven Consumes the Sacrifice/James Tissot

I will espouse you to me forever:
I will espouse you in right and in justice,
in love and in mercy;
I will espouse you in fidelity,
and you shall know the LORD. (Hos 2:21, 22)

THE COVENANT OF CREATION

As His arms open wide to gather His children into His embrace, our loving Father welcomes His sons and daughters into His family—the Trinity—to enjoy the intimacy of their unconditional love. From the dawn of life in the Book of Genesis to its final consummation in the Book of Revelation, God reveals Himself and His love in ever-deepening ways. The Genesis story in which God created everything out of nothing is a love story, written, produced and directed by God! God *is* and "God is love" (1 Jn 4:16). While there is only one God, He is a Trinity of Persons—the Father, the Son and the Holy Spirit—who share one divine nature in a Divine Family.

Our Father's Plan. Our loving Father is deeply involved in the daily lives of His children. He patiently proves His love by giving Himself to us time and again despite our sin and frailty. He invites us into the bosom of His family, and the manner in which His divine plan is realized is known as salvation history. It is the story of our salvation in which God calls each of us—His sons and daughters—to holiness. He created us to share His divine nature and to have complete access to Him, our Father, through Jesus Christ, the Word made flesh in the Holy Spirit.

Two Creation Accounts. There are two accounts of creation in the Bible. The Book of Genesis opens with a story of creation known as the priestly narrative in which God, named *Elohim*, creates the universe out of primeval chaos, giving it structure, order and beauty just by the power of His Word. He is actively creating a home for the crown of His creation, man and woman, whom He created in His image and likeness. Pope John Paul II writes in *The Gospel of Life* that "the creation of man is presented as the result of a special decision on the part of God, *a deliberation to establish a particular and specific bond with the Creator.* 'Let us make man in our image, after our likeness' (Gn 1:26). The life which God offers to man is a gift by which God shares something of Himself with His creature."

The second narrative (Gn 2:4-25) describes *Yahweh* (a more personal name for God) at work like an artist, creating the first human couple and adorning their environment. We see Him as a God personally invested in His creation, tending to the physical, spiritual and emotional needs of His children. By His actions He loves us into life and is mainly concerned about the relationship of man and woman to each other and to the world. In these stories humanity is the culmination of creation, having dominion over all animal and plant life.

Covenants. Throughout Biblical history God showed His love by making covenants with His people, pledging His unconditional love. He was the initiator of the covenants—or promises—through which He guarantees His children life and blessings—land, fertility, descendents—asking only that they show they have accepted the covenant and are faithful to Him. Covenants were more binding than contracts because they signified a permanent bond with another, a union like marriage. The history of the Chosen People is the history of the covenant, which on God's part is guided by mercy and faithfulness, and on the people's part by a response of faith.

Covenant Love. The covenant is the core of God's relationship with His people—a way of personalizing His relationship by showing how precious each and every life is to Him. To understand "covenant" is to begin to grasp the depth of our Father's love for us. His unconditional love is a gift which His children can't earn or merit by good works or virtue. God keeps His promises even when we have done everything wrong, even when we have done nothing, even when we have sinned. The idea of covenant helps us, especially in today's Godless world, to rediscover a personal God who enters our history and our lives and calls us each by name. Covenant is about love, about presence, about union—gifts from the heart of a God who wants us to know and experience His boundless love so that we can rejoice in our identity as His sons and daughters.

Eucharist Fulfills All Covenants. God placed His sons and daughters in their home in the world, an oasis of love and plenty, called paradise. God made a covenant with all of creation, Pope John Paul II writes in his encyclical *Redeemer of Man,* promising blessings in return for their allegiance and love. The Holy Father sees this as the foundational covenant from which all of the others in Scripture spring—culminating in the New Covenant sealed by Jesus, whereby God's original covenant plan is fulfilled and renewed. In the covenants of the Old Testament, God used words and symbols to show His love and presence and to bond with His children. In the New Testament, He used a chalice of blood, "the Blood of the new and everlasting covenant," the Blood of His Son, Jesus Christ, in order to unite us completely to Himself.

Dr. Scott Hahn, professor of theology at Franciscan University of Steubenville, explains "covenant love" by relating it to the family. Just as flesh and blood and a common name unite the members of a family, Hahn says, so are the members of God's universal family, the Church, united through baptism and the sacrificial family banquet of the Eucharist—Christ's Flesh and Blood. Through the Eucharist, Jesus invites His beloved children to become intimate members of *His* family, the Trinity, the eternal and original covenant family.[1]

Story of Genesis: The Creation of the Animals/Raphael

*At the time when the L*ᴏʀᴅ *God made the earth and the heavens—while as yet there was no field shrub on earth and no grass of the field had sprouted, for the L*ᴏʀᴅ *God had sent no rain upon the earth and there was no man to till the soil, but a stream was welling up out of the earth and was watering all the surface of the ground—the L*ᴏʀᴅ *God formed man out of the clay of the ground and blew into his nostrils the breath of life, and so man became a living being.* **(Gn 2:4-7)**

THE COVENANT WITH ADAM

nto this covenant family were born man and woman. Yahweh first created Adam, who as an individual represents the whole of humanity. Like a potter, God forms man from the dust of the soil and breathes into him the "breath of life" (Gn 2:7). The word in Hebrew for "breath," *ruah,* is the same as "spirit." The Church Fathers understood this to mean that God breathed His own spirit into Adam. Endowed with the Holy Spirit and not just a rational soul, Adam was gifted with the grace of divine sonship.[2] As the first human being and the father of the human race, Adam was a type of Him who was to come, Christ the Lord, the new Adam.

Adam: Touched by God. St. Augustine wrote that Adam's name in Greek signifies the whole world. "For there are four letters, A, D, A and M, and with the Greeks the four quarters of the world have these initial letters. They call the East, "Anatole"; the West, "Dusis"; the North, "Arctur"; and the South, "Mesembria," and these letters spell Adam. Adam is thus scattered throughout the globe."[3]

In Michelangelo's portrayal of God endowing man with life, the hand of God is charged with life, while Adam's hand lies helpless, awaiting God's touch. We see his soul's aspiration toward his heavenly Father in whose image he is made. Adam gazes in wonder and gratitude at his Creator who is about to give him the gift of life by which he will become a living soul.

A Marital Covenant. God made His first covenant with Adam (representing the people of Israel) a marital bond. "I will make a covenant for them on that day. . . . /I will espouse you to me forever: /I will espouse you in right and in justice, in love and in mercy; /I will espouse you in fidelity, /and you shall know the LORD" (Hos 2:20-22). As a husband and wife promise themselves to each other in the covenant relationship of marriage, so did God promise to wed *Himself* to Adam in a marital relationship that would last forever. God made the continuance of Adam's blissful state, including the privilege of immortality, dependent upon one command: that he must not eat the fruit from the tree of the knowledge of good and evil.

Woman and Man. Because it was not good for man to be alone, God forms woman from Adam's rib. "Eve" is a form of the Hebrew word for "life"; she recognizes that she will be the "mother of all the living" (Gn 3:20).[4] Eve was brought to Adam to be his wife, eliciting a cry of wonder and love from him: "This one, at last, is bone of my bones and flesh of my flesh" (Gn 2:23). The taking of Adam's rib for the creation of Eve foretells the unbreakable union between man and wife. Man sees the woman as another "I,"

sharing the same human nature. Created *together* and willed each for the other, the two are created to become one body— literally, one flesh. Equal as persons and complimentary to each other, they are united by God in marriage so that by forming "one flesh" they can transmit human life: "Be fertile and multiply; fill the earth and subdue it" (Gn 1:28). As spouses and parents they can cooperate in a unique way in the Creator's work of transmitting human life.[5]

Love Desires Union. God wants to give Himself to His people. He invites them to be His bride. He has stamped the entire universe with His seal of love, a love that finds its fulfillment in union with the beloved. He betrothed Himself to Adam extending His promise of never-ending love to him and to each of His beloved children, giving all people the gift of being His children. He sealed His promises in covenants, life and death oaths—bonds in blood—which bind us to an irrevocable partnership with our God.

The Bible is the story of the marriage of Israel and Yahweh. Even when Israel sins and behaves like an unfaithful wife, God remains faithful and desirous of winning back His bride. He loves His people passionately—as a husband loves his wife. The marriage will reach its fulfillment in the New Covenant established by Christ— the Eucharist—the wedding of Christ with the souls of His beloved.

The Sabbath. On the seventh day when God finished His work of creation, He sanctified the Sabbath by making it a day of rest. The Sabbath symbolizes God's covenant with creation, by which He calls His children to the end for which He made us—to rest in our Father's blessing and holiness, now and for all eternity.[6] Perhaps the real significance of the Sabbath rest is sacrificial. It enables us to offer to God a portion of our time, a piece of our lives. We keep one day a week free from contact with work—it has no commercial value—to show that it is being dedicated to God. It is His day, no longer ours.

Worship: Our Response. Response to God's love is expressed through worship. Emmanuel—God is with us in the Eucharist! Just as families show their love for each other by spending time together, so do the members of God's family assemble in Church on Sundays to "keep holy the sabbath day" (Dt 5:12), to express their faith and gratitude for His presence in their lives. Between its inauguration and its completion at the Parousia, when Christ returns to establish the eternal Eucharistic banquet, the marriage of Christ with His bride continues in the sacramental life of the Church. On Sunday, and even daily for many, God's faithful have the privilege of renewing their covenant with God through the Sacrament of the Eucharist, the visible sign of our union with Christ.

Creation of Adam/Michelangelo

What are humans that you are mindful of them,
mere mortals that you care for them?
Yet you have made them little less than a god,
crowned them with glory and honor.
You have given them rule over the works of your hands,
put all things at their feet:
All sheep and oxen,
even the beasts of the field,
The birds of the air, the fish of the sea,
and whatever swims the paths of the seas.
O LORD, our Lord,
how awesome is your name through all the earth! **(Ps 8:5-10)**

ADAM AND EVE BREAK GOD'S COVENANT

Adam and Eve lived in a state of wedded bliss in the garden of Eden until they yielded to the temptation of pride and disobedience and ate the fruit of the "tree of knowledge of good and bad" (Gn 2:17). This was the one tree in the center of the garden their heavenly Father had told them not to touch, for "the moment you eat from it you are surely doomed to die" (Gn 2:17).

Satan and Sin. Satan, in the form of a serpent, challenged God's authority by saying to them, "You certainly will not die! No, God knows well that the moment you eat of it your eyes will be opened and you will be like gods who know what is good and what is bad" (Gn 3:4-5). They didn't die, but their eyes were opened and they saw for the first time that they were naked, and they were ashamed of their nudity. By believing the serpent rather than God, they seriously sinned, thus breaking God's covenant and separating themselves from Him so that they were no longer entitled to the perfect life that the garden had offered.

Hiding from God. While trying to hide themselves from God in their shame, Adam and Eve were called by God. They showed their sinfulness by trying to evade responsibility for what they had done. Adam blamed Eve and Eve blamed the serpent. Placing the blame for one's wrongdoing on someone else is as old as the garden of Eden!

Pride was the first sin which lies at the root of all sin. It says, "Not Thy will, but my will be done." It was pride that prevented Adam from telling the truth and taking responsibility for his sin. In spite of their sin and its consequences, Yahweh does not stop loving Adam and Eve. He clothes them with leather garments to hide their guilt and shame. But because of their sin, they are denied access to the tree of life— immortality—and expelled from the garden.

Consequences of Sin. Adam and Eve were created sinless. Just as a transgression of children against their father might cause them to lose their inheritance, so did the disorder of Adam and Eve affect their genealogy. Through them all future generations lost their inheritance and the grace of God's presence. This privation of privilege and grace is called original sin. In order to regain our lost inheritance, we must be brought into a new family relationship with God.[7]

Immediately after the fall, Adam and Eve brought upon themselves the curses of their sin—punishments resulting from their unfaithfulness to the covenant. Relegated to a life of suffering, the woman would now feel the pain of childbirth; she also would become subservient to her husband (reflecting the place of women in ancient society). The man would continue to farm the land, but now the soil would be barren and both would ultimately suffer death. According to author Peter Kreeft, professor of philosophy at Boston College, the punishments are really mercies; they are like tourniquets, he writes, stemming the flow of blood, or like quarantines, stopping the spread of the disease. When we suffer as a result of our sinful choices, we often have a change of heart—and a change of behavior. When we know what is good and continue to choose evil, death is the ultimate consequence.

Christ Replaces the Old Law. Covenant blessings and curses remained in effect until the New Testament, when Jesus would replace the old covenants of the law with the new covenant of His love, in which He would take the curses on Himself and offer His own life as payment for the sins and guilt of humanity. St. Paul explains that "Christ ransomed us from the curse of the law by *becoming* a curse for us" (Gal 3:13) (emphasis added). Dr. Scott Hahn maintains that God in His justice and mercy had allowed the Israelites to bear curses symbolically until the "fullness of time" (Gal 4:4) when He would send His Son to bear them redemptively.[8] Through Christ's sacrificial suffering on Calvary and His resurrection from the dead, God showed that the Law was no longer necessary. "For just as in Adam all die, so too in Christ shall all be brought to life" (1 Cor 15:22). Now it is faith in Christ—and not the Law—which will bring us life.

New Order of Creation. All of humanity was affected by the sin of our first parents and the original plan of salvation was frustrated. But God did not cast us off for our unfaithfulness, says Fr. Bill McCarthy, author and Director of My Father's Retreat House in Moodus, CT. Instead, God strengthens our spousal relationship with Him by beginning a new order of creation, this time with a new Eve, Mary, and a new Adam, Jesus. From them we would get a new nature—God's own nature, God's own Spirit and God's own Son living within us.[9]

This would take place with the establishment of the New Covenant. St. Thomas Aquinas taught that in the tradition of the Church, the Eucharist is compared to matrimony in that both are signs of the one profound and mysterious reality—the union between Christ and His Church.[10] The Eucharistic Banquet is the marriage supper of the Lamb, as the words before Communion state: "Happy are those who are called to His supper" (based on Rev 19:9). The covenant which brings us life is Jesus Himself, given to us in the Eucharist as a sign of His betrothal to us. Our union with Him in the Eucharist is a marriage; it is the fulfillment of all the covenants through which God pledges our complete restoration—by drawing us into union with Himself.

*Expulsion from Paradise/*Tapestry, Brussels

When they heard the sound of the LORD God moving about in the garden at the breezy time of the day, the man and his wife hid themselves from the LORD God among the trees of the garden. The LORD God then called to the man and asked him, "Where are you?" He answered, "I heard you in the garden; but I was afraid, because I was naked, so I hid myself." Then he asked, "Who told you that you were naked? You have eaten, then, from the tree of which I had forbidden you to eat!" The man replied, "The woman whom you put here with me—she gave me fruit from the tree, and so I ate it." The LORD God then asked the woman, "Why did you do such a thing?" The woman answered, "The serpent tricked me into it, so I ate it." **(Gn 3:8-13)**

THE SACRIFICE OF CAIN AND ABEL

This is the first account of sacrifice in the Bible, offered by Cain and Abel, the sons of Adam and Eve. In the Old Testament, sacrifice was the central form of worship. The word "sacrifice" comes from the Latin words *sacrum* and *facere*, to make a thing sacred. The ancient Israelites sacrificed animals and crops to worship God, to obtain His forgiveness, to express their devotion to Him, and to return to a state of purity. The offering of sacrifice continued to be the chief means of establishing communion with God until Jesus Christ offered His life as a perfect sacrifice, redeeming us from our sin and winning for us our eternal salvation.

Familial Priesthood. The Book of Genesis shows the patriarchs building altars in Canaan and offering sacrifices. They exercise the "familial" priesthood practiced among the majority of ancient peoples.[11] During the age of the patriarchs, the priestly functions (such as offering sacrifice) were carried out by the father of a family, and were passed on from father to son, especially to the firstborn son, who became the head of the family after his father's death. St. Jerome would later teach that before Aaron and the establishment of the Levitical priesthood, firstborn sons discharged the office of priests, clothed in priestly vestments in which they offered sacrifices to God.[12]

In Genesis, patriarchal authority—and therefore the priesthood—is handed on from father to firstborn son through a blessing. St. Thomas Aquinas discussed the priesthood of the firstborn sons in his great theological work, *Summa Theologiae*, saying "priesthood also existed before the Law among the worshippers of God in virtue of human institution, for that dignity was allotted to the first-born."[13]

The Sacrificial Ritual. "Cain and Abel," says St. Athanasius, a fourth century Doctor of the Church, "learned religion and the rite of sacrificial worship from their father, Adam."[14] Eve's firstborn son, Cain, a farmer, offered God the fruits of his fields while Abel, his shepherd-brother, offered a firstling of his flock. Although both brothers offered sacrifice, God approved of Abel's gift of animal flesh over Cain's gift of crops. Cain murdered his brother out of jealousy. When the Lord asks him where his brother is, Cain replies, "I do not know. Am I my brother's keeper?" (Gn 4:9). Like his parents who refused to take responsibility for their sin, Cain is also unwilling to be accountable before God.

First Fruits. Abel had offered God the firstlings of his flock which symbolized a pledge of the entire flock or harvest. Abel, then, was generously offering everything—not just one lamb, but in symbol his whole flock of sheep—to the Lord God.[15] It is possible that God accepted Abel's sacrifice not only because it was the firstborn of his flock, but because he offered it in faith. To be acceptable to God, an inner spirit of thanksgiving, adoration, petition and atonement are needed to accompany the exterior rite. The Letter to the Hebrews says that it was Abel's faith which made his sacrifice greater than Cain's (Heb 11:4). The shedding of blood was a religious act; a solemn appeal to God, which, by its expiatory character, pointed to the great shedding of blood on the Cross. "According to the law almost everything is purified by blood, and without the shedding of blood there is no forgiveness" (Heb 9:22).

To the Fathers of the Church, Abel, the shepherd sacrificing the first-born of his flock, prefigured Christ the Good Shepherd. St. Ambrose sees Abel's pure sacrifice as an image of the Eucharist, and the lamb offered up as a first fruit—as the archetype of Christ's sacrifice on Calvary.[16]

Sin Multiplies. The story of Cain and Abel shows how quickly after Adam and Eve's transgression sin gained a foothold in the world. Cain is the first example of the moral disorder resulting from his parents' sin. Cain, fearing for his life, is banished from the soil to become a restless wanderer over the earth. But God in His mercy reaches out to protect him from the threat of murder by putting a mark on him showing that he belonged to God, was under His protection and therefore could not be touched.

Marked with the Sign of Faith. Just as God marked Cain with a protective sign to assure his safe journey through the wilderness, so does our baptism as Christians mark us as belonging to Christ. French Cardinal Jean Danielou devotes a chapter to this special mark in his book, *The Bible and the Liturgy. Sphragis* was a word which designated a seal used to impress a mark on wax. Seals had a variety of applications. In the Early Church the ceremonies of Baptism included the rite of *sphragis,* the imposition of the sign of the Cross on the forehead of the candidate at Baptism. The *sphragis* also sealed official documents, and it was the mark the shepherds used to brand the beasts of their flock to distinguish them. The *sphragis* signified that the catechumen belonged to Christ and was incorporated into the flock of the Good Shepherd. It was also a mark of protection. The Fathers of the Church taught that Christians are like sheep who bear the same mark and belong to the same Master, Christ, who is able to recognize *His own*. Through this sign we are reborn, St. Cyril of Jerusalem said, forgiven from the original sin of our first parents and all personal sins, and incorporated into the Church, the Body of Christ.[17]

"Marked with the sign of faith," we pray in the Eucharistic Prayer before the Consecration at Mass. Through this sign we are thus raised to the dignity of the royal priesthood and consecrated to serve God by worshipping Him as a Eucharistic community. Our new life is nourished through the Body and Blood of Christ in the Eucharist.

The Sacrifice of Cain and Abel/Edward Gover

The man had relations with his wife Eve, and she conceived and bore Cain, saying, "I have produced a man with the help of the LORD." Next she bore his brother Abel. Abel became a keeper of flocks, and Cain a tiller of the soil. In the course of time Cain brought an offering to the LORD from the fruit of the soil, while Abel, for his part, brought one of the best first-lings of his flock. The LORD looked with favor on Abel and his offering, but on Cain and his offering he did not. Cain greatly resented this and was crestfallen. (Gn 4:1-5)

SACRIFICE

t. Thomas Aquinas in his *Summa Theologiae* writes that "Adam, Isaac, and other just men offered such sacrifices to God as were fitting for the times when they lived. . . . For in ancient times," he continues, "original sin was remitted through offering sacrifices. In every age and among all nations sacrifices have always been offered."[18]

Sacrifice Binds Us to God. Sacrifice is a universal ritual as old as religion and born of an instinct deeply imbedded in human nature. Although there are diverse types of sacrifices, they all share a common purpose—to establish contact with God and give something back to Him. People of all nationalities, cultures and religions offer sacrifice to proclaim the supremacy of God through adoration and thanksgiving, while at the same time acknowledging their dependence on Him by asking for their needs and making amendments for their sins.[19] The Israelites ritualized the offering of their lives to God through the act of sacrifice, in which they offered bread, wine, oil, salt, incense and animals.[20] The gift or object sacrificed was always a sign of the interior disposition of offering and surrender. The Psalmist prayed, "My sacrifice, God, is a broken spirit; /God, do not spurn a broken, humbled heart" (Ps 51:19).

Priesthood. After the Israelites broke their covenant with God in the golden calf incident, the Levites, who remained loyal to God and were not idolaters, assumed the Israelite priesthood, replacing the firstborn sons of the families and tribes. Even though Aaron, a Levite and Moses' brother, had yielded to pressure and cooperated in the creation of the golden calf, God called Aaron and his sons to be priests. Thus was the Levitical priesthood instituted. Scott Hahn adds that worshipping the golden calf was an act of covenant apostasy which released the dreaded curses. From then on, God required Israel to offer Him animal sacrifices as a punishment and a cure for their idolatry—and as a sign of their homage to Yahweh. The sacrificial slaughter of cattle, sheep and goats became an everyday ritual. By a holy mixture of justice and goodness, God elected certain figures (priests) to bear Israel's curse *symbolically,* until He sent the One—Christ—who was both willing and worthy to bear it *redemptively.*[21]

Types of Sacrifice. The priest's role as a mediator between God and His people was to offer sacrifices—which were of various kinds. There were animal sacrifices known as whole burnt offerings or holocausts in which the animal was entirely consumed by fire. This was chiefly a sacrifice of praise and worship of God, a ritual of supreme adoration. There were partially burnt offerings known as "peace offerings" in which a portion of the flesh was burned and another part was eaten at the sacrificial meal shared by both priest and those who had offered it. (A third part was reserved for the priests.) Of all forms of sacrifice, this peace offering and its ritual bears the closest analogy to the Sacrament of the Eucharist. Then there were offerings of atonement, also called sin or debt-offerings, in which a portion of the flesh was burned and the remainder consumed by the priests. These sacrifices were intended to appease the wrath of God and to obtain the pardon of sin.[22]

Only a Clean Oblation. Only ritually clean domesticated animals—such as cattle, sheep and goats—were used for sacrifice. Sacrifice typically involved the shedding of blood as a way of purifying people from their sins. The victim had to be perfect, without blemish. Except for a holocaust, one part was to be burnt and one part eaten. The animal was slain by the priest, and the most sacred part of the victim, the blood, was poured on the ground before the altar. The altar was a symbol of divinity; the offering was brought into contact with the altar to signify the transfer of ownership over the gift. Blood was a symbol of life, and the spilling of the animal's blood represented the attitude of the person offering sacrifice. People passed on their contrition, thanksgiving, adoration or petition to God through the victim.

Sacrifices Prefigure the Cross. Ancient sacrifices of the Old Law are important because they prefigured the sacrifice of Christ on the Cross. The ancient sacrifices were figures and types of that one sacrifice which was to succeed and replace them in the New Law, a sacrifice that was to be complete and perfect in itself—the sacrifice of Christ. The author of Hebrews says: "if the blood of goats and bulls and the sprinkling of a heifer's ashes can sanctify those who are defiled . . . how much more will the blood of Christ . . . cleanse our consciences. . . ." (Heb 9:13, 14).

Just as Aaron had been called by God, so too Jesus, in a more exalted way, is called by God to mediate and intervene in the lives of His people, and to offer the sacrifice of His life for our sins. Although Jesus Himself never claims the title of priest, He is the priest of His own sacrifice.[23]

Saul Sacrifices the Oxen/James Tissot

So all the people went to Gilgal, where, in the presence of the LORD, they made Saul king. They also sacrificed peace offerings there before the LORD, and Saul and all the Israelites celebrated the occasion with great joy. (1 Sm 11:15)

THE COVENANT WITH NOAH

en generations after the creation of Adam and Eve, the earth was overcome with depravity and lawlessness. God resolved to destroy evil by allowing a flood to cover the land which would destroy all people and living creatures. He instructed Noah, "a herald of righteousness" (2 Pt 2:5), blameless among his peers, and a man who "walked with God" (Gn 6:10), to build an ark to escape the flood. Noah did as God commanded. It rained for forty days and forty nights. The flood came and all living things died.

God Renews His Creation. After 150 days the flood waters began to subside and the ark came to rest on solid ground on Mount Ararat, thought to be in Armenia. When the dove he sent out no longer returned to the ark, Noah knew that it had found dry ground and that it was safe to disembark. Noah and his family were saved as were the representatives of all the animals and creeping things of the earth. After almost a year, Noah, his sons and their families set out to build a new world in which justice and righteousness would prevail.

God made a covenant with Noah to reconcile the world to Himself, renewing all of creation—a blessing which extended to all of Noah's descendents. Noah is like a new Adam who will eventually be realized in the person of the Messiah. The Just One will save the world as Noah once saved it at the time of the Flood, when "the hope of the universe, who took refuge on a raft, /left to the world a future for his race, under the guidance of your hand"[24] (Wis 14:6).

God's first words to Noah and his sons when they disembarked were a reiteration of the blessings given at creation: "Be fertile and multiply" (Gn 9:1). The blessing of procreation continues in effect. What is altered is humanity's relationship to the animals. God permits animals to be killed and eaten, but the blood, because of its association with life, which belongs to God alone, must not be eaten. The prohibition against the taking of human life continues because humanity is created in the image of God (cf. Gn 1:27).[25]

Noah Offers Sacrifice. When Noah disembarked, he offered sacrifice to God in thanksgiving for His protective care during the long period of the Deluge. "Then Noah built an altar to the LORD, and choosing from every clean animal and every clean bird, he offered holocausts on the altar" (Gn 8:20). The "LORD smelled the sweet odor" (Gn 8:21), which is an expression drawn from a primitive notion that food offered to the gods was actually eaten by them, an idea which Israel later rejected. But here it shows that the sacrifice was accepted by Yahweh and thus reconciliation with humanity was effected.[26] Noah represents all who are saved through Christ; the salvation granted to Noah foreshadows the salvation of all people through the waters of Baptism.

Sign of the Covenant. A rainbow symbolized God's pledge never to destroy the world by a flood again. "As the bow appears in the clouds, I will see it and recall the everlasting covenant that I have established between God and all living beings. . . ." (Gn 9:16). The rainbow is a sign which shows God's desire for union between heaven and earth, and His mercy in saving a remnant of humanity, with whom He makes a new historical beginning.

The Flood in History. Dr. Warren Carroll, author and founder of Christendom College, writes in *The Founding of Christendom* that the report of an immense deluge is much too widespread and deeply imbedded in the traditions of ancient peoples to deny that it reflects the memory of an event that really happened.[27] St. Isidore of Seville (c. 560-636), theologian and archbishop of Seville, wrote an encyclopedic compilation of human and religious knowledge. In it he wrote, "Ararat is a mountain in Armenia where the historians testify that the Ark came to rest after the Flood. So even to this day wood remains of it are to be seen there."[28]

In the 1970s a book and then a movie became popular: *In Search of Noah's Ark.* The authors report that in 1883 the Turkish government announced its discovery of what some believed to be Noah's ark. A considerable amount of research concluded, they wrote, that the story of the Genesis Flood which has survived 5,000 years can be found in more than two hundred different accounts of past and present civilizations. There is enough anthropological evidence, one modern scientist writes, to support the theory that the Book of Genesis gives an eyewitness account of the Flood.[29]

Flood Foreshadows Paschal Mystery. The ark is a symbol of the Church and the great Flood is a foreshadowing of the Paschal Mystery, the death and resurrection of Christ, through which humanity is saved from eternal destruction. The sign of God's covenant today is His Body and Blood, poured out for us on the Cross and given to us in the Eucharist, to nourish and strengthen our relationship with God and with one another.

Like Noah, we can offer a sacrifice of thanksgiving, the most perfect of all sacrifices—the holy Sacrifice of the Mass. Through the Mass we are washed clean and redeemed, not by the blood of animals, but by the Blood of Christ. "With faith in Your love and mercy I eat Your Body and drink Your Blood. Let it not bring me condemnation, but health in mind and body," the priest prays before Communion during Mass. Just as the Flood destroyed evil but saved the people in the ark, so do Baptism and the Eucharist destroy sin and recreate us into the people God called us to be. We rejoice with St. Paul: "So whoever is in Christ is a new creation: the old things have passed away; behold, new things have come. And all this is from God. . . ." (2 Cor 5:17, 18).

The Animals Entering the Ark/Jacob Savery

"I, on my part, am about to bring the flood [waters] on the earth, to destroy everywhere all creatures in which there is the breath of life; everything on earth shall perish. But with you I will establish my covenant; you and your sons, your wife and your sons' wives, shall go into the ark. Of all other living creatures you shall bring two into the ark, one male and one female, that you may keep them alive with you. . . . I will establish my covenant with you, that never again shall all bodily creatures be destroyed by the waters of a flood; there shall not be another flood to devastate the earth." **(Gn 6:17-19, 9:11)**

THE COVENANT WITH ABRAHAM

hen Abraham was seventy-five years old, God asked him to leave his home in Mesopotamia to become a wanderer in foreign lands among unknown peoples. God made a covenant with him, promising to lead him to a new land, to make of him a great nation, to make his name great and finally promising to bless all the families of the earth through him. We see God at work in the lives of the Israelites, molding them into His Chosen People, uniting them into His family through Abraham, whom He chose to father the nation of Israel.

Open to God. Abraham is regarded as the greatest of the Patriarchs, not because he was holier than his contemporaries (he considered himself "dust and ashes," Gn 18:27), but because he was open to God's call and willing to follow divine instructions. Because of his "yes," God's plan to re-unite all people to Himself began to unfold. Abraham gathered his family together, with his nephew Lot accompanying them, and set out for the land of Canaan in blind faith, trusting his future to God. He built an altar each night and as the fire rose up in the night sky, so did the prayers of this devout nomad beg God for courage to see his family through the tragic hardships and famine that befell them.

Father of Nations. In view of Abraham's new task to be "father of a host of nations" (Gn 17:4), God changed Abram's name to Abraham and promised him a son through Sarah. Abraham is elderly and a nomad like Cain, and Sarah is barren and no longer of childbearing age. God's promises, therefore, stretch Abraham's faith to the extreme. When hearing this Abraham fell on his face and laughed to himself: "Can a child be born to a man who is a hundred years old? Or can Sarah give birth at ninety?" (Gn 17:17).

Cutting the Covenant. When Abraham asks what signs he may expect to show that the fulfillment of God's promise is imminent, he is instructed to prepare the ritual by which a covenant is established. God said to Abraham, "Bring me a three-year-old heifer, a three-year-old she-goat, a three-year-old ram, a turtledove, and a young pigeon" (Gn 15:9). Abraham brought the animals and split them in two (except the birds). Known as "cutting the covenant," these rather dramatic sacrificial rituals were practiced all over the Near East. Animals were cut in two, the halves were laid at each side of a pathway, and the parties to the treaty walked between them carrying a fire pot and a flaming torch. This signified that if one person failed to keep the treaty, he would be cut in two as the animals were.[30]

While Abraham slept and it was dark, "there appeared a smoking brazier [oven] and a flaming torch, which passed between those pieces" (Gn 15:17). The fire and torch were visible signs of God Himself who cut the covenant with Abraham, promising him descendents and land—gifts from the heart of God to Abraham.

Circumcision. Then God instructed Abraham to perform the ritual of circumcision on all the males in his household to show his good faith that he accepted the covenant. Circumcision was the mark of this covenant, a sign of belonging to God's chosen people. The shedding of blood was the symbol of the continuous consecration of the nation to God from one generation to another. Through this symbolic act, the covenant is ratified, the people are reminded of their covenant obligations, and their membership in the covenant community is sealed.[31] Circumcision distinguished the sons of Israel from other tribes and any male who was not circumcised was cut off from his people because "he has broken my covenant" (Gn 17:14). Circumcision signified a bond in blood—a bond of life and death.

Baptism and Eucharist. Just as God's people were set apart and the covenant sealed in the blood of circumcision, so are Christians set apart today by the Sacraments of Baptism and the Eucharist. St. Paul in his letter to the Colossians describes Baptism as the symbolic ritual replacing the Old Testament rite of circumcision, through which one gained entry into the community. We die to the old self through Baptism, which, according to St. Paul, is a circumcision of our flesh (Col 2:11).

In the New Testament, Jesus came to fulfill the promise of blessings God made to Abraham by making a New Covenant of the greatest possible intimacy with us—Abraham's descendents. He did this at the Last Supper and on Calvary when He "cut" a covenant with His own Blood, offering Himself, the Lamb of God, as the sacrifice to seal the promise of redemption for His beloved children. Through the Mass we are able to unite ourselves to Christ in the sacrificial offering of His life to the Father and seal our commitment to Him, our Covenant Partner. As members of the Church we walk to Calvary with Christ in the Mass, bonding ourselves to Him and to one another in a union of unconditional love. Then we, like Abraham, become a blessing to the world.

The Caravan of Abraham/James Tissot

The LORD **said to Abram: "Go forth from the land of your kinsfolk and from your father's house to a land that I will show you.**
I will make of you a great nation,
and I will bless you;
I will make your name great,
so that you will be a blessing.
I will bless those who bless you
and curse those who curse you.
All the communities of the earth
shall find blessing in you. . . .
Between you and me I will establish my covenant. . . ." (Gn 12:1-3, 17:2)

Abraham and Melchizedek

In the days of Abraham, foreign kings plundered the cities of Sodom and Gomorrah, taking Lot, Abraham's nephew, captive with all his possessions. As soon as Abraham heard that Lot had been captured, he pursued the kings, rescued Lot and brought him back with all his possessions.

Melchizedek. When Abraham returned from battle he was met by Melchizedek—King of Salem. Salem, which means "peace," was traditionally the site of the city of Jerusalem where the first Eucharist would be offered. Melchizedek was the first person to be called a "priest" in the Bible.[32] Melchizedek blessed Abraham and offered him bread and wine, the food that Jesus, our eternal High Priest, would offer at the Last Supper, which would become His Body and Blood poured out for us as a sign of His new and everlasting Covenant.

Melchizedek: Noah's Son. Fr. Pablo Gadenz, a priest of the diocese of Trenton, New Jersey, traced the Old Testament origins of the priesthood. He presents the finding of Biblical scholarship which interprets Melchizedek as Shem, the firstborn son of Noah. According to this interpretation, the blessing that Noah extended to his son Shem-Melchizedek (Gn 9:26) was the patriarchal priestly blessing which he (Melchizedek) then passed on to Abraham. Hence Melchizedek, the firstborn son of Noah, is the chief priest and patriarch (father figure) over his house, that is, over all of his extended family which through ten generations includes Abraham as well. Abraham, after receiving the blessing from Melchizedek, is designated to become the new chief priest and patriarch over all his descendants.[33]

St. Jerome, and many other biblical scholars, were familiar with the identification of Melchizedek as Shem, as seen in Jerome's commentary on Melchizedek blessing Abraham: "They say that he [Melchizedek] was Shem, the son of Noah, and calculating the years of his life, they declare that he lived to the time of Isaac, and that all the firstborn [from] Noah until Aaron exercised the priesthood, were high priests."[34]

Melchizedek Prefigures Christ. Melchizedek is a type of Christ through his twofold dignity as priest and king, and through his name, which signifies "King of Righteousness." Jesus, like Melchizedek, is also a priest/king ("Like Melchizedek, /you are a priest forever" Ps 110:4). The Messiah in Psalm 110 is linked to Melchizedek, says Fr. Bill McCarthy. This is because Christ is the firstborn son of the Eternal Father and He established a priesthood not based on family lineage through one of the tribes—such as the Levitical priesthood established under Aaron—but upon a call from God given to the righteous son of any family.

Due to the weakness of the Levitical priesthood, Father McCarthy says, it was necessary that another priest according to the order of Melchizedek arise, our Lord Jesus Christ, who could lead all who were to be sanctified to perfection. Christ's priesthood would put an end to the ancient priesthood. Melchizedek is a type of Christ who restored the familial priesthood by establishing the new family of God—namely, the Church.[35]

Melchizedek in Art. Throughout the history of Christian art, Melchizedek is represented both as a historical figure and as a type of the New Testament priesthood offering the sacrifice of bread and wine to God. He is often shown dressed as a royal priest, sometimes with miter or tiara in addition to his kingly crown, and offering up to God bread (even at times in the form of the Eucharistic host) and wine. These images are often combined with a representation of Abel's and Abraham's sacrifices and the Last Supper.[36]

Priesthood and Eucharist. Melchizedek's name appears in the Roman Missal in the first Eucharistic prayer, a prayer which links the Mass of today with the sacrifices of the Old Testament. "Look with favor on these offerings and accept them as you once accepted the gifts of your servant Abel, the sacrifice of Abraham, our father in faith, and the bread and wine offered by your priest Melchizedek."[37] As a mediator between God and His people, the priest of today is called to stand *in persona Christi*—in the person of Christ—at the altar of the Cross at Mass, to offer himself in union with Christ to the Father. A high priest "is taken from among men and made their representative before God, to offer gifts and sacrifices for sins" (Heb 5:1).

Ordination. "The Eucharist is the principal and central *raison d'etre* of the sacrament of the priesthood, which came into being at the moment of the institution of the Eucharist," writes Pope John Paul II in his encyclical, *The Mystery and the Worship of the Eucharist.* "Through our ordination—the celebration of which is linked to the holy Mass from the very first liturgical evidence—we are united in a singular and exceptional way to the Eucharist. In a certain way we derive *from* it and exist *for* it."[38]

The ordination ceremony of a Catholic priest today includes the anointing of his hands, performed by the bishop. As the bishop anoints the palms of the priest with chrism, the bishop prays: "The Father anointed our Lord Jesus Christ through the power of the Holy Spirit. May Jesus preserve you to sanctify the Christian people and to offer sacrifice to God." Then, the antiphon (taken from Psalm 110) is sung: "Christ the Lord, a priest forever in the line of Melchizedek, offered bread and wine."[39]

Abraham and Melchizedek/Mosaic/St. Mary Major Basilica

Melchizedek, king of Salem, brought out bread and wine, and being a priest of God Most High, he blessed Abram with these words:
"Blessed be Abram by God Most High,
the creator of heaven and earth;
And blessed be God Most High,
who delivered your foes into your hand." **(Gn 14:18-20)**

THE SACRIFICE OF ISAAC

rom his initial call to leave his homeland and set out for the Promised Land, Abraham hoped to bear a son to carry on his family line. Abraham had acquired riches—cattle, gold and silver and many servants—but he had never ceased praying for the greatest of riches, a son.

Sons were considered a great blessing because they were needed to tend the flocks and herds. When Abraham's wife, Sarah, was elderly and beyond child-bearing age, God miraculously granted them a son, Isaac. Later, Abraham was put to the ultimate test of faith, to offer to God what was most precious to him, his own son. God had promised Abraham descendents through the son whom He was now asking him to sacrifice.[40]

Abraham's Obedience. Obeying God, Abraham set out on a three-day journey to Mount Moriah, accompanied by Isaac and two servants, where he built an altar and piled wood upon it. Isaac asked where the sheep was for the holocaust. "God himself will provide the sheep for the holocaust" (Gn 22:8), replied Abraham. In great inner torment, Abraham bound Isaac, laid him on the wood and when he raised the knife to kill Isaac, an angel intervened to stay his hand. God was pleased with Abraham's trust and obedience, and allowed him to substitute a ram caught in a thicket to sacrifice in place of Isaac.

Isaac: A Type of Christ. In Jerusalem there are two mountains, Mt. Moriah, where Solomon built his Temple, and Mt. Calvary, where the crucifixion took place. Abraham, who offered to sacrifice his son on Mt. Moriah, foreshadows the sacrifice of the Son of God who was offered by His Father for the sins of the world. Like Isaac, the Son of God climbed a hill and God "provided the sheep," Himself, the Lamb of God, who takes away the sins of the world.[41] Isaac is a figure of Jesus Christ who carried His cross to Calvary to be offered by His heavenly Father for the sins of the world. God confirmed His promises to Abraham and "blessed him in every way" (Gn 24:1). Scripture tells us that he "kept his glory without stain" (Sir 44:19) and, because Abraham did not withhold his son Isaac, his glory would be seen in his offspring through whom "all the nations of the earth shall find blessing" (Gn 22:18).

Promises Fulfilled. We are Abraham's descendents and among all the families of the earth who share in the blessing promised to him nearly four thousand years ago. God reached out through Abraham to all generations, forming us into His family. From Abraham would come the Chosen People, from them would come Christ, and from Christ would spring the new People of God, His Church. It is through the Church—the Body of Christ—that we are bound to Christ and to one another in a new and everlasting covenant which He sealed with the sacrifice of His life. As Catholic Christians (Catholic comes from the Greek *katholikos,* which means universal) we are able to participate in this covenant through the Eucharist—the ultimate and eternal blessing—an intimate sharing in the divine life of God Himself.

Saying Yes to Christ. Jesus invites us to respond to His call—like Abraham—by following Him in blind faith and obedience. Jesus showed the depth of His love for us when, at the Last Supper and in the Garden, He said *yes* to the will of His Father, offering His Body and Blood for us.

In a homily he gave at the closing Mass of a Forty Hours Devotion, Jesuit Fr. Paul Cioffi, Director of the Georgetown University Institute of Pastoral Renewal, said "On the night He was handed over, He handed Himself over (Eucharistic Prayer II) believing God wanted Him to enter into His death and that God would rescue Him from it. *Nothing could shake Jesus' confidence in the Father.*" Father Cioffi continues: "That key moment of human history—Jesus' sacrifice—was saved for us in the Mass because it sheds light on human suffering and the problem of evil. God did not take away the Passion and death from Jesus. We can expect no more from God the Father than He did for His Son. Jesus wants us to focus on His *act* and invites us to take the very same risk in faith He took. The cost of discipleship, He told us, is to lose one's life in order to find it; to take up our cross daily" (cf. Mk 8:34).[42]

The Narrow Way. Through the Sacrifice of the Mass we can, like Abraham, offer our lives and our loved ones to the Father. To live in a covenant relationship with Christ is to enter the narrow way. What does that mean if not to live a crucified life with our Savior? Christ is Emmanuel, God with us. His Real Presence in the Eucharist is a continuation of His Real Presence on earth. God sent His Son into our world and into our lives in order to lead us to life—eternal life.

"Christ assures us we are not trapped in hopelessness—in suffering and evil," Father Cioffi adds. "He came into our prison in the Incarnation and opened the door from the inside—calling us forth into the fresh air of the freedom and joy He now knows. Jesus failed to win over the religious institution of Israel, and even His apostles deserted Him during the Passion. Then He instituted the Eucharist. 'I have much more to tell you, but you cannot bear it now' (Jn 16:12). He leaves the Eucharist to preach for Him now."[43]

Isaac Bears the Wood for the Sacrifice/James Tissot

**Some time after these events, God put Abraham to the test. He called to him,
"Abraham!" "Ready!" he replied. Then God said: "Take your son Isaac,
your only one, whom you love, and go to the land of Moriah. There you
shall offer him up as a holocaust on a height that I will point out to you."
Early the next morning Abraham saddled his donkey, took with him his son
Isaac, and two of his servants as well, and with the wood that he had cut for
the holocaust, set out for the place of which God had told him. (Gn 22:1-3)**

THE PASSOVER OF THE JEWS

 he Egyptians were an idolatrous people who worshiped the gods of nature, and of wealth, power and fertility. Even the Pharaoh was worshiped as divine. God wanted the Israelites freed from the influence of the Egyptians, so He sent Moses and Aaron to ask Pharaoh to release them. Pharaoh's heart was so hardened that it took ten plagues before he finally let them go. Each plague was directed against a specific Egyptian god.

Finally, in order to break the physical stranglehold Pharaoh had over the Israelites, God ordered the slaying of all the firstborn Egyptians, from the firstborn of Pharaoh to the firstborn of the slave girl to the firstborn of the animals. St. John Chrysostom, a fourth century Bishop and Doctor of the Church, preached a sermon saying that God wanted to slay the Egyptian firstborn because they held in slavery His firstborn, the Chosen People.

The Passover. The death of the firstborn became the basis of the most important feast in Israel's history, the Passover. The name of the feast (in Hebrew *Pesach*) is derived from a verb meaning "pass over." On the evening of the fourteenth day of the month of Nisan (which fell roughly during our March and April), every Israelite family in Egypt was to kill a lamb and, with a spray of hyssop, brush the blood of the lamb over the lintel and two doorposts to mark the Israelite home so the destroying angel would pass over it. At their Passover meal the Israelites hastily roasted and ate the lamb in their travelling dress with sandals on their feet and staff in hand, prepared to flee Pharaoh's vengeance. They were so rushed that the dough in their bread was unleavened! (Bread to which no yeast has been added).

The Sacred Meal. God asked the Israelites to perpetuate this sacrificial meal for their descendants so that when their children would ask them, "What does this rite of yours mean?" (Ex 12:26) they would reply: "This is the Passover sacrifice of the LORD, who passed over the houses of the Israelites in Egypt; when he struck down the Egyptians, he spared our houses" (Ex 12:27). The narrative that shapes the ritual feast is initiated by a question from the youngest who asks why this night is different from all other nights. The head of the household then explains that the Israelites had been slaves of Pharaoh in Egypt when God mercifully led their people out of Egypt into the freedom of a new life. Had God not done that, their children and their children's children would still be in bondage.

A Journey to Freedom. By freeing the Israelites from slavery in Egypt and saving their firstborn from death, the Passover was a prefigurement of our liberation from the slavery of sin and our salvation from eternal death. Theologian Fr. Raniero Cantalamessa, OFM CAP., also author and preacher to the papal household, writes that from the beginning of the exodus of the chosen people out of Egypt God was contemplating the Eucharist, preparing to give us the true Lamb. He refers to St. John Chrysostom who questioned what it was the Lord saw over the Jews' houses that was so precious to make him "pass over" and tell his angel not to destroy them saying, "Seeing the blood, I will pass over you" (Ex 12:13). His conclusion was: "He saw the Blood of Christ, he saw the Eucharist!"[44]

Eucharist: The Christian Passover. The first Passover was to be commemorated annually by a sacred meal, a meal involving worship and thanksgiving to Yahweh for His saving work. The paschal atmosphere of the first Eucharist which Christ instituted at the Last Supper would be the new Passover of the Church (*pasch* is the Christianized *pesach*). Onto the ritual Passover blessings intended for bread and wine, Jesus grafts the institution of the Eucharist.[45] By celebrating together the final *Pasch* and the first Eucharist in the upper room, Christ forged a visible ritual link between the two Testaments, joining together the old sacrifice of Israel and the new sacrifice of the Christian era of grace.[46]

Just as the ancient Passover was a memorial which conferred on the Israelites the actual benefits of their deliverance, so does the Eucharist memorialize and renew the saving death and resurrection of Jesus. In giving His Body to eat and His Blood poured out to drink, the Evangelists describe Christ's death as the sacrifice of the Passover of which He is the new Lamb.

Eucharist is Our Liberation. Just as an extended family gathers together periodically to share memories and dinner at a family reunion, so does our Church family unite at the Easter Vigil to relive and renew our beginnings, through Baptism and the Eucharist. At Easter we remember the deliverance of the Israelites from slavery and our deliverance through Christ's death and resurrection. Christ Himself presides over the paschal Eucharist, sharing His triumph over sin and death with the newborn sons and daughters of the Church.

In the Easter Eucharist we meet Christ directly, not merely in His power present, as in Baptism or the other sacraments; the Eucharist makes Him present in substance. On Holy Saturday we keep vigil with the Church as we await Christ's resurrection where we encounter Him in His risen Flesh and Blood in the Easter liturgy.[47] The Eucharist is the Christian Passover liberation from sin and death.

Signs on the Door/James Tissot

"It is the Passover of the Lord. For on this same night I will go through Egypt, striking down every firstborn of the land, both man and beast, and executing judgment on all the gods of Egypt—I, the Lord! But the blood will mark the houses where you are. Seeing the blood, I will pass over you; thus, when I strike the land of Egypt, no destructive blow will come upon you." (Ex 12:11-13)

THE MANNA IN THE DESERT

After the slaying of the firstborn Egyptians, the Pharaoh summoned Moses and Aaron in the middle of the night and ordered them out of Egypt. Taking their unleavened dough and their kneading bowls wrapped in their cloaks, the Israelites set out in haste—600,000 men on foot, not counting women and children—to find freedom in a new land. The Lord accompanied them in a pillar of cloud by day and a column of fire by night, leading them toward the Red Sea by way of the desert.

The Sea Opens. With the Egyptians in close pursuit, Moses stretched out his hand over the sea, which parted by means of a strong wind to allow their safe crossing. When the Egyptians attempted to follow the Israelites through the Red Sea, Yahweh let the sea swallow them. The Israelites celebrated yet another deliverance—and the majesty and power of Yahweh. But the people grew hungry and thirsty on their march through the desert toward Sinai, and complained to Moses saying they would rather have died back in Egypt eating their fill of bread than die of famine in a foreign desert.

Once again God came to their rescue. He told Moses that He would rain down bread from heaven for them in daily allotments which would be enough to feed their families. Moses and Aaron told the people that the Lord would respond to their complaints and in the morning they would see the glory of the Lord.

Manna. God fed them with quail and manna. Quail is a bird of the partridge family, normally migrating across that region in the springtime. Manna is a bread-like substance which fell on the ground like frost, white and sweet like sugar.

The Bible derives the word manna from the question "Man hu?" (Hebrew for "What is it?"), which the Israelites asked when they first saw the "fine flakes like hoarfrost on the ground" (Ex 16:14). Moses told them that this was the bread which the Lord had given them to eat. It would keep overnight until the heat of the morning sun melted it, and it did not fall on the Sabbath. (More than enough fell on the previous day to feed them on the Sabbath). It could be ground like meal, boiled or made into cakes.[48] For forty years, God rained down manna in such quantity as to sustain each family with a daily supply of two quarts—and there were thousands of families.

Chemical analysis. Manna consists of the dried remains of a type of insect found under tamarisk trees. Modern Bedouin Arabs still call this substance "manna." Chemical analysis of manna shows it to contain sugar and important nutrients needed for a healthy diet. These wonders follow the same pattern as the whole miracle tradition connected with the Exodus. The food in itself is natural, but it took the all-seeing eye and the all-achieving power of God to accomplish the miracle of coincidence by which the food was present at the time, and in the quantity, necessary for the survival of the Israelites.[49]

Living Bread. This example of God interceding for the needs of His people with "bread from heaven" (Ps 78:24) is a type of the true bread from heaven, the Sacrament of the Eucharist, our spiritual food nourishing us on our journey through life. The multiplication of the loaves and fishes in the New Testament has been compared to this Exodus story. The Jews, alluding to the manna, the "bread from heaven," ask Jesus what sign He, the new Moses, will give them comparable to the manna. Jesus contrasts the manna with the "living bread that came down from heaven" (Jn 6:51) given by His Father. He leads them from physical bread (the loaves multiplied for them) to divine teaching, and finally, to the Sacrament of His flesh.

The Lord commanded Moses to keep some of the manna in reserve as a sign for future generations of the way God fed the Israelites in the wilderness. Moses instructed Aaron to put some manna in a vessel (about a tenth of a bushel)[50] which was then stored in the tabernacle (Ex 16:32-34).

Jesus, Bread of Eternal Life. Jesus commissioned His disciples to preach the Gospel to the whole world saying, "Behold, I am with you always, until the end of the age" (Mt 28:20). He fulfills His pledge to be with us through the Sacrament of the Eucharist. Our Manna is Jesus in the Blessed Sacrament.

Jesus would spend the final year of His life teaching people that only God could fill their hunger—the hunger of the human heart for love. The full meaning of these words will not become evident until the night before He dies when He will feed us with His love which He gives to us as Bread, the Bread of eternal life. Jesus is the Living Bread, the Food of our souls. When Jesus died, He left us something which no other person had been able to give, namely, His Body, Blood, Soul and Divinity, for the life of the world.

The Gathering of Manna/James Tissot

**In the morning, a dew lay all about the camp, and when the dew evapo-
rated, there on the surface of the desert were fine flakes like hoarfrost on the
ground. On seeing it, the Israelites asked one another, "What is this?" for
they did not know what it was. But Moses told them, "This is the bread
which the Lord has given you to eat. . . ." The Israelites called this food
manna. It was like coriander seed, but white, and it tasted like wafers made
with honey. (Ex 16:13-15, 31)**

THE MOSAIC COVENANT

In leading His people to the Promised Land, God was patient and compassionate, teaching His chosen people to rely on Him alone. God was constantly manifesting His presence to them, going before them in a pillar of cloud by day and a column of fire by night, meeting their every need, forming them into a community of worship dedicated to His service and ruled by His law.[51]

Encamped at the base of Mt. Sinai, Moses went up the mountain to meet with God who gave him a new set of laws—the Ten Commandments—through which they would consecrate themselves to His service. Like the covenant with Abraham, this Sinai covenant was initiated by God who named Israel as His own possession, His priestly people, "dearer to me than all other people . . . a kingdom of priests, a holy nation" (Ex 19:5, 6).

The Altar of God. Implicit in God's promises to His people were conditions which they had to fulfill, the first one being the worship of God alone. "Hear, O Israel! The LORD is our God, the LORD alone!" (Dt 6:4). The Lord God instructed the Israelites to make an altar of acacia wood, plated with bronze and covered with a grating. Like a hollow box, it featured horns at the four corners (symbolizing the deity) with poles on either side which were put through rings so it could be carried. The altar symbolized God in the sacrificial ritual; the offering was made by applying the blood of the victim (which symbolized its life) to the altar.[52]

Covenant Sacrifice. The Israelites bound themselves to observe the conditions of the covenant by a solemn ritual in which the altar was sanctified to Yahweh; blood from the bulls was placed in bowls. After he proclaimed Yahweh's covenant love and code of obedience and received the people's assent, Moses sealed the agreement by the sprinkling of blood, half on the altar (which represented Yahweh), and half on the people, saying:[53] "This is the blood of the covenant which the LORD has made with you in accordance with all these words of his" (Ex 24:8). The rite signified that if one of the parties broke the covenant, their blood would be shed, and above all, it showed that the two were "of the same blood."[54] Since blood is a carrier of life (Lv 17:11), the mutual sprinkling of the blood signified that God was sharing His very life with these people; that from this moment on, the Israelites became His own people. The covenant sacrifice sealed, ratified and proclaimed their entry into God's own life as a "holy nation" (Ex 19:6), a redeemed race, a free and responsible people—the people of God.[55]

The Blood. The words "This is the blood of the covenant" are a prefiguration of the words used by Jesus at the Last Supper—words now said by the priest at Mass during the Consecration: "This is the cup of My Blood, the Blood of the new and everlasting covenant." As Moses proclaimed the old covenant, so Christ the new. The chosen people, with its twelve tribes, corresponds to the new covenant, represented by the twelve apostles. Blessed Sacrament Scripture scholar Fr. Eugene LaVerdiere explains: "The cup of the Lord's supper was not just a renewal of the Sinai covenant. It was the new covenant, a reference to Jeremiah (31:31-34) which announced a new covenant with the law inscribed not on tablets of stone but on people's hearts and with God forgiving peoples' sins. The new covenant established by Christ would not be in the blood of animals, but in His own blood, 'which would be shed for you.' It would be established in the sacrificial blood of Christ, the Passover Lamb."[56]

Covenant Meal. The covenant sacrifice was concluded with a sacred banquet to which God invited Moses, Aaron and his sons and seventy elders up the mountain where they "beheld the God of Israel" (Ex 24:10) and shared a meal with their Divine host. This sacred banquet testifies to the intimacy God wished to enjoy with His chosen family. The meal symbolized the union between the God of the covenant and the people of God and promised a continuation of God's covenant blessings, His enduring friendship, protection and constant care for Israel.

Covenant Renewal. The meal also was a foreshadowing of the final sacrificial meal Jesus would share with His apostles, the Last Supper, the paschal banquet in which God would unite His children to Himself in an intimate bond of love through the Blood of His Son, Jesus Christ. Throughout all future generations God's faithful would be able to share in this sacrificial meal through a sacred rite which came to be called the holy Sacrifice of the Mass, enabling them to renew their covenant with God sacramentally.

When we receive the Body and Blood of Christ we experience a true encounter with the person of Jesus. God's presence in the Eucharist is not just a sign as in the days of Moses. He comes to us *in person.* This is the real meaning of the Eucharist. When we say "Amen" after we receive His Body and Blood in Holy Communion, we also must say "Amen" to the responsibilities of living as a covenant partner with Christ.

THE ALTAR OF BURNT-OFFERING.

The Altar of Burnt Offering/Mary Evans Picture Library

Moses then wrote down all the words of the Lᴏʀᴅ and, rising early the next day, he erected at the foot of the mountain an altar and twelve pillars for the twelve tribes of Israel. Then, having sent certain young men of the Israelites to offer holocausts and sacrifice young bulls as peace offerings to the Lᴏʀᴅ, Moses took half of the blood and put it in large bowls; the other half he splashed on the altar. . . . Then he took the blood and sprinkled it on the people, saying, "This is the blood of the covenant which the Lᴏʀᴅ has made with you in accordance with all these words of his." **(Ex 24:4-6, 8)**

THE ARK OF THE COVENANT

he covenant of Sinai made a people out of the Israelite tribesmen. Up to that time they had been a nomadic clan who settled in Egypt as foreigners and finally were reduced to the status of slaves. With the Sinai covenant, the Israelite exiles won a new freedom, gaining national religious identity as Yahweh's people in addition to political independence.[57]

Design of the Ark. While the Israelites camped at the base of the mountain, Moses spent forty days and nights on Mt. Sinai. During that time God gave him specific instructions on the construction of the Ark, which symbolized His absolute love for His Chosen People and the union between them. Like a mobile sanctuary, it was to be a chest made of acacia wood overlaid inside and outside with gold. The Ark contained the stone tablets of the Sinai Covenant (which explains why the Ark was called the "Ark of the Covenant"), the blossoming staff of Aaron and even manna which Moses stored as a perpetual memorial to the fact that God feeds His people (Heb 9:4). The Ark was the seat of the invisible God who sits enthroned upon the cherubim.

Mercy Seat. The mercy seat was the throne of Yahweh who manifested Himself to His people, received their prayers and offerings and led them in their expeditions. It was a lid made of pure gold and decorated with two cherubim who covered it with their outstretched wings. The cherubim were symbols of the presence of the Lord who was believed to dwell between them. The Ark was a memorial of the covenant, a symbol of Yahweh's personal presence and the place where atonement was received.

Attached to the Ark on each side were rings through which wooden poles overlaid with gold were placed to equip it for travel. Once a year on the Day of Atonement (the feast of Yom Kippur), the high priest entered the Holy of Holies where the Ark was kept and sprinkled blood from sacrificial animals onto the mercy seat (Lev 16:14, 15) to cleanse Israel from its sins.[58] The Ark accompanied the Israelites through the wilderness as they crossed the Jordan into the Promised Land (Jos 3:14).

The Ark at Jericho. The Ark usually accompanied the Israelite army into battle to symbolize Yahweh's kingship and leadership. Its presence is attested at the siege of Jericho (Jos 4:5) where it was carried on the shoulders of the priests in ritual procession. Before attacking Jericho,

the Israelites performed an unusual rite. The Ark was carried around the strongly fortified city daily for seven days. Seven priests walked before the Ark of Yahweh sounding their trumpets as they went. On the seventh day they marched around seven times and at the seventh time the trumpets sounded, after which the city walls miraculously fell down (Jos 6:6-21). The Israelites then captured the city.[59] When the Temple of Solomon was constructed in Jerusalem, the Ark was placed in its Holy of Holies. It was probably destroyed along with the Temple in 587 BC.[60]

The Ark in Revelation. The last time the Ark is mentioned in Scripture is in the Book of Revelation where John, on the Isle of Patmos, in mystic ecstasy, looks up and sees in the heavens the Ark which has been missing for five hundred years.[61] "Then God's temple in heaven was opened, and the ark of his covenant could be seen in the temple" (Rv 11:19). A woman clothed with the sun appeared in the sky (the Blessed Virgin), about to give birth, while a red dragon (Satan) waited to devour the child. After giving birth to a son, who was destined to rule all nations, she fled into the desert where God took care of her. Satan was enraged with her and went off to make war with the rest of her offspring—those who keep God's commandments (the Church) and bear witness to Jesus.

Mary, Ark of the Covenant. Mary is the new Ark, says Fr. Bill McCarthy, leading the Church into the fullness of the kingdom. Just as Joshua would only go into battle with the Ark leading the way, so now will we, the Church, battle Satan and evil, with Mary leading the way as Mother of the Church. Father McCarthy encourages devotion to Mary "especially since she is returning so often to earth in these days with countless appearances all over the world. She is urging her children to 'Do whatever He tells you' and to live her messages of peace, purity, prayer, Eucharist, Confession, fasting, love, forgiveness and zeal."[62]

Our Lady is the privileged human sanctuary chosen by the God of the New Covenant as His dwelling place on earth. Whereas the former Ark had housed inanimate manna, the new Ark, Mary, enclosed within herself for nine months that Person who is the living bread from heaven. This made Mary in effect the first-ever tabernacle of the Real Presence.[63] Before King David brought the Ark to Jerusalem, it rested in a mountain village near Jerusalem. Today that village is crowned with a great statue of the Virgin and Child and is the site of the Church of Our Lady, Ark of the Covenant.[64]

The Seven Trumpets of Jericho/James Tissot

"In the ark itself you are to put the commandments which I will give you. There I will meet you and there, from above the propitiatory, between the two cherubim on the ark of the commandments, I will tell you all the commands that I wish you to give the Israelites." **(Ex 25:21, 22)**

TENT OF MEETING

The Ark was sheltered under a tent known as the "Tent of Meeting," which stood in the center of the Israelite camp. Solomon's later temple in Jerusalem was merely an elaborate facsimile in stone and timber of this crude tabernacle of the desert. The Tent of Meeting was the first "house of God" on earth, the first church where the people of God assembled. It meant to the Hebrews what all the soaring cathedrals of the Middle Ages meant to Christian Europe. It was more than a place of prayer—it was the center of gravity of their whole religious life.

Purpose and Design. Like a miniature portable temple, the Tent of Meeting was set up by Moses whenever the Israelites pitched camp as a sacred space where anyone who wished could go to consult the Lord. The twelve tribes of Israel positioned themselves around the tent, at a slight distance from it. The Tent represented God's abiding presence in the midst of His people.

Enclosed within an outer court, the Tent was seventy-five feet wide and 150 feet long. It was made of curtains hung on pillars of brass. The entrance of both the court and the tabernacle was to the east. The Tent was built in such a way that it could be taken apart and carried with them on their march to the land of Canaan.

The Tent of Meeting was made of acacia wood and fine-twined purple and scarlet linen. Other materials that went into the making of the Tent were spices, oil, gold, silver and precious stones, ram skins, the skins of fish (perhaps porpoise) and strong leather. These materials were volunteered as gifts by the Israelites, and a Sabbath Day had been set aside to receive their offerings.[65] The Tent was called "the tent of the commandments" (Num 9:15) and "the Dwelling of the meeting tent" (Ex 40:2). For the Lord said, "I will set my Dwelling among you" (Lev 26:11).

Furnishings. The ground plan was similar to that of the Temple Solomon would later erect. A door at one end led into an outer court in which there was an altar and a laver, a basin in which the priest purified his hands and feet. Within the Tent (which had two sections) was a Holy Place containing the lampstand and the Table of Showbread (bread of offering). According to God's instructions, a table was made of the finest wood overlaid with pure gold, upon which were set twelve loaves of unleavened bread. They were constantly exposed before the Most High, six on each side of the table, and were carefully renewed each week to prevent corruption. These loaves were a type of the bread placed on our altars today, a prefigurement of the Eucharist.

Holy of Holies. A great veil, measuring sixty by thirty feet, divided the Holy Place from the Holy of Holies, which contained the Ark of the Covenant and the Altar of Incense. This sacred place was reserved exclusively for the high priest, which he entered once a year to offer sacrifice. It is a striking symbol of the Catholic sanctuary, which the priest enters to offer the holy Sacrifice of the Mass.[66]

The Ark is represented by the tabernacle in Catholic churches, which encloses the true "manna," the most Blessed Sacrament—Christ, Himself. God dwelt in the *Holy of Holies,* gave audience to His priests in the holy place, and received the homage of His people in the Court.

The Shekinah Presence. Moses worked diligently to build the tabernacle according to a heavenly model given to him by God. Nineteen times in the building of the Tabernacle, Scripture relates, Moses did as the Lord commanded him.[67] When Moses finished all the work, the people saw a marvelous sight. The pillar of cloud and fire that had been with them from Egypt, rose and moved directly over the Holy of Holies, filling it with light:

"Moses could not enter the meeting tent, because the cloud settled down upon it and the glory of the LORD filled the Dwelling. Whenever the cloud rose from the Dwelling, the Israelites would set out on their journey. But if the cloud did not lift, they would not go forward; only when it lifted did they go forward. In the daytime, the cloud of the LORD was seen over the Dwelling; whereas at night, fire was seen in the cloud by the whole house of Israel in all the stages of their journey" (Ex 40:35-38).

Centuries later, scholars named this light the "Shekinah" (Hebrew *shakan*, literally "tabernacle").[68] The Shekinah cloud of glory through which God manifested His presence was so strong that one literally could see it as a "cloud" by day and a "fire" by night.

The Glory of the Lord. Just as God's presence was visible to the people in the Old Testament and the "glory of the LORD filled the Dwelling" (Ex 40:34), so is God present to us now through His Son Jesus, who is the new way into the glory of God. Jesus is the fulfillment of God's promise of His intimate and everlasting presence through a new covenant in which "the nations shall know that it is I, the LORD, who make Israel holy, when my sanctuary shall be set up among them forever" (Ez 37:28).

The tabernacle (Tent of Meeting) prefigures the spirituality of the Church today, God's sanctuary, where Christ resides in the midst of His people. The glory of the Lord shines upon His people through Christ when "The Word became flesh and made his dwelling among us" (Jn 1:14). Emmanuel—God is with us in His Eucharistic Real Presence! He replaces the Ark of the Covenant with Himself in the New Covenant of His Body and Blood, present now in all the tabernacles of the world.

*The Israelites Encamped about the Tabernacle/*Mary Evans Picture Library

"They shall make a sanctuary for me, that I may dwell in their midst. This Dwelling and all its furnishings you shall make exactly according to the pattern that I will now show you." **(Ex 25:8-9)**

THE COVENANT WITH DAVID

 amuel was divinely instructed by Yahweh to anoint David as king. This he did in the house of David's father, Jesse, in Bethlehem of Judea, which St. Luke calls "the city of David" (Lk 2:4).[69] The youngest of eight sons, David was a shepherd blessed with many gifts and talents. "He was ruddy, a youth handsome to behold and making a splendid appearance" (1 Sm 16:12). He was a poet and a musician (he wrote many of the Psalms), a ferocious and resourceful fighter, a wise ruler with a real concern for his people and considered Israel's greatest king.

David: Israel's Hope of Salvation. David was a man of deep faith and prayer who valued the religious aspect of his kingly office. He established his royal palace in Jerusalem, thus making the city the religious center of the twelve tribes of Israel. Jerusalem was the site of the celebration in which Melchizedek and Abraham shared bread and wine in thanksgiving for Abraham's victory. Jerusalem was also the site of Abraham's sacrificial offering of his son, Isaac.

The figure of David, as priest and king, stands out in such a way that he still remains for Israel the model of the Messiah who is to be born of his race. He is consistently the "blessed of God," the one whom God assists with His presence. In his struggle with Goliath, in all the wars he conducts to free Israel, "The LORD brought David victory in all his undertakings" (2 Sm 8:14).[70] God promised David through the prophet Nathan that the Messiah would be descended from him.

David's Sin. The turning point in David's life came when he committed adultery with Bathsheba and arranged the murder of her husband. "His sin caused tragic consequences for his family and the nation," writes Peter Kreeft. In recounting the story of David, Kreeft says "There exists an unavoidable law of spiritual cause and effect as universal and as objective as the law of gravity: the only road to blessing is obedience, and the road to judgment is disobedience of God's laws."[71] God sent the prophet Nathan to threaten David with the retribution that would result from David's sin—evil would befall his own house. The first consequence of David's sin was the death of the child born from their union. Then David's own son turned against him and David had to flee Jerusalem.

David Repents. David's repentance restored him to God's favor. Fr. John Power, Irish biblical scholar and missionary, comments at length on David in his book, *The History of Salvation.* He writes that David had to endure many humiliations and pay dearly for his faults. "But David was magnanimous, big in heart and mind," he says. David's repentance for his sins was great and public, forming the basis of our Psalm 51, the *Miserere*. "For I know my offense; /my sin is always before me. /Against you alone have I sinned; /I have done such evil in your sight. . . ." (Ps 51:5, 6). Among the cruel and sensual oriental kings of the time, Fr. Power asserts that David stands out as a noble figure, whose long and turbulent life was spent in active devotion to Yahweh.[72]

David and the Ark. David, who was trying to unite a divided Israel, had a deep reverence for the Ark of the Covenant. He had his warriors bring it to Jerusalem which he wanted to make a religious as well as geographical capital. He revered the Ark as the presence of Yahweh, the God of Israel, and as a symbol of Israel's ancient unity. While enroute to Jerusalem, David, the priest-king, was wearing a priestly garment and danced with joy in front of the Ark of the Covenant. David wanted to build a temple for Yahweh in Jerusalem to house the Ark but was told that, because he had "shed much blood" (1 Chr 22:8), his son, Solomon, would actually build it.

God's Covenant with David. God rewarded David's desire to honor Him by making a covenant with him, promising that instead of David building a house for the Lord, the Lord would build a house for David—that is, a dynasty. He promises that his house and his sovereignty will remain forever; it is Jesus who will fulfill this promise. King David prophesied that the Messiah will be a priest, not according to the Mosaic rite of Aaron and the Levites which is not "forever," but according to the order of Melchizedek: "Like Melchizedek you are a priest forever" (Ps 110: 4).

The Israelites thought of the coming Messiah as another David, Fr. Power adds, one who would restore glory and honor to the royal house of the shepherd boy from Bethlehem. And it is in these terms that Gabriel announced the birth of Christ to Mary: "He will be great and will be called Son of the Most High, and the Lord God will give him the throne of David his father, and he will rule over the house of Jacob forever, and of his kingdom there will be no end" (Lk 1:32, 33). And when the enthusiastic crowd swirls around Christ on Palm Sunday they shout: "Hosanna to the Son of David!" (Mt 21:9).[73]

Jesus is Priest, Prophet, King. Abraham was the father of all Israelites and the one with whom God initiated the covenant with the Chosen People, and Moses was the mediator through whom God bound His people to Himself in the Sinai Covenant. But David was the king through whom God chose to found the eternal and universal kingdom. Into this kingdom would come the Mediator of the new and everlasting covenant, Jesus Christ, who would sign and seal His covenant not with the blood of bullocks, but with the precious Blood of the true Lamb of God on Calvary.[74]

Transporting the Holy Ark/Giambattista Maganza, Jr.

"I have made a covenant with my chosen one;
I have sworn to David my servant:
I will make your dynasty stand forever
and establish your throne through all ages." **(Ps 89:4-5)**

ELIJAH IS VISITED BY AN ANGEL

The whole career of Elijah is summed up in his Hebrew name which means "my God is Yahweh." Elijah is one of the great Biblical prophets who has been compared to a type of John the Baptist in the New Testament—whom Jesus calls the greatest of all (Mt 11:11). When Peter, James and John went to the mountain they witnessed the transfiguration of Jesus. "Elijah appeared to them along with Moses" (Mk 9:4) announcing that the prophets and the law were being fulfilled in Jesus.

Elijah Despairs. Elijah was crushed because his campaign to reestablish the pure worship of Yahweh and to repudiate the cult of false gods seemed to have failed. He is forced to flee from his kingdom by the hostility of Ahab, the King of Israel, and his wife, Jezebel, the Phoenician princess who was leading the people of Israel to worship false gods. She threatened Elijah who feared for his safety. He fled to the desert where he sat under a broom tree and prayed for God to take his life.

Theologian Msgr. James O'Connor, writing in *The Hidden Manna,* compares Elijah to "so many in all ages who, having striven for the good and defended the truth, find themselves alone, friendless, and apparently without any hope for success in their efforts. But God strengthens Elijah by sending an angel to provide the prophet with food."[75]

An Angel Offers Sustenance. The fact that God sent an angel to feed a despairing prophet—"Get up and eat, else the journey will be too long for you" (1 Kgs 19:7)—is a message for all God's children who are discouraged and have lost their way. Elijah had lost faith and was ready to give up, yet the Lord invited him to eat and drink to strengthen him for his mission—which led him to Mt. Horeb (Sinai), the mountain of God. There God revealed to him his Presence and gave him the assurance that he was not alone, that a remnant in Israel, seven thousand in all, had not worshiped Baal. Monsignor O'Connor concludes that the bread and water is a foreshadowing of the Eucharist which strengthens us on our journey and is, for us, Viaticum (Communion for the dying)—the Eucharistic Flesh of him who is the source of all life.[76]

Eucharist is Nourishment. God gives us the Eucharist to fill us with hope and purpose for our journey through life. The bread and water given to Elijah symbolized the Bread and Wine of the Eucharist. Jesus Himself is our food—our nourishment for the journey. St. Thomas Aquinas, the great "Eucharistic Doctor," draws an analogy between food that nourishes our bodies, and Jesus, the Bread of Life, Who nourishes the life of our souls: "The body needs nourishment to restore what is lost daily through the action of natural heat. In the life of the soul, too, something is lost in us every day through venial sin which lessens the warmth of charity. But the Eucharist confers the virtue of charity, because it is the sacrament of love."[77] St. Thomas explains that every effect produced for physical life by material food and drink—that is, sustenance, growth, regeneration and pleasure—all of these effects are produced by the Eucharist for the spiritual life.

Food for Our Journey. As we wander through the deserts and dark times of our lives, we pray that God will reach out with His mercy just as He did to Elijah, who "went a day's journey into the desert [and]. . . prayed for death" (1 Kgs 19:4). Hungry and tired, we resemble the multitudes on whom Jesus took pity because "they were like sheep without a shepherd" (Mk 6:34). Jesus, who "welcomes sinners and eats with them" (Lk 15:2), mercifully invites us to refresh ourselves at His table where He will "feed with the finest wheat, satisfy them with honey from the rock" (Ps 81:17).

When Elijah reached Mt. Horeb, God made His presence known, not in the wind or the earthquake or the fire, but in a "tiny whispering sound" (1 Kgs 19:12). So does Jesus, the Bread of Life, come to us in a little white Host in Communion, silently restoring our strength and whispering His unconditional love.

Our Final Journey. The Eucharist is also our companion and source of strength for our final journey of life, Monsignor O'Connor concludes, the one that will end our exile and bring us to the mountain of God, where we shall enter into His rest and "dwell in the shelter of the Most High (Ps 91:1). God Himself is our refuge. "Then will I ever dwell in your tent, take refuge in the shelter of your wings" (Ps 61:5). The same Lord present in the Eucharist is our companion on the way to that shelter where, journey done, we shall see Him face to face.

The Church considers Viaticum so necessary for this final journey that canon law legislates: "Christ's faithful who are in danger of death, from whatever cause it may proceed, are to be refreshed by Sacred Communion in the form of Viaticum." It is through Viaticum that we shall pass beyond appearances and behold the Lord face to face in heaven. It is there that we shall receive the Manna, hidden now under the appearances of bread (Rev 2:17).[78]

Elijah Visited by an Angel/Alessandro Moretto

[Elijah] went a day's journey into the desert, until he came to a broom tree and sat beneath it. He prayed for death: "This is enough, O LORD! Take my life, for I am no better than my fathers." He lay down and fell asleep under the broom tree, but then an angel touched him and ordered him to get up and eat. He looked and there at his head was a hearth cake and a jug of water. After he ate and drank, he lay down again, but the angel of the LORD came back a second time, touched him, and ordered, "Get up and eat, else the journey will be too long for you!" He got up, ate and drank; then strengthened by that food, he walked forty days and forty nights to the mountain of God, Horeb. (1 Kgs 19: 4-8)

THE PROPHET MALACHI

hen the Babylonian armies destroyed the capital city of Jerusalem in 587 BC, many citizens of the country, including civic and religious leaders, were taken to Babylon. The temple, which had served as the religious center since the days of Solomon, was demolished. Forty-six years after the fall of Jerusalem, the Babylonian Empire itself capitulated to Cyrus the Great who issued a decree releasing the Jews from their captivity so that they could return home to rebuild their temple.

Over the course of several generations, groups of Jewish exiles in Babylon made their way back to their homeland. Of the two to three million exiles, only a remnant of roughly fifty thousand made the nine hundred mile trek back to Palestine. Fr. John Power notes that the Jewish exiles were a tight-knit minority of the ancient twelve tribes, the promised "remnant" of the house of David. Driven by a deep religious fervor, they would no longer be called Israelites but *Jews* (the word *Yehudi* means a descendant of the people who formerly occupied Judah), through whom God's plan of salvation will be realized.[79]

Malachi Confronts Evil. Malachi is considered the last of the Old Testament prophets, but his place in the chronology of this period of restoration continues to confound scholars. Historically, he is writing around the same time as Ezra and Nehemiah or possibly before them. All three were ministering to the returning Jewish exiles, helping them rebuild the spiritual and moral foundation of their covenant relationship with God. Malachi, whose name means "my messenger," was a staunchly patriotic Jew. He was a no-nonsense prophet who roused the hearts of his people to remember the faithful God of the covenant: "Remember the law of Moses . . . all Israel" (Mal 3:22). He faced a lethargic priesthood and community in which serious religious and social abuses went unrecognized. Malachi questioned God about the evils of his day.

A New Liturgical Sacrifice. Many of the priests were unfaithful to their covenant relationship with God. They dishonored God by their flawed sacrifices and by failing to live up to their responsibilities as teachers and leaders. A pure intention and a clean heart were not expressed by the unworthy victims offered by the priests—"polluted food on my altar!" (Mal 1:7). The offering in sacrifice of a blind, sick or lame animal was forbidden in the law.

Malachi foretells the rejection of Jewish sacrifices and predicts a new liturgical sacrifice in which people of every nationality would participate (Mal 1:10, 11).[80] In place of all the holocausts and bloody sacrifices so favored in the Old Law will come a "pure offering" (Mal 1:11), more acceptable to God than all the ancient sacrifices. "For from

the rising of the sun, even to its setting, /my name is great among the nations; /And everywhere they bring sacrifice to my name, /and a pure offering; /For great is my name among the nations, /says the Lord of hosts" (Mal 1:11). The Council of Trent interpreted this as a prophecy about the Holy Sacrifice of the Mass in which Christ would become the universal "pure offering."[81]

Malachi's vision of a worldwide sacrificial worship of Yahweh is one of the high points of the messianism of the Old Testament. The nations will not only recognize the divinity of Yahweh but will offer acceptable sacrifice. Christian theology has long seen in this verse a prediction of the Eucharist, arguing in particular from the word *minhah,* which designates an offering of meal in the priestly ritual.[82] Jesus would share that meal with His apostles at the Last Supper when He instituted a new and perfect sacrifice—that of His Body and Blood—which He substituted for the sacrifices of the Old Law. The sacrifice of Our Lord's Body and Blood is now represented in the Holy Sacrifice of the Mass all over the world, day and night, "from the rising of the sun, even to its setting" (Mal 1:11).

Addressed Complaints. Malachi addressed the complaints of those who questioned whether it paid to obey God since evil seemed to triumph. Peter Kreeft describes the people as smug—as having a false sense of security which showed in their materialistic attitudes and legalistic way of thinking. Some four hundred years later, Jesus would condemn these same attitudes in the Pharisees and Sadducees. Malachi tells them that though they have neglected God, God has not neglected them. Evil will not go unpunished. The "day of the Lord" (Mal 3:23) will come, and then it will be clear that it is not "vain to serve God" (Mal 3:14).[83]

John the Baptist. Malachi foretells the coming of John the Baptist, "my messenger /to prepare the way before me; /And suddenly there will come to the temple /the Lord whom you seek." (Mal 3:1). God's silence during the next four hundred years is broken by John the Baptist's voice quoting Isaiah 40:3: "A voice of one crying out in the desert, /'Prepare the way of the Lord, /make straight his paths'" (Mt 3:3). Jesus declared John the Baptist to be the greatest of prophets who filled the role of Elijah, the one who would prepare the world for "the great and terrible day" (Mal 3:23) of the coming of the Lord. That day will dawn in the Temple of Jerusalem where the Lord will be wondrously present among His people (Mal 3:1, 2), completely burning away all uncleanness (Mal 3:3, 19), and granting the fulfillment of all His promises (Mal 3:20). Through John the Baptist we have a portrait of Jesus the Paschal Lamb, who was led like a lamb to the slaughter and gave his life as an offering for sin (Is 53: 7, 10)—the victim whose sacrifice would save the world.

The Prophet Malachi/James Tissot

"*I have no pleasure in you, says the Lord of hosts;*
neither will I accept any sacrifice from your hands,
For from the rising of the sun, even to its setting,
my name is great among the nations;
And everywhere they bring sacrifice to my name,
and a pure offering;
For great is my name among the nations,
says the Lord of hosts." (**Mal 1:10-11**)

RENEWAL OF THE COVENANT WITH EZRA

zra was one of the leading figures in the restoration of the Jewish community in Palestine after their return from the Babylonian exile. He has been called the father and founder of Judaism. The people in Babylon spoke Aramaic, and Ezra, whose name in Aramaic means "help," traced his descent from the priestly line of Aaron, the first high priest and the brother of Moses. He was also "a scribe, well-versed in the law of Moses" (Ezr 7:6).

Ezra is a Christ-symbol just as Moses was, leading the people out of captivity, Peter Kreeft writes. One reason why the Jews had to return from captivity, Kreeft says, was because in God's providential plan, Israel, not any other land, was to be the land of promise—the land of the Messiah for Christians. It was the place God had prepared for the fulfillment of His supreme promise of salvation to the world.[84]

Ezra Restores Faith. "Ezra had set his heart on the study and practice of the law of the LORD and on teaching statutes and ordinances in Israel" (Ezr 7:10). Many scholars believe that the synagogue, or "place of assembly," originated in Babylon as the place where Ezra and the scribes met with small groups of people to read to them and instruct them in the Law of Moses. When many of these people returned to Jerusalem with Ezra, they established synagogues there as well. Part of Ezra's commission from the Persian King Artaxerxes was to regulate religious matters. While Ezra's ally, Nehemiah, cup-bearer to the king and eventually governor of Judah, organized the Jews to rebuild the walls of Jerusalem, Ezra set about rebuilding the temple and the people's faith.

The Temple. The significance of the temple was that it foreshadowed Christ's salvation in the liturgy, notes Peter Kreeft, adding that the temple was to literally and physically receive the Messiah when He came (in the Eucharist). The temple foreshadows the liturgy of the Eucharist, in which God continues to be really present with His people— a temple of flesh rather than of stone. The tabernacles on our altars are not little images of the great Solomonic temple in Jerusalem; Solomon's temple is a mere image of the tabernacle that we know.[85] Ezra and Nehemiah focused their lives on restoring the temple and the worship life of the returning exiles. They displayed great courage and devotion to their faith under trying circumstances and gave their all in the service of their community and their God.

Nehemiah. Ezra and Nehemiah were faithful to their religious tradition and lived the covenant relationship with

God that they preached. When Nehemiah returned to Judah to undertake his second term as governor, he saw Jews conducting business as usual on the Sabbath. He instructed the people to stop trading on the Sabbath. The prophets Jeremiah and Ezekiel had attributed the fall of Jerusalem and the Babylonian exile to Jewish profanation of the Sabbath. Now Nehemiah tells Jewish officials that their neglect of the Sabbath might well have the same result. He ordered the city gates closed on the Sabbath (from sundown to sundown). When vendors continued to appear at the city gates, Nehemiah drove them off with threats of violence. He appointed Levites to monitor the gates so that the sacred character of the day would be maintained.[86]

Renewal of the Covenant. Afraid that his people would be drawn into pagan superstitions by marrying gentiles (for which God would punish them), Ezra put a stop to the mixed marriages and led the people in repenting and recommitting themselves to the law. Jewish exclusiveness was important because Israel had been chosen by God to be holy ("set apart"). They were called to be different from the "world" in order to accomplish God's plan of salvation.[87] Ezra organized feasts during which Nehemiah read the law of Moses to the people of Jerusalem, who wept over their failures. But Ezra urged them to rejoice in the law "for rejoicing in the LORD must be your strength!" (Neh 8:10). In his priestly role, Ezra led the people to renew the Mosaic covenant with Yahweh. The entire community took an oath to come into a new relationship with the Lord and abide by the covenant under penalty of a curse should they break their word.

New Era of Jewish Worship. The Jews were now in the Promised Land, no longer a nation ruled by a king, but a community of worshippers dedicated to Yahweh. In the temple which they built amidst extreme poverty and the scorn of their neighbors, it became the place of their religion where they centered their hopes for the future. In the temple they gathered all their sacred songs to form the hymnbook for the second temple—the Book of Psalms.[88]

The Jews experienced a profound conversion to the Lord through prayer, deeper worship and obedience to God's law. For the first time in Israel's history, many Jews were awarded the crown of martyrdom (1 and 2 Maccabees).[89] It would take the martyrdom of Jesus of Nazareth, who came along five hundred years later and who offered His Blood on a cross for the sins of humanity, to finally free the Jews and all people from the burden of sin and guilt they carried on their shoulders.

Nehemiah Looks on Ruins of Jerusalem/James Tissot

"The rest of the people . . . join with their brethren who are their princes, and with the sanction of a curse take this oath to follow the law of God which was given through Moses, the servant of God, and to observe carefully all the commandments of the L<small>ORD</small>*, our Lord, his ordinances and his statutes."* **(Neh 10:29, 30)**

THE PROPHET ISAIAH

reeminent among the Old Testament prophets was Isaiah, a citizen of Jerusalem who gave the people hope and promised that their longings would be fulfilled. A married man with two sons, he held a high position in the royal palace as adviser to King Ahaz and his successor, King Hezekiah. According to experts in the Hebrew language, Isaiah had an exquisite command of the language and a splendid literary style.[90] He was a poet who composed oracles and songs of great beauty.

Isaiah Warns Israelites. Isaiah's vision of the Lord in glory made an indelible impression on his ministry. A religious man, he was consumed with the awareness of God's holiness and majesty while at the same time distraught over the sinfulness of his people. For many years he warned the Israelites that Yahweh would punish them for abandoning the covenant. During his lifetime he witnessed the collapse of the northern kingdom of Israel. According to tradition, Isaiah was eventually tortured and murdered.

The Coming of Emmanuel. The later chapters of the Book of Isaiah, known as Deutero-Isaiah or Second Isaiah, were probably written by the prophet's disciples after his death. Composed of poems filled with hope, these prophecies looked to the end of the Babylonian captivity and the rebuilding of the holy city of Jerusalem. They promised the coming of Emmanual, born of a virgin, a divinely appointed king whose reign would bring peace. "The Lord himself will give you this sign: the virgin shall be with child, and bear a son, and shall name him Immanuel" (Is 7:14).

The Suffering Servant. According to Fr. John Power, Deutero-Isaiah sketched, more eloquently and more accurately than any other Old Testament writer, a portrait of Christ—humble, suffering, but eternally triumphant. The prophet's messianic vision reached its apex in four splendid pieces of poetry known as the Servant Songs. Sometimes the "Servant" seems to be simply the Israelite nation, as in "You are my servant . . . Israel" (Is 49:3). But in other passages the Servant is an individual, a man of sorrows. The fourth song, which is found in the Good Friday readings of the Passion of the Lord, describes the sinless Servant of God as a "man of suffering" (Is 53:3) who would voluntarily suffer for the sins of His people and save them from God's punishment. The suffering Servant, Jesus Christ, in whom this prophecy is fulfilled, is portrayed as one who achieves victory through suffering, not defeat.

For many years Israel had looked upon undeserved suffering as a punishment for sin. Second Isaiah is the first to break this biblical tradition and teach that suffering itself is not a punishment, but atonement. "[H]e was pierced for our offenses, /crushed for our sins, /Upon him was the chastisement that makes us whole" (Is 53:5). The Servant of the Lord would undergo intense suffering to pay the price for our sins; His pain brings healing and salvation to sinners.

This was a hard and almost incomprehensible message to oriental people, writes Fr. John Power, because these people knew victory only as military domination, and recognized triumph only in the pretensions of royalty.

The "Fifth Gospel". The Book of Isaiah is sometimes called the "Fifth Gospel" because, according to St. Jerome, Isaiah recounts the life of the Messiah in such a way as to make one think he is "telling the story of what has already happened rather than what is still to come."[91] Isaiah is most often quoted in the New Testament and the prophet leaves the Church a rich legacy of language and imagery which is still popular today. (The *Sanctus*, the Emmanuel prophecy, the key of David, the suffering Messiah, the winepress, the New Jerusalem, the Jesse tree motif in Christian art and Handel's *Messiah* are based on excerpts from Isaiah.)[92]

Jesus Fulfills Prophecies. The number of prophecies from Isaiah found in the New Testament which are fulfilled by Christ number over three hundred. The prophecies concerning the Suffering Servant were among the great resources which enabled people at the time of Christ to begin to understand the mystery of Christ's passion and death.

At the beginning of His Galilean ministry when Jesus travelled to Nazareth, he went into the synagogue according to custom on the Sabbath day. He was handed a scroll of the prophet Isaiah from which He read:

> The spirit of the Lord is upon me,
> because he has anointed me
> to bring glad tidings to the poor.
> He has sent me to proclaim
> liberty to captives
> and recovery of sight to the blind,
> to let the oppressed go free,
> and to proclaim a year acceptable to the Lord.
> (Lk 4:18-20)

When He handed back the scroll, everyone was looking intently at Him. He said, "Today this scripture passage is fulfilled in your hearing" (Lk 4:21).

Isaiah/James Tissot

Yet it was our infirmities that he bore,
our sufferings that he endured,
While we thought of him as stricken,
as one smitten by God and afflicted.
But he was pierced for our offenses,
crushed for our sins,
Upon him was the chastisement that makes us whole,
by his stripes we were healed.
We had all gone astray like sheep,
each following his own way;
But the Lord *laid upon him*
the guilt of us all. (**Is 53:4-6**)

THE NEW TESTAMENT

The Eucharist Established

Christ Pantocrator

ehold, the days are coming, says the Lord,
when I will conclude a new covenant with the house of
Israel and the house of Judah.
It will not be like the covenant I made with their fathers
the day I took them by the hand to lead them forth from the
land of Egypt;
for they did not stand by my covenant
and I ignored them, says the Lord.
But this is the covenant I will establish with the house of Israel
after those days, says the Lord:
I will put my laws in their minds
and I will write them upon their hearts.
I will be their God,
and they shall be my people. (Heb 8:8-11)

THE ANNUNCIATION

he world awaited the coming of the Messiah, whose arrival had been foretold in the Old Testament. The Psalmist announced that this Child would sit on the throne of David, His father. Daniel prophesied that His reign would last forever, and the great prophet Isaiah sang of the Virgin who would bring forth Immanuel, "God with us." "Therefore the Lord himself will give you this sign: the virgin shall be with child, and bear a son, and shall name him Immanuel" (Is 7:14).

Mary's Faith. The Angel Gabriel's words to Mary repeated these ancient prophecies—that she was to conceive and bear a son whom she is to name Jesus—which means "Yahweh is salvation."[1] Mary's faith was so great that it caused her cousin Elizabeth to remark, "Blessed are you who believed that what was spoken to you by the Lord would be fulfilled" (Lk 1: 45). "Upon Mary's act of faith and acceptance," Pope John Paul II says, "depended nothing less than the redemption of the world."[2]

The Virgin Birth. Troubled by the vision of the angel and filled with humility, Mary questioned how she would give birth because she was a virgin. According to one Scripture scholar, "Mary was already united to Joseph by a bond which was a true marriage, and her words would be absolutely devoid of meaning if she were not expressing her determination to remain a virgin."[3] St. Augustine enlightens us further: "Mary would not speak thus if she had not vowed her virginity to God. It is because Jewish customs demanded it, that she was betrothed to a just man, who, far from ravishing her virginity, would be its guardian."[4]

Overshadowed by the Holy Spirit. To Mary's inquiry of how this birth would take place, the angel tells her that divine favor is to be shown her through a virginal conception of the child by the divine presence residing within her—"the Holy Spirit will come upon you, and the power of the Most High will overshadow you" (Lk 1:35). Like the pillar of cloud (God's presence) that overshadowed the tabernacle in the Old Testament, through the power of the Holy Spirit, Mary would also be overshadowed. She would become the new Ark or Temple of the Spirit, the Dwelling-place of the Most High.

Mother of God. Spiritual writers see a similarity between Mary and Abraham's wife Sarah—between Mary's virginity and Sarah's age and barrenness—and the answer the angel gave to both: "Nothing will be impossible for God" (Lk 1:37). Just as Abraham believed that Sarah would bear a son and that all the families of the earth would be blessed through his seed, so did Mary believe God when He told her that she, a virgin, would give birth to a son who would be the heir of all God's promises.[5] Abraham's "yes" to God earned him the title of "father of all of us" (Rm 4:16). Mary's "yes" would earn her the title "Mother of God," her oldest and most important title, which was defined as a truth of faith to be believed by all Christians at the Council of Ephesus in 431 AD. This, the Church teaches, is the basis of Mary's greatness.[6] In the eighth century, St. John Damascene wrote that when Mary became the Mother of the Creator, she became Queen of the Universe.

Mary's "yes" led one of the early Fathers of the Church, St. Irenaeus, to say, "Just as Eve being disobedient became the cause of death for herself and for the whole human race, so Mary . . . being obedient became the *cause of salvation* for herself and for the whole human race."[7]

Mary and Eucharist. St. Thomas Aquinas taught that at the Annunciation a mystical marriage took place—a marriage between God and humanity in Mary. He says that through the Annunciation the world awaited the consent of the Virgin acting in the place of humanity. St. Thomas calls Mary the "go between" of the spiritual union that Christ progressively achieves with all those who will become one Flesh with Him in the Eucharist. Mary's consent to the Incarnation of the Word is the condition that makes our partaking of the Eucharist possible.[8]

Bread is My Flesh. The Eucharist is a mystical renewal of the incarnation of the eternal Son of God. Jesus, the Word of God, prepared the minds of His followers in the year preceding the Last Supper to accept Him as their Bread saying, "The bread that I will give is my flesh for the life of the world" (Jn 6:51). It is Mary who has provided the Flesh for our Bread—the Eucharist. As she nourished the Child of her womb, "giving milk to our Bread" (St. Augustine), so she nourishes those who are being born of her spiritually by providing them with Jesus—the Fruit of her Womb.

From Mary's flesh the sacred Body of Jesus was formed—the Body which we adore in the Blessed Sacrament and receive in Holy Communion. As the divine Word became flesh through the overshadowing of the Holy Spirit, so the same divine Word is really and substantially present when the words of consecration are said during Mass through the power of the Holy Spirit. "It is clear that the Virgin gave birth to Christ beyond the order of nature," wrote St. Thomas Aquinas, "and that which we consecrate is the Body born from the Virgin."[9]

The Annunciation/Carl Bloch

"Hail favored one! The Lord is with you." But she was greatly troubled at what was said and pondered what sort of greeting this might be. Then the angel said to her, "Do not be afraid, Mary, for you have found favor with God. Behold, you will conceive in your womb and bear a son, and you shall name him Jesus. He will be great and will be called Son of the Most High, and the Lord God will give him the throne of David his father, and he will rule over the house of Jacob forever, and of his kingdom there will be no end." **(Lk 1:28-33)**

THE SAVIOR IS BORN

ver since the fall of Adam and Eve, people looked up to God with "fear and trembling." When God entered the world as a child in a manger, the faithful were drawn to His love. The sign given to Mary in confirmation of the angel's announcement to her is the pregnancy of her elderly cousin, Elizabeth. If a woman past the childbearing age could become pregnant, why, the angel implied, should there be doubt about Mary's pregnancy, for "nothing will be impossible for God" (Lk 1:37). She was the person God chose to fulfill the prophecies concerning the promised Messiah, the one who would save His people. Jesus is God's gift for the salvation of the world.

Mary's Yes. Then Mary freely and humbly agreed to be the Mother of God, saying, "Behold, I am the handmaid of the Lord. May it be done to me according to your word" (Lk 1:38). With those words, theologian Warren Carroll says "the Incarnation was accomplished." For the next nine months Mary Immaculate carried God in her womb. During that time she visited her cousin Elizabeth who welcomed her as "the mother of my Lord" (Lk 1:43) and John the Baptist in Elizabeth's womb "leaped for joy" (Lk 1:44). It is good to remember, Carroll adds, that the drama of the Incarnation began with the prayer of Zechariah.[10] In God's plan it was his child, John the Baptist, whose mission it was to "prepare a people fit for the Lord" (Lk 1:17).

Bethlehem. Luke the Evangelist dates the birth of our Savior to the time of a census of the Roman Empire ordered by the Emperor Caesar Augustus. Joseph and Mary traveled south from their hometown of Nazareth in Galilee to Bethlehem in Judea, the birthplace of King David. As Mary's firstborn son, Jesus is heir to David's throne. The Early Church attached considerable importance to Jesus' descent from David but, more significantly, Bethlehem was the expected birthplace of the Messiah, according to the prophet Micah. "But, you Bethlehem-Ephrathah, /too small to be among the clans of Judah, /from you shall come forth for me /one who is to be ruler in Israel" (Mi 5:1).

"House of Bread." The creator and Savior of the world was born in a cave-stable. How fitting that in Bethlehem, a town whose name means "house of bread," Jesus, the Bread of Life, was placed in a manger. Scripture scholar Robert Karris writes that Jesus did not come to His people like a stranger from a foreign land who was passing through. He takes up permanent residence among them. "Jesus, who lies in a feeding trough, is food for the world."[11]

Luke related the Eucharist to Jesus' birth, writes Biblical scholar Fr. Eugene LaVerdiere. When the city of David denied Him hospitality, Mary, the servant of the Lord, laid Him in a manger, thereby offering Him as nourishment for the flock (Lk 2:7). The story of Jesus' birth pointed to the end of Jesus' life, when the city of David again rejected Jesus. The One who was denied hospitality at birth offered hospitality at death—giving Himself as nourishment in the Last Supper.[12]

Historical Jesus. The Good News of the Incarnation was given to us through the gospels which attest to the historical reality of Christ's birth, teaching, miracles, death and resurrection. All the Evangelists as well as Peter and Paul and a host of others introduce us—through precious eye-witness accounts—to the living, breathing, loving, suffering Jesus Christ. St. John writes: "The Word became flesh and made his dwelling among us, and we saw his glory, the glory as of the Father's only Son, full of grace and truth" (Jn 1:14). Christ came as a whole person who, in effect, "pitched His tent among us," a reference to the Tent of Meeting that was the place of God's presence in the Old Testament. The incarnate Word is the new mode of God's presence among His people; the "glory" which once filled the tabernacle and the temple is now centered in the Eucharist.

Independent Historical Data. The Jewish historian, Flavius Josephus, was also writing in the first century AD. In *The Antiquity of the Jews* he corroborates many of the points in the gospel accounts about the life of Christ.

> Now about this time arises Jesus, a wise man, if indeed he should be called a man. For he was a doer of marvelous deeds, a teacher of men who receive the truth with pleasure; and he won over to himself many Jews and many also of the Greek (nation). He was the Christ. And when, on the indictment of the principal men among us, Pilate had sentenced him to the cross, those who had loved (or perhaps rather "been content with") him at the first did not cease; for he appeared to them on the third day alive again, the divine prophets having (fore)told these and ten thousand other wonderful things concerning him. And even now the tribe of Christians, named after him, is not extinct.[13]

Nativity Today. This "doer of marvelous deeds" who was born in Bethlehem, who lived and walked in the Judean hills, who dined with sinners and fed hungry people with real bread and His healing love, is with us two thousand years later, feeding us with His presence in the Sacrament of the Eucharist. We are like the shepherds and the magi who go to the manger—the Mass—where Christ is born anew on our altars. There we celebrate the nativity of the Word—and our spiritual rebirth through Him. Thus we sing at the Christmas liturgy: "Today a new day dawns, the day of our redemption, prepared by God from ages past, the beginning of our never ending gladness."[14]

Nativity/Federico Barocci

Now there were shepherds in that region living in the fields and keeping the night watch over their flock. The angel of the Lord appeared to them and the glory of the Lord shone around them, and they were struck with great fear. The angel said to them, "Do not be afraid; for behold, I proclaim to you good news of great joy that will be for all people. For today in the city of David a savior has been born for you who is Messiah and Lord. And this will be a sign for you: you will find an infant wrapped in swaddling clothes and lying in a manger." And suddenly there was a multitude of the heavenly host with the angel, praising God and saying: "Glory to God in the highest and on earth peace to those on whom his favor rests." (Lk 2:8-14)

PRESENTATION OF JESUS IN THE TEMPLE

ver since God had spared the life of the Israelites when He slew the firstborn of the Egyptians, the custom arose of presenting the firstborn male child to God to perpetuate the memory of the night in which Yahweh "killed every firstborn in the land of Egypt, every firstborn of man and of beast" (Ex 13:15). From then on every firstborn male child belonged to the Lord.

In patriarchal societies the firstborn male child was the head of a family and exercised a priestly responsibility of offering sacrifice and leading the family in worship. Even when the priestly tribe of Levi was given this office, firstborn sons continued to be consecrated to God and had to be bought back at a set price.

The Firstborn. Obedient to the demands of this Jewish religious custom, Mary and Joseph dutifully brought their firstborn son to the temple. They came for the purification of Mary, forty days after His birth. According to Mosaic Law, a woman who gave birth to a male was considered unclean and unable to worship for forty days. She was required to offer a year-old lamb as a burnt offering and a turtledove as an expiation of sin. Mary, who could not afford a lamb, offered two young pigeons or doves, the gift of the poor. Then she and Joseph presented Jesus in the temple and consecrated Him to God.

Jesuit theologian Hans Urs von Balthasar suggests that Mary's sacrificial offering is reminiscent of Hannah, the mother of Samuel in the Old Testament, who returned to God the son she asked for and received from the Lord (1 Sm 1: 24-28). Hannah brought him to the temple to express her gratitude and gave him back to God.[15]

Simeon. The Holy Spirit promised Simeon, a faithful elderly prophet from Jerusalem, that he would not die before seeing the Messiah. "This man was righteous and devout, awaiting the consolation of Israel, and the holy Spirit was upon him" (Lk 2:25). Simeon recognized Jesus as the long-awaited Messiah and embraced Him in the Temple court where he expressed his joy in a canticle of thanksgiving, the *Nunc Dimittis*: "Now, Master, you may let your servant go /in peace, according to your word, /for my eyes have seen your salvation, /which you prepared in sight of all the peoples, a light for revelation to the Gentiles, /and glory for your people Israel" (Lk 2:29-33).

A Sign of Contradiction. Anna, a faithful elderly widow and prophetess, who prayed daily in the Temple, also "gave thanks to God and spoke about the child to all who were awaiting the redemption of Jerusalem" (Lk 2:38). Simeon foretold of the rejection and passion of Jesus and that Mary's soul would be pierced by a sword. "Behold, this child is destined for the fall and rise of many in Israel," he said to Mary and Joseph, "and to be a sign that will be contradicted (and you yourself a sword will pierce) so that the thoughts of many hearts may be revealed" (Lk 2:34, 35). Simeon's prophecy associates the sorrows of Mary with the suffering which her Son is to undergo. Scripture scholar Fr. Ferdinand Prat in his *Life of Christ* writes that Mary's sorrows will be principally caused by the sufferings of Jesus, while the most excruciating torment of Jesus will be to see His Mother's anguish at the foot of the Cross.[16]

Pope John Paul II. Simeon's words prefigure the rejection of Jesus, writes Pope John Paul II. This rejection, he says, will reach its culmination on Calvary. "'Standing by the cross of Jesus' (Jn 19:25), Mary shares in the gift which the Son gives of himself: she offers Jesus, gives him over, and begets him to the end for our sake." The Holy Father adds further that "the 'yes' spoken on the day of the Annunciation reaches full maturity on the day of the Cross, when the time comes for Mary to receive and beget as her children all those who become disciples, pouring out upon them the saving love of her Son."[17]

Mary's Sacrificial Offering. Mary symbolically offered her firstborn Son to God in the temple, a sacrifice which would lead them *both* to the Cross, He to die and she to witness His redemptive act by the sword that pierced her heart. Mary is intimately united with Jesus in His work of salvation. Of this union, Vatican II's *Dogmatic Constitution on the Church* says: "thus the Blessed Virgin advanced in her pilgrimage of faith, and faithfully persevered in her union with her Son unto the cross. [There] she stood, in keeping with the divine plan and enduring with her only-begotten Son the intensity of his suffering. She associated herself with His sacrifice in her mother's heart, and lovingly consented to the immolation of this victim which was born of her."[18]

Sacrifice of the Mass. It is this sacrificial act of Christ which is renewed today in the Mass, where Mary is present as the "Mother of the Eucharist." In the entrance chant to the Mass for the Feast of the Purification we sing, "We welcome your love, O God, in the midst of your temple." The same Child is present at Mass who was blessed by Simeon and presented by the Blessed Mother in the Temple to the Eternal Father. Jesus, our Paschal Lamb, is offered to the Father for our salvation to be immolated on the altar of the Cross. At every Mass, Mary, inseparable from her Son, unites her heart with her offering, saying, "I pray that my sacrifice and my Son's may be acceptable to You." *And thine own soul a sword shall pierce.* Her sacrifice—and ours—is one with His.

The Presentation in the Temple/Rembrandt

"Now, Master, you may let your servant go
in peace, according to your word,
for my eyes have seen your salvation,
which you prepared in sight of all the peoples,
a light for revelation to the Gentiles,
and glory for your people Israel." **(Lk 2:29-32)**

THE BAPTISM OF JESUS

hen John the Baptist sent word to Jesus asking if He was "the one who is to come" (Lk 7:19), Jesus responded by revealing His understanding of their relationship. Jesus identified John as His precursor, saying, "Behold, I am sending my messenger ahead of you, he will prepare your way before you" (Lk 7:27). John is the messenger foretold by Isaiah (Is 40:3) and whom the prophet Malachi identified as Elijah (Mal 3:23). Then Jesus commended John to the crowds: "I tell you, among those born of women, no one is greater than John; yet the least in the kingdom of God is greater than he" (Lk 7:28). Theologian Jean Cardinal Danielou identifies John as "the last and the greatest of the prophets of the old covenant, and the herald of the new."[19]

John Prepares the Way. John was "A voice of one crying out in the desert: 'Prepare the way of the Lord, make straight his paths. . .'" (Lk 3:4). He summoned people to repentance, to prepare for the judgment of God which he said was like an axe laid at the root of a tree which will be cut down if it does not produce good fruit (Lk 3:9). His words had a sense of urgency and were heightened by his dress, which recalled the prophet Elijah, and by the asceticism of his life. Some who heard him speak wondered whether he was not the Messiah, to which John replied that he was unworthy to even carry Jesus' sandals.

Rite of Baptism. The rite of Baptism was a symbol of purification and rebirth. It was prefigured in the waters of the Deluge, which purified and renewed the world; in the waters of the Red Sea which "gave birth" to the Chosen People by saving them from the Egyptians; in the waters of the Jordan which the Israelites crossed in order to enter the Promised Land.

Jesus Begins Public Life. Jesus was still relatively unknown when He presented Himself among the penitents at the Jordan river to be baptized by John. By submitting to John's baptism, Jesus identified Himself with the people of Israel. John knew that the baptism he was administering was symbolic, expressing the repentance of the sinner, but effecting of itself no interior sacramental change. Jesus, he said, would baptize with fire and the Holy Spirit.

Father Acknowledges Son. When He came out of the water, Jesus "saw the heavens being torn open and the Spirit, like a dove, descending upon him. And a voice came from the heavens, 'You are my beloved Son; with you I am well pleased'" (Mk 1:10). With those words, God the Father acknowledged His Son in public for the first time and confirmed His mission of salvation.

Baptism Unto Death. Those who were baptized became God's own—His favored sons and daughters. Christ's faithful saw how He let the Spirit of His baptism lead Him to drink the cup of suffering at the end of His life. They understood that Jesus looked upon His impending death as a second "baptism" which His disciples would share. "Can you drink the cup that I drink or be baptized with the baptism with which I am baptized?" (Mk 10:38). Jesus spoke of His crucifixion and death as a "baptism" for the salvation of the human race.

Early Christians. It is our privilege as Christians to be baptized with Jesus "into His death" so that we can rise with Him to new life. The Early Christians were stripped of their clothes, anointed with oil, and then plunged three times into the baptismal pool, an action which represented an immersion into Christ's death and burial. When they came out of the purifying waters they were clothed in a white robe, shining with the radiance of grace, and, according to St. Cyril of Jerusalem, surrounded by choirs of angels!

Nuptial Mystery. The Early Fathers viewed the process of the sacramental initiation in the Church as a deepening of the nuptial mystery—the wedding of Christ with His beloved Church. Baptism purifies and incorporates the soul into the Church, the Bride of Christ. Christ, the Bridegroom, now invites His Bride to the wedding feast, which is the Eucharist. For each of us who are baptized, a spousal fidelity must be maintained in the living out of our baptismal commitment. It is the Eucharist that provides us with the daily strength for that living.

In a homily on the Feast of the Lord's Baptism, Fr. Lawrence Hennessey, Dean of the Ecclesiastical Faculty at St. Mary of the Lake Seminary, Mundelein, IL, said that Baptism and the Eucharist are the Savior's way of making us part of His living Body in the world—the Body we call the Church. Says Father, "'Marked with the sign of faith' we are drawn into God's own unending life and given a share of God's own Spirit-life. The Holy Spirit is the source of all gifts and talents found in our lives which are given to us for the sake of others. To share these gifts and talents in our everyday life is our path to holiness. We must beg God for the grace to *live* our Baptismal and Eucharistic commitment so that He can also say to us, 'Here is my servant whom I uphold, /my chosen one with whom I am pleased, / Upon whom I have put my spirit'" (Is 42:1).[20]

The Baptism of Jesus/Carl Bloch

It happened in those days that Jesus came from Nazareth of Galilee and was baptized in the Jordan by John. On coming up out of the water he saw the heavens being torn open and the Spirit, like a dove, descending upon him. And a voice came from the heavens, "You are my beloved Son; with you I am well pleased." **(Mk 1:9-11)**

THE WEDDING FEAST OF CANA

Sacred Scripture often compared the relationship between God and His people to that of a bridegroom and his bride. Jesuit Biblical scholar Fr. Ignace de la Potterie instructs that from the first prophets up to the Book of Revelation, God seeks to establish a covenant with His people, and this covenant is described under the image of marriage. God is the Groom and Israel the Bride—though many times unfaithful. What is said in the Old Testament between the relation of Yahweh and Israel is found again in the New Testament in the relationship between Christ and His Church. The wedding at Cana thus signifies fundamentally the "beginning" of the messianic (Spirit-anointed) manifestation of Jesus.[21]

A Country Wedding. Because Jesus came to unite Himself to His people in a covenant relationship like marriage, it was fitting that He should begin His public ministry by attending a wedding. Cana was a small town nestled on a gentle slope extending eastward toward the Sea of Galilee where the apostle Nathaniel lived. It was about five miles from Mary's home in Nazareth and where Jesus passed through enroute to Capernaum. Jesus and His mother were invited to a wedding reception in Cana, a simple country wedding (which in those times lasted eight days!) comprised of ordinary folk with whom Jesus shared a meal at this festive banquet. John the Evangelist portrays this episode as the beginning of His public ministry, and the first of many encounters in which Jesus would dine with people.

Jesus' "Hour". At the Wedding Feast of Cana, Jesus performed the first of His miraculous signs when His mother called her Son's attention to the dwindling supply of wine. "They have no wine" (Jn 2:3) she said, and Jesus responded, "Woman, how does your concern affect me? My hour has not yet come" (Jn 2:4).

The hour to which Jesus refers relates to His future glory—His crucifixion, resurrection and ascension. Jesus' response meant the appointed time for beginning His redemptive act was not yet at hand. His mother was asking for a miracle; He was implying that a miracle worked as a sign of His divinity would be the beginning of His death. The moment He showed Himself before people as the Son of God, He would draw down upon Himself their hatred, for evil can tolerate mediocrity, but not supreme goodness. The miracle she was asking for would be unmistakably related to His act of redemption.[22]

"Woman." It was not the custom to address one's own mother as "woman," and by doing so, Jesus is signifying something special. "It is from this moment that Jesus begins to manifest Himself as Messiah" writes Father de la Potterie, "and by that very fact the relationship between Him and Mary is no longer the simple relationship of a son to his mother. Jesus now takes upon Himself a messianic role and in addressing His mother as 'Woman,' He involves her in His mission which is beginning." This will add a new dimension to their relationship, one which is "beyond the maternal and familial."[23]

The next time Jesus would address His mother as "Woman" would be from the Cross where the new covenant, prefigured at Cana, will be sealed and where His mother again will be at His side. At Cana, the prophecy of Simeon to Mary in the Temple was confirmed—from now on, whatever involved her Son would involve His mother. Mary would no longer just be the mother of Jesus, but the mother of all whom the Savior would redeem.

Cana Points to Eucharist. All true prophecies were accompanied by signs. The word of Elijah had brought down fire from heaven (1 Kgs 18:38) and the word of Moses changed water into blood (Ex 7:14-24). It was expected that the Messiah would work similar deeds of power. At Cana Jesus changed some 150 gallons of water in six great stone jars into the finest wine, a sign which signaled His divinity and from the sheer abundance of the wine, the abundance of His love for us in the Eucharist.

"The primary focus of the wedding feast of Cana is on the new era or covenant brought by Jesus," writes Father LaVerdiere. "A number of elements, beginning with the setting—a wedding feast—and the symbol of wine, but especially the proximity to the Jewish feast of Passover and the reference to Jesus' 'hour,' evoke the Eucharist as a symbol of the new era."[24]

Eucharist: Our Banquet. Jesus, Himself, is the greatest of God's signs. In laying down His life for us on Calvary, Jesus gave us a taste of His infinite love—His own Body and Blood, sealed in the gift of the Eucharist. The water that He changed into wine at Cana becomes transformed into the *best* wine for us—the Blood-Wine of Communion to sustain and nourish us on our faith journey. At Mass we are given a foretaste of the wedding feast in the Father's kingdom, where we will be given to drink of the new wine of the Blood of Christ, served by Jesus Himself, our Messianic Bridegroom.

The Wedding at Cana/Carl Bloch

Now there were six stone water jars there for Jewish ceremonial washings, each holding twenty to thirty gallons. Jesus told them, "Fill the jars with water." So they filled them to the brim. Then he told them, "Draw some out now and take it to the headwaiter." So they took it. And when the headwaiter tasted the water that had become wine, without knowing where it came from (although the servers who had drawn the water knew), the headwaiter called the bridegroom and said to him, "Everyone serves good wine first, and then when people have drunk freely, an inferior one; but you have kept the good wine until now." (Jn 2:6-10)

BANQUET AT THE HOME OF LEVI

he Gospel of Luke recounts the many meals Jesus shared with people. They each reflected in different ways the meaning of Emmanuel, God with us—the gift and privilege of being His disciples. Jesus used meals as an opportunity just to be with people in order to listen to them and love them, as well as to teach them about forgiveness, to heal, to call sinners to conversion and repentance, to offer reconciliation and salvation, and to reveal His messianic identity. These meals point to the covenant meal of the Eucharist as Jesus' ultimate gift through which He unites His beloved faithful to Himself and to one another.

A Sign of the Messiah. The solemn meal was a sign of the Messiah who would come "eating and drinking." "For John the Baptist came neither eating food nor drinking wine, and you said, 'He is possessed by a demon.' The Son of Man came eating and drinking, and you said, 'Look, he is a glutton and a drunkard, a friend of tax collectors and sinners.'" (Lk 7:33, 34). Sharing a meal with someone represented mutual acceptance. "By eating with outcasts, Jesus is saying in dramatic form that God shares life with them," writes Robert Karris. "Jesus' apostasy is eating with tax collectors and sinners—social and religious outcasts, people regarded as apostates by the standards of religious leaders."[25] For this He was vilified.

Levi the Tax Collector. At the very beginning of His public ministry, Jesus was walking along the shoreline of the Sea of Galilee at Capernaum when He came upon Levi, a tax collector, who worked for the Roman government. Levi was a common Jewish name, after the founder of one of the twelve tribes of Israel. Levi and others like him practiced extortion, demanding more money from people than the actual percentage the government had levied. People resented their abuse and hated them for it.[26]

Jesus Calls Levi. When Jesus saw him He said, "Follow me" (Lk 5:27), an invitation to intimate love and friendship. Levi immediately left everything behind and hosted a great reception for Jesus, which his wealth allowed. "Leaving everything behind," writes Fr. LaVerdiere, "meant leaving his way of life as a tax collector along with the concerns and preoccupations it involved—all this as a necessary prerequisite for spiritual conversion." To dine with people, Father LaVerdiere adds, especially in their homes, was to show solidarity with them, a solidarity expressed and confirmed in the breaking of the bread. It is the kind of unity that brings healing, a metaphor Jesus used to justify dining with tax collectors and those referred to by the Pharisees as sinners.[27] "Those who are healthy do not need a physician, but the sick do. I have not come to call the righteous to repentance but sinners" (Lk 5:31, 32). The banquet at the home of Levi points to the Eucharist as a call to conversion; to accept—and give—forgiveness.

Witness of Reconciliation. The Pharisees did not dine with Jesus at Levi's dinner and persisted in their attitude of superiority and self-righteousness, refusing to recognize their own need of repentance. Yet leading Pharisees continued to ask Jesus to dinner. When Simon the Pharisee hosted Jesus in his house, Simon's hardness of heart is contrasted with the sinful woman who enters the dinner and wipes the feet of Jesus with her tears. She had probably experienced a spiritual conversion through Jesus and sought Him out in order to thank Him. Grateful that Jesus has forgiven her sins, "she has shown great love" (Lk 7:47). She had accepted Jesus' call, repented and been forgiven, while the host stood aloof and questioned whether Jesus was indeed a prophet. In a sense the Gospel points to all people (in the person of the Pharisee) whom God wants to bless with faith and forgiveness, but who are not open to His love.

Eucharist and the Poor. During another dinner at the home of a Pharisee, Jesus used the occasion to tell a parable about the need for humility, entreating His listeners to refrain from choosing places of honor at the table. Then He urged the host to make up a guest list and invite to his dinner table not friends, brothers and sisters and wealthy neighbors, but "the poor, the crippled, the lame, the blind" (Lk 14:13). These were the people for whom Jesus preached the gospel. "At this meal even the poorest and the most helpless would have an honored place at table in the kingdom of God," Father LaVerdiere writes. The message here is that "The church must be a source of hope for all, even the least of human beings, and the Eucharist must be a visible expression and a proclamation of that hope."[28] Thus would Jesus fulfill His Eucharistic mission—to bring the gospel to the poor, to proclaim liberty to captives, to bring sight to the blind and to free the oppressed, in fulfillment of the prophecy of Isaiah.

Eucharist: the Great Banquet. St. John the Evangelist compared the kingdom to a wedding feast or a great banquet. "Blessed are those who have been called to the wedding feast of the Lamb" (Rev 19:9). This is the great feast of the blessed in the kingdom of God through which salvation history will reach its consummation.

Jesus' meals with sinners were His way of announcing God's salvation to people here and now, and not only in the future. Jesus shows us how our Father and Creator wants the whole of creation to participate in the great banquet of life, "to which all are equally invited by God."[29] We need not worry what we will eat, or drink or wear, for "your heavenly Father knows that you need them all" (Mt 6:32).

The Feast in the House of Levi/Veronese

After this he went out and saw a tax collector named Levi sitting at the customs post. He said to him, "Follow me." And leaving everything behind, he got up and followed him. Then Levi gave a great banquet for him in his house, and a large crowd of tax collectors and others were at table with them. The Pharisees and their scribes complained to his disciples, saying, "Why do you eat and drink with tax collectors and sinners?" Jesus said to them in reply, "Those who are healthy do not need a physician, but the sick do. I have not come to call the righteous to repentance but sinners." (**Lk 5:27-32**)

MULTIPLICATION OF THE LOAVES & FISHES

As a result of His teaching and healing, enormous crowds were pressing upon Jesus and the disciples. This prompted Jesus to take the Twelve away by boat to a quiet spot known today as Tabgha, a town on the edge of the Sea of Galilee. There they could rest from their labors. Mark notes that they had been so busy they couldn't even eat in peace. Passover was drawing near. Caravans, en route to celebrate the great feast in Jerusalem, were lining up around the lake.

Jesus Tends His Flock. The crowds took note of where Jesus was headed and followed on foot. Jesus was touched with compassion because "they were like sheep without a shepherd" (Mk 6:34). Sheep are weak and defenseless animals who are known to stand still while an attacking wolf devours them. They are paralyzed by fear which causes their death. By comparing the people to sheep, the Lord was characterizing them as defenseless, needy, and unable to hide their pain or their hunger. These are the people to whom the Lord reaches out, to share Himself, His love, His time, His heart.[30] Jesus "healed those who needed to be cured" (Lk 9:11), then He spoke to them about the kingdom of God. There were about five thousand people who followed Jesus to the mountainside.[31]

Mission of Apostles. It was twilight and time to eat. In Luke's account, the apostles ask Jesus to dismiss the crowds so they could tend to their own needs. Instead, Jesus encourages them to "Give them some food yourselves" (Lk 9:13). Father LaVerdiere sees this as an encouragement for them to nourish the crowds, not just in word but in deed, with the bread Jesus gave them. As the Church of the Twelve, their mission was to serve at the banquet of the kingdom of God.[32]

Buy Bread for Them? Even though Jesus knew what He would do, in John's Gospel He questioned Philip about buying bread for them. Philip estimates that the wages of a laborer working six days a week for eight months would not suffice to procure a little for each of the many gathered there! Jesus asked the crowd to recline in groups of fifty or a hundred on the grassy slopes.

Bread Broken by Jesus. The words that Luke uses in reference to the ritual of Jesus "taking," "looking up to heaven," "blessing," "breaking," and "giving" are liturgical words intended to remind us of the Last Supper when Jesus would "take, bless, break and give" Himself to us in the Eucharist. From the loaves and fishes, each received not the "little [bit]" (Jn 6:7) envisaged by Philip, but a full meal, so that they filled up twelve wicker baskets with leftover fragments—a transparent allusion to the Twelve who formed the church which draws its nourishment from the bread broken by Jesus. Their mission was to continue proclaiming the gospel as well as Jesus' offer of hospitality at the table of the kingdom of God, a practice centered around the Eucharist, the sacramental meal to which all are invited.[33]

Jesus Feeds His People. The Hebrews once murmured, "Can God spread a table in the desert?" (Ps 78:19). The multiplication of the loaves and fishes recalls God's feeding of His people in the wilderness (manna) and Elisha's feeding of one hundred men with twenty barley loaves at which there were some leftovers (2 Kgs 4:42-44).

Jesus' Intention. Jesus' intention was to show people the superabundance which God wants to heap upon those who rely on Him. Above all, as St. John's gospel explains, His intention was to urge them to seek a food that does not perish. This food was symbolized by the manna in the wilderness. Jesus uses His gift of material bread to direct our attention to one who will give *Himself* as food: "Whoever eats my flesh and drinks my blood has eternal life, and I will raise him on the last day. For my flesh is true food, and my blood is true drink. Whoever eats my flesh and drinks my blood remains in me and I in him" (Jn 6:54-56). Christians see in the bread they break both ordinary food and heavenly food; they recognize in it the Bread which is itself alive and gives life to them.[34]

Jesus' Challenge. Like the great banquet at the house of Levi and the dinner in the home of Simon the Pharisee, the breaking of the bread shows Jesus challenging the disciples. He speaks to their missionary responsibility as the church of the Twelve. Jesus' admonition to "give them some food yourselves" applies to the Church celebrating Eucharist today, just as it did to the Church in Luke's time. The Eucharist is a call to conversion, *metanoia.* The Eucharist requires a loving welcome for all who embark on the way of metanoia in the community of the Twelve: it is an event of reconciliation.[35]

God Fills Us. The Eucharist *is* the Presence of God. It is Jesus who comes into the desert of our lives and fills us to overflowing with His unconditional, bountiful love in the Eucharist. Jesus had given the crowds at Tabgha the gift of His compassionate loving food, satisfying their needs. He shared a meal with them. He spent time with them. He spent Himself.[36] They were beginning to see that their Lord was powerfully present in the "breaking of the bread" (Lk 24:35), a term that would come to signify Jesus' sacramental presence. Jesus was preparing them to acknowledge *Him* as their Living Bread.

The Feeding of the Five Thousand/Hendrik de Clerck

Then [Jesus] said to his disciples, "Have them sit down in groups of [about] fifty." They did so and made them all sit down. Then taking the five loaves and the two fish, and looking up to heaven, he said the blessing over them, broke them, and gave them to the disciples to set before the crowd. They all ate and were satisfied. And when the leftover fragments were picked up, they filled twelve wicker baskets. (Lk 9:14-17)

BREAD OF LIFE

fter ministering to the multitudes at Tabgha, Jesus went to Capernaum where the crowds descended on Him the next day. What disappointment and rejection Jesus must have experienced when He read their hearts and saw that they were not looking for Him because of who He was, but because of what He could give them—free food.[37]

Bread of Eternal Life. Reproaching them with the truth, Jesus admonishes them to look instead for food that lasts, the eternal Food that He would give them. Biblical scholar Fr. Raymond Brown writes that Jesus did not come simply to satisfy earthly hunger but to give a bread that would nourish people for eternal life. Jesus points out that His revelation constitutes teaching by God, so that one must believe in the Son to have eternal life. And to have eternal life one must feed on His flesh and blood, language which evokes the Eucharist. "The bread that I will give is my flesh for the life of the world" (Jn 6:51) might well be St. John's Eucharistic formula comparable to "This is my body, which will be given for you" (Lk 22:19; 1 Cor 11:24). This Bread of Life discourse reveals that Jesus feeds His followers both through His revelation and His Eucharistic flesh.[38]

Jesus Asks For Faith. The crowds press Jesus for details as to how they may obtain this Food. "This is the work of God, that you believe in the one he sent" (Jn 6:29). The promised Food is theirs on one condition: that they have faith in Him. Unconvinced, they want a sign by which He could prove His mission as Moses did, who fed the people with manna in the desert. Jesus' miraculous feeding of the multitudes the day before was not sign enough! After pointing out the superiority of the bread which He is about to give them over the manna given to their ancestors, Christ says: "And the bread that I will give is my flesh for the life of the world" (Jn 6:51). According to Viennese Liturgist and Professor of Sacramental Theology Fr. Johannes Emminghaus, in the Aramaic language which Jesus spoke there is no equivalent of the verb "to be." So that when Jesus said, "I am the bread of life," He really said, "I—the bread of life."[39] Jesus identifies *Himself* as the Bread of Life.

Living **Bread.** While He was speaking, the Jews began to murmur among themselves. They challenged His claim to divinity since they knew His mother and father— "Is this not Jesus, the son of Joseph?" (Jn 6:42). Jesus understands and reiterates that His authority comes from His Father in heaven who gave Him power to raise people to life on the last day. He reminds them that the people who ate the manna in the desert died. *That* bread did not have the power that He was talking about. The *Living* Bread which Jesus was offering would give them freedom from death; it would give them eternal life.

True Food and Drink. Whenever anyone correctly understood what Jesus said, but found fault with it, He repeated His words. Jesus reiterated "to eat My flesh and drink My blood" five times.[40] It is impossible any longer to mistake the meaning of those words. To put an end to their doubt Jesus says that the flesh of the Son of Man is a true food, comparable to the manna with which the Israelites nourished themselves in the desert, and that His blood is a true drink, as were the miraculous waters of Horeb.

Jesus Speaks Literally. If Christ wished to be understood figuratively, theologian Fr. John O'Brien suggests that it would have been His duty not only as the Son of God, but even as an honest Teacher, to correct the Jews and say to them: "You misunderstand me. You think that I am referring to my flesh, whereas I am speaking figuratively and am referring only to a symbol."[41]

An instance in which Jesus did speak figuratively happened after a discourse with the Pharisees. Jesus and His disciples departed by boat and, in their haste, the disciples had forgotten to bring bread. Jesus said to them, "Look out, and beware of the leaven of the Pharisees and Sadducees" (Mt 16:6). The disciples thought at first that Jesus meant the leaven of the Pharisees' bread. He gently rebuked them. He was not referring to bread—by "leaven" He meant the corrupting influence of the teaching of the Pharisees and Sadducees.

But at Capernaum, Jesus makes it quite clear that His words are literal and not figurative. He emphasizes what He is saying by using the double expletive, "Amen, amen," indicating that the words which follow are especially important. Jesus exhausts all the possibility of human language in making His meaning unmistakably clear.[42]

Eucharist Divides Followers. Jesus was giving His very Self to His followers, more intimately than a mother gives life to a child at her breast. Yet He was crucified. As Archbishop Fulton Sheen points out, Jesus asked a faith that most people did not have. When He multiplied the loaves and fishes, the crowds followed Him because they were interested in wonders and in security. They wanted Him to become a king but Our Lord would have no kingship based on the "economics of plenty." He offered Himself to the intellectual and religious leaders, says Archbishop Sheen, but they only wanted a meek, gentle reformer who would not upset their authority.

Christ lost both the chaff and the wheat when He spoke of Himself as the Bread of Life. The announcement of the Eucharist "cracked His followers wide open and divided them," says the Archbishop, each person deciding for himself whether he would accept all of Christ's message or only parts of it.[43]

Seek Me Because Ye Eat from the Loaves/James Tissot

"Amen, amen, I say to you, whoever believes has eternal life. I am the bread of life. Your ancestors ate the manna in the desert, but they died; this is the bread that comes down from heaven so that one may eat it and not die. I am the living bread that came down from heaven; whoever eats this bread will live forever; and the bread that I will give is my flesh for the life of the world." **(Jn 6:47-52)**

THE *LIVING* BREAD

henever anyone misunderstood Christ, He corrected them, as when Nicodemus thought "born again" meant re-entering his mother's womb. But now, in the synagogue at Capernaum when Jesus promised that He was going to give His disciples His own flesh and blood as their food and drink, Jesus was speaking *literally*. "Amen, amen, I say to you, unless you eat the flesh of the Son of Man and drink his blood, you do not have life within you. Whoever eats my flesh and drinks my blood has eternal life, and I will raise him on the last day. For my flesh is true food, and my blood is true drink" (Jn 6:53-55). He states He is the Bread of Life twelve times, and repeats six times that His flesh and blood are to be consumed.

Figurative Meaning. His listeners wanted to believe that He was speaking metaphorically—that eating His flesh and drinking His blood merely meant believing in Him. But, as Father O'Brien explains, the phrase "to eat the flesh and drink the blood," when used figuratively among the Jews, as among the Arabs of today, meant to inflict upon a person some serious injury, especially by calumny or false accusation. To interpret the phrase figuratively would make our Lord promise life everlasting to someone for slandering him, which would reduce the whole passage to utter nonsense. Unless the words of Christ are taken at their face value, they become meaningless. Worse than that, Christ would be an archdeceiver![44]

Purposeful Words. Some thought Jesus was demanding cannibalism, for the word He used for "eat" (*phagein*) was very blunt. The noun *phagos* derived from this verb means "glutton." After the mention of drinking His blood, Jesus used a different verb. While *phagein* means "to eat," *trogein* means "to gnaw or crunch." They will not eat as their ancestors did, they will gnaw and crunch on His flesh, the true bread. There is no mistake here. Jesus spoke purposefully. The evangelist portrays Jesus as re-empasizing his prior statement about eating His flesh (*phagein*). But then, so that there can be no mistake about His meaning (He is not using a metaphor!), the evangelist uses the more graphic word *trogein*.

> "Amen, amen, I say to you, if you do not eat (*phagete*) the flesh of the Son of Man and drink his blood, you do not have life in you. The one who eats (*ho trogon*) my flesh and drinks my blood has eternal life and I will raise him up on the last day. For my flesh is real food and my blood is real drink. The one who eats (*ho trogon*) my flesh and drinks my blood remains in me and I in him" (Jn 6:53-56).[45]

Anticipating their thoughts of cannibalism, Jesus was saying that when they saw the ascension of His visible body into heaven, they would realize that the Eucharistic Meal would not be cannibalistic eating. Jesus' Flesh and Blood are made present in a sacramental way, not in a crudely physical sense.

Jews Scandalized. The Jews were shocked at the idea of human sacrifice and by the further demand to drink His blood, which was especially forbidden (Lv 3:17). The fact that Jesus said they must drink His blood meant that He considers Himself the source of life because blood was considered the source of life. Instead of being externally righteous according to the Law, they will be internally pure, cleansed, holy. But to be that, they must drink His blood.[46] This tried their faith, and "many [of] his disciples returned to their former way of life and no longer accompanied him" (Jn 6:66). Had Jesus defended Himself by saying that He was only speaking symbolically, we are led to believe that some of the disciples would have remained with Him. Fr. Eugene LaVerdiere points out that to believe Jesus, people had to be open to the Spirit, since the words Jesus spoke were Spirit and life (Jn 6:63).

The Twelve. Jesus, seeing the struggle of the Twelve, asked: "Do you also want to leave?" (Jn 6:67) Jesus was willing to allow His own apostles to leave Him rather than modify the promise He had just made to them. Peter was the first to proclaim his faith saying, "Master, to whom shall we go? You have the words of eternal life" (Jn 6:68). The apostles would spend the rest of their lives giving witness to the Real Presence of Christ in the Eucharist—all except one, Judas Iscariot. At this promise of the heavenly Bread, Jesus knew that Judas had abandoned all faith in Him.[47] Showing Judas that He knew this, Jesus said: "Did I not choose you twelve? Yet is not one of you a devil?" (Jn 6:70).

Our Invitation. *The Catechism of the Catholic Church* teaches that the Eucharist and the Cross are stumbling blocks—a mystery which never ceases to be an occasion of division. Today, as then, Jesus offers Himself to us as real food and drink which will satisfy our inner hunger and thirst for meaning. "I am the bread of life," Jesus told them, "whoever comes to me will never hunger, and whoever believes in me will never thirst" (Jn 6:35). When the woman at the well said, "Sir, give me this water, so that I may not be thirsty" (Jn 4:15), Jesus offered *Himself* to quench her thirst. "All who are thirsty, /come to the water!" (Is 55:1) the prophet Isaiah cried. Jesus is the water. Jesus is the bread. He gives Himself to us in the Eucharist to fill our hunger and quench our thirst.

The Lord's question "Will you also go away?" echoes through the ages as a loving invitation to discover that Jesus is the *Living* Bread and that to receive in faith the gift of His Eucharist is to receive the Savior Himself.

The Pharisees Question Jesus/James Tissot

The Jews quarreled among themselves, saying, "How can this man give us [his] flesh to eat?" Jesus said to them, "Amen, amen, I say to you, unless you eat the flesh of the Son of Man and drink his blood, you do not have life within you. Whoever eats my flesh and drinks my blood has eternal life, and I will raise him on the last day. For my flesh is true food, and my blood is true drink. Whoever eats my flesh and drinks my blood remains in me and I in him. Just as the living Father sent me and I have life because of the Father, so also the one who feeds on me will have life because of me." (Jn 6:52-58)

PREPARATIONS FOR THE PASSOVER

 esus and His disciples had been on the road for some days traveling to Jerusalem to celebrate the great feast of the Passover. The disciples anticipated sharing in the celebratory aspects of such a feast with their Lord, while Jesus prepared for His upcoming role, as yet not fully known to the disciples. Scripture tells us that Jesus eagerly desired to eat the Passover with His disciples. Thousands flocked to the city for the feast, and because Jesus was so well-known, He was constantly in demand. Scripture tells us that "all the people were hanging on his words" (Lk 19:48) and crowds "would get up early each morning to listen to him in the temple area" (Lk 21:38).

Origin of Feast. Fr. John Power writes that the liberation of the Israelites from slavery in Egypt which took place in the thirteenth century BC marked the beginning of Israel as the Chosen People. As an historical event, it dominated the whole history of salvation. It is only natural that Israel should recall it and celebrate it in some solemn manner, and the most special manner they knew of was by sacrifice. They borrowed the rite from an existing paschal feast—a spring sacrifice of lambs held to acknowledge the return of life after winter—which the Israelites turned into a communion sacrifice to the true God. The ancient sacrifice is given a new and nobler meaning when the paschal lamb becomes Christ and the paschal supper becomes the Eucharist.[48]

Preparatory Rites. At the time of Christ the memorial feast was the most important religious and political festival of the year, celebrating the covenant relationship of God with the Israelites. John tells how Christ drove out the sellers of the lambs on the first Pasch of His public ministry (Jn 2:14-16). The lamb was generally bought in the temple courtyard and was killed by the priest, who sprinkled its blood on the altar of holocausts. Then the lamb was brought back to the community to which it belonged. These were some of the preparations that Christ sent Peter and John to carry out before the Last Supper.

Jesus in Jerusalem. Jesus sent Peter and John into the city to make preparations for the Passover. Jesus told them that a man carrying a water jar would meet them. They were to follow this man to the house he enters, then ask the master of the house for use of the guest room for the Teacher, who wanted to eat the Passover there with His disciples.

There were plots against Jesus' life, but He was not a blind victim of betrayal. Luke showed Him fully aware of the course of events and consciously prepared to fulfill the Israelite Passover with the sacrifice of His own life. Jesus was aware of every detail, even how someone carrying a water jar would meet them on entering the city.[49]

The "Guest Room". Some theologians think Peter and John waited near the wall of the Sion quarter, where legend has it a street led down to an ancient well. There the water was considered the purest in Jerusalem, best suited for making the unleavened bread used in the Passover. Women generally carried the water so it would be easy to notice the few men who returned from the well. John, the beloved and trusted friend of Jesus, recognized the man immediately. The disciples followed him to a large upper room.[50]

The Greek word for the room where they ate the Passover is *kataluma*, a term much broader than "guest room," and is commonly used to indicate a place of hospitality for those on a journey. Houses in Jerusalem often had a room built as a second story which could be accessed from stairs in the inner courtyard. It is there in the *kataluma,* the upper room of a house in the city, that Jesus would take His place at table with His disciples.[51]

Passover and Eucharist. Jesus made a Paschal meal the occasion of the institution of the Eucharist, deliberately joining together the final Pasch and the first Eucharist. In this way the Pasch is one of the strongest links between the Old and New Testaments, and thus we of the New Testament can refer to the heart of our Christian liturgy as "the Paschal Mystery."[52]

At the first Passover, God saved His people from death. In its celebration, the Jewish people commemorate this great act of salvation. At His last Passover, Jesus saved the whole world from death. In their celebration of the Lord's Supper on Holy Thursday, Christians commemorate His act of universal deliverance. The first Passover led to the covenant at Sinai and the creation of the Israelite people. The Lord's Supper celebrates the New Covenant and the creation of the Christian people.[53]

The Pasch Continues. Jesus Himself would become the Passover of the Church. St. Paul teaches that the Eucharist is the new Pasch, grace is the new Exodus, and Baptism is our crossing of the Red Sea. How blessed we are today to have the history and the traditions of our Jewish and Christian ancestors on which to build. We are connected to all of sacred history—but most especially to Christ and to one another in the Eucharist—our Paschal celebration of unity and thanksgiving.

Man Bearing a Pitcher/James Tissot

When the day of the Feast of Unleavened Bread arrived, the day for sacrificing the Passover lamb, he sent out Peter and John, instructing them, "Go and make preparations for us to eat the Passover. . . . When you go into the city, a man will meet you carrying a jar of water. Follow him into the house that he enters and say to the master of the house, 'The teacher says to you, "Where is the guest room where I may eat the Passover with my disciples?"' He will show you a large upper room that is furnished. Make the preparations there." (Lk 22:7-9, 10-12)

JESUS WASHES THE DISCIPLES' FEET

There is only one gospel, the gospel of Jesus Christ, telling the good news of the Savior's life, death and resurrection. As a memorial of the death and resurrection of Jesus and as the Lord's Supper, the Eucharist is at the very heart of that gospel.[54] In his account of the Last Supper, John focuses on the Paschal mystery—the death and resurrection of Jesus—and on the meaning behind Jesus' action of washing the apostles' feet. In place of Jesus' words over the bread and wine, John describes the washing of the feet.

John's Gospel. John alone of the Evangelists does not write a literal account of the institution of the Eucharist, but gives it to us in an allegorical form in the foot-washing scene. It is conjectured that when he was writing his Gospel around the year 90 AD, the Eucharist and its founding was well-known and its reiteration would be unnecessary. What was needed was a deeper grasp of the nature and purpose of the Eucharist—which John already related in Jesus' discourse on the Bread of Life. Scripture scholars point out that the foot-washing prelude to the Paschal dinner is indeed Eucharistic, and is so essential to the Christian life that without it one cannot be a disciple of Christ.[55]

The Inner Circle. The apostles were mostly uneducated fishermen from Galilee. They were simple, good men and Jesus valued them. They were His "inner circle" with whom He wished to share His life and His final Passover meal. The love of God lifted them up and made them who they were. Jesus took the time during this meal to reveal to them the nature of who God is. Jesus served them.[56]

Peter's Protest. The act of washing another's feet was usually delegated to the lowliest of slaves. "What I am doing, you do not understand now, but you will understand later" (Jn 13:7), Jesus said as He prepared to wash Peter's feet. "You ought to wash one another's feet. I have given you a model to follow, so that as I have done for you, you should also do" (Jn 13:14, 15). When Peter protested, Jesus told him that unless he allowed Him to wash his feet, He would have nothing to do with him.

Jesus Models Service. In this dramatic scene, Jesus, servant of the Father, becomes the servant of His people. Jesus' entire life was one of service. The Eucharist is a profound gesture of love expressed in service—Jesus giving Himself to His disciples and the disciples giving themselves to Him and to each other.

Our Lord told Peter that a refusal to accept His divine cleansing would prevent them from having an intimate relationship. Not to understand that divine love means sacrifice was to separate himself from the Master. The idea of having no part with Our Lord humbled Peter, as he committed not his feet, but his whole being to the Master, saying, "Master, then not only my feet, but my hands and head as well" (Jn 13:9).[57] After explaining the meaning of what He had just done, Jesus challenged His apostles to imitate Him.

Foreshadowing of Calvary. There was an additional meaning in Jesus' act. His washing of His disciples' feet foreshadowed what happened on Calvary, where Jesus was stripped of His garments and humbled Himself to accept the Cross. Crucifixion was a slave's death. The Son of God "emptied himself, /taking the form of a slave. . . /he humbled himself, /becoming obedient to death, /even death on a cross" (Phil 2:7, 8). And by way of the Cross Jesus, the perfect Servant of God, draws His followers after Him to His Father's house—where servants will sit at a banquet table eternally.[58]

True Discipleship. Pope John Paul II reinforced the meaning of Christ's action during a Holy Thursday Mass, saying, "Love reaches its peak in the gift the person makes of himself, without reserve, to God and to his brothers and sisters. By washing the Apostles' feet, the Teacher presents them with an example of service. By this act, Jesus reveals a distinctive feature of his mission: 'I am among you as the one who serves' (Lk 22:27). Thus a true disciple of Christ can only be someone who "takes part" in Christ's actions, making himself, as he was, prompt in serving others even with personal sacrifice."[59]

The Church has preserved the rite of the "Washing of the Feet" which takes place during the Holy Thursday liturgy, in memory of what Jesus did, modeling a life lived for others. Jesus asks His disciples to serve Him in this world by extending His love to everyone. He fills His beloved children with Himself so that they can love with His love, see with His eyes, hear with His ears, heal with His hands. In this way will others experience God's great love for them.

Our lives can be a Mass, a Eucharist for others. We are joined to Christ in the unification of life, and we become a living sacrifice to give glory to the Father. We, the People of God, become His presence in the world, continuing the work of Redemption.

Jesus Washing Peter's Feet/Ford Madox Brown

. . . he rose from supper and took off his outer garments. He took a towel and tied it around his waist. Then he poured water into a basin and began to wash the disciples' feet and dry them with the towel around his waist. He came to Simon Peter, who said to him, "Master, are you going to wash my feet?" Jesus answered and said to him, "What I am doing, you do not understand now, but you will understand later." Peter said to him, "You will never wash my feet." Jesus answered him, "Unless I wash you, you will have no inheritance with me." **(Jn 13:4-8)**

THE LAST SUPPER

he Last Supper was the culmination of a long history of sacrificial meals in Israel's history, meals in which part of the sacrifice was given back to the family that offered it to be shared with family and friends. The feast of the Passover commemorated the Mosaic Covenant and the deliverance of the Israelites from slavery—God's saving action which was sealed in the blood of animals. Jesus had all this in mind when He introduced a new sacrifice—the New Covenant which was sealed in the sacrifice of His own Body and Blood. The Last Supper is the historical and religious fulfillment of the Pasch. Christ is the new and eternal Paschal Lamb Who offered His Body and Blood in the Eucharist, the paschal meal of the New Covenant.

Passover *Seder*. On the night before His crucifixion, Jesus ate His last Passover meal with His apostles. Matthew, Mark and Luke describe the meal as a Passover *seder*. The *seder* was comprised of four parts, and each part was completed by drinking a cup of wine. During the third course, the Paschal lamb and unleavened bread were eaten, known as the bread of affliction from the Exodus story. Instead of the customary words, Jesus "took bread, said the blessing, broke it, and giving it to his disciples said, 'Take and eat; this is my body'" (Mt 26:26). Then he raised the cup of wine, called the cup of blessing (the third cup), "gave thanks, and gave it to them, saying, 'Drink from it, all of you, for this is my blood of the covenant, which will be shed on behalf of many for the forgiveness of sins'" (Mt 26:27, 28).

Adaptation of Rite. Father Power draws a parallel between the Jewish Pasch and the new rite Jesus established. To the washing of hands, which opened the meal, Christ added the washing of His apostles' feet. The dish of bitter herbs gave Him the opportunity of announcing His approaching death and the betrayal of Judas. As head of the community of the Twelve it was His duty to tell the story of the Exodus, and to this He added the explanation of His death—the extended sermon in John 14-17. He pronounced the sacred words of consecration over the unleavened bread and the ceremony concluded with the singing of the Hallel Psalms (psalms of praise): "Then after singing a hymn, they went out to the Mount of Olives" (Mk 14:26).

Meaning in Aramaic. When Jesus declared the bread to be His body and the wine to be His blood, Father Emminghaus explains that what He really said was "This—My Body" and "This—My Blood" because, again, in Aramaic there is no verb "to be." To insert the word "symbolizes" or "represents" or some such word in place of "is" is simply impossible. The bread *is* Jesus' flesh and the wine *is* Jesus' blood.

Separate Consecration. Some theologians speculate that Jesus put His imminent death before the apostles' eyes by showing them His Body and Blood under the separate signs of bread and wine. On the Cross He would die by the separation of His Blood from His Body. Hence He did not consecrate the bread and wine together, but separately, to foreshadow his death—the separation of Body and Blood. Scott Hahn writes that Jesus didn't finish the Passover until Calvary—where He fulfilled it. Calvary began with the Eucharist, while the Eucharist ended with Calvary. They are one and the same sacrifice.[60]

Priesthood. "Do this in memory of me" (Lk 22:19), Jesus said to His apostles after He offered them His Body and Blood. Certainly the apostles could not have dared to repeat this rite unless the Master had told them to do so. The liturgical formula was already almost fully fixed by the time of the composing of the gospels. Such an early practice could not have been established except in accordance with the express directive of Christ.

The apostles became the first participants in Christ's priesthood, derived entirely from Christ. The community of believers were not its creators but its beneficiaries. The apostles had successors in the person of bishops, and each one was associated with a "presbyterium," a group of priests united around them. "Your presbyterium is united with its bishop like the strings of a lyre," wrote St. Ignatius of Antioch (d. 107) to the Christians of Ephesus.[61]

Priesthood and Eucharist. The Second Vatican Council reaffirmed Christ's teaching when it spoke of the ordained priest as a sign of Christ the head of His Body, the Church.[62] The priest is the link with the whole Church in time and space, writes Jesuit Fr. Raymond Maloney, Professor of Systematic Theology and Liturgy at the Milltown Institute in Dublin. Without the priest, he says, the congregation remains simply a local assembly. It is true that the faithful are all priests belonging to a "royal priesthood" in the words of St. Peter, who worship and intercede and "offer to God the Father the divine Victim."[63] But, in the words of Pope John Paul II, "the priest alone consecrates and only he offers the sacrifice *in the person of Christ*."[64] The Liturgy of the Eucharist is offered by the priest in imitation of Christ, in union with the assembly.

The Last Supper/Carl Bloch

Then he took the bread, said the blessing , broke it, and gave it to them, saying, "This is my body, which will be given for you; do this in memory of me." And likewise the cup after they had eaten, saying, "This cup is the new covenant in my blood, which will be shed for you." (Lk 22:19, 20)

THE COMMUNION OF THE APOSTLES

hrist refers to the covenant meaning of the Last Supper in all four gospels. The Lord's Supper marked the beginning of the New Covenant, a covenant which the prophet Jeremiah had foretold as one of deepest intimacy. It would not be written on stone, like the tablets of the law, but on the heart. (cf. Jer 31:33). Jesus is the mediator of this covenant, a love relationship so intimate that it would move St. Francis of Assisi to exclaim: "Our whole being should be seized with fear, the whole world should tremble and heaven rejoice, when Christ the Son of the living God is present on the altar in the hands of the priest."

Priest and Victim. Jesus is the priest and victim of His own sacrifice, the new and eternal Paschal Lamb who perfects and brings to fulfillment all the sacrifices and covenants of the Old Testament. The purpose of the Passover was to restore communion with Israel which was accomplished not only by killing the lamb and sprinkling its blood on the doorposts—but also by eating the lamb. "This day shall be a memorial feast for you" (Ex 12:14). Scott Hahn explains that Christ's sacrificial death which began in the Upper Room and was completed on Calvary wasn't the end of His Passover sacrifice. Since God's purpose is to restore communion, we too have to eat the Lamb. This, he believes, is why Jesus instituted the Eucharist.[65]

Vine and Branches. The disciples had been profoundly moved by the washing of their feet by the Lord. The mysterious words Jesus had just pronounced over the bread and wine must have stirred deep emotions within them. Jesus had taught them in so many words and by example how much He loved them and wanted to be one with them. He had used the image of the vine and the branches to illustrate the kind of intimate relationship He wanted with His followers (Jn 15: 1-17). United to Him as branches to a vine, His Blood would be like sap giving life to the limbs, enabling them to bear fruit. "By this is my Father glorified, that you bear much fruit and become my disciples" (Jn 15:8). He wants His disciples to share His very life—a life which is more intimate even than that between a husband and wife.

"The truth is that Eucharistic Communion is so profound that it goes beyond any human comparison we could make," writes Fr. Raniero Cantalamessa. "A married couple may form one flesh," he says, "but they cannot form one spirit." The strength of Communion is that we become one spirit with Jesus and this "one spirit" is ultimately the Holy Spirit—a sharing in God's own life.[66]

Life-giving Presence. The Jesus described in the gospels is someone who drew all types of people to Himself, especially children. His very presence filled peoples' needs—physical, emotional and spiritual. Now that He was going to leave them, He wanted to remain with them in a way that they would continue to experience His life-giving presence. At this sacrificial meal, His apostles learned that Jesus would *always* remain with them in the breaking of the bread. "As the living Father sent me and I have life because of the Father, so also the one who feeds on me will have life because of me" (Jn 6:57). He taught them that just as He lives because of and for the Father, so would His disciples, by partaking in the sacred mystery of His Body and Blood, live because of and for Jesus. Jesus is the Bread of Life who nourishes those who receive Him by transforming them into Himself. "He calls Himself the 'Bread of Life,' Father Cantalamessa says, "precisely to make us understand that He doesn't nourish us as ordinary food does, but that, as He possesses life, He gives it to us saying, 'the one who feeds on me will have life because of me'" (Jn 6:57).[67]

The Body of Christ. When the apostles received the Body of Christ in Communion, they were united in a new and deeper way to Him—and to one another. What the bread and wine visually symbolize—through the unity of many grains of wheat and the crushing of the grapes—we must say *Amen* to with our lives. The word "Amen" means "truly" or "it is true."

To acknowledge the gift of His presence which Jesus gave to the apostles and gives to His disciples today in the Mass, the faithful respond "Amen!" when the priest says, "The Body of Christ." Thus we say *Amen* to His Mystical Body, the Church, and precisely to those close to us in life or at the Eucharistic table. Jesus knew how difficult it would be to die to ourselves and live for others, especially for those who oppose or criticize us, who make life difficult for us. When we want a more intimate communion with Jesus or we need forgiveness or a special grace from Him, Father Cantalamessa suggests a way to obtain it. "Welcome Jesus in Communion together with that particular brother or sister and say to Jesus: 'Jesus, I receive You today together with (name the person); I'll keep him or her in my heart with You; I shall be happy if You bring him or her with You.'" This little act is very pleasing to Jesus, Father says, because it causes us to die a little.[68]

We Are Beloved! To share in the covenant meal of the Eucharist is also to share in the sacrifice of Christ. The Mass enables us to unite ourselves to Christ's sacrifice, so that we might share in His glory. As disciples of Christ today we are called—like the "Beloved Disciple"—to become one with the crucified and risen Lord. Jesus invites us to "see and believe" in the gift of the Eucharist and through it to share the same intimacy with Him that St. John enjoyed. Christ's disciples of today are those "witnesses chosen by God in advance, who ate and drank with him after he rose from the dead" (Acts 10:41). We are the Beloved Disciple!

Communion of the Apostles/James Tissot

"Just as the living Father sent me and I have life because of the Father, so also the one who feeds on me will have life because of me." **(Jn 6:57)**

THE CRUCIFIXION OF JESUS

he procession of a man condemned to crucifixion was usually preceded by a trumpeter to clear the road, followed by a herald announcing the name of the criminal. Sometimes the criminal's name and the reason for his condemnation were written on a board which hung around his neck. A centurion mounted on horseback, along with a detachment of soldiers, formed part of the procession. Two thieves were part of Our Lord's procession, to be crucified with Him.[69]

The Way of the Cross. Jesus was already very weak from the torture of the crown of thorns and the scourging, which had been carried out with straps covered with iron hooks which penetrated to the bone and tore off pieces of flesh at every blow. Bearing the full weight of the heavy crossbeam on His back and shoulders, Jesus fell many times as He made His way about a third of a mile up steep hills to Golgotha, the "Place of the Skull." Arriving at the place of execution, Jesus' body was a raw wound. It is likely that He was stripped naked according to the Roman custom.

Legend has it that Golgotha was the burial place of Adam. Representations of the Crucifixion often show a skull at the foot of the Cross to indicate that the new Adam was dying for the old Adam. It was a place where dead bones were thrown after executions.

Crucifixion. This was the most terrible—and painful—death inflicted in the ancient world. A nail was driven through a hollow just below the heel of the hand, so the hand would support much of the weight of a hanging body. On its way through this space the nail pierced a major nerve, causing intense pain.[70] The Roman writer Seneca reported that those who were crucified cursed the day of their birth, the executioners, even their mothers, and spat upon those in the audience. Cicero recorded that at times it was necessary to cut out the tongues of those who were crucified to stop their terrible blasphemies. Surely the executioners expected Christ to curse—hadn't everyone else? They didn't expect the cry that they heard:[71] "Father, forgive them, they know not what they do" (Lk 23:34).

An "Eyewitness" Account. Sr. Anne Catherine Emmerich (1774-1824), a German mystic and visionary, experienced ecstasies during which she witnessed the details of Our Lord's Passion. Through these visions she gives us an "eyewitness" account:

> They placed the cross on the ground and then seizing his right arm, they dragged it to the hole prepared for the nail, and having tied it down with a cord, one of them knelt upon his sacred chest, a second held his hand flat, and a third, taking a long thick nail, pressed it on his hand, and with a great iron hammer drove it

through the flesh and far into the wood of the Cross. Our Lord uttered one deep but suppressed groan, and his blood gushed forth and sprinkled the arms of the executioners.

> When the executioners had nailed the right hand of Our Lord, they perceived that his left hand did not reach the hole they had bored to receive the nail, therefore, they tied ropes to his left arm and pulled the hand violently until it reached the place prepared for it. They drove the second nail into his left hand.

> The agony which Jesus suffered from this violent tension was indescribable. The words "My God, my God" escaped His lips. . . .They then fastened his left foot onto his right foot. . . . Next, they took a very long nail and drove it completely through both feet into the Cross below, which operation was more than unusually painful on account of his body being so unnaturally stretched out. I counted at least thirty six blows of the hammer.[72]

Christ's "Hour". "This is my Body, which will be given for you" (Lk 22:19). Less than twenty-four hours had passed since Jesus had uttered those words. The apostles, silent witnesses to His execution, now understood their meaning. Christ's sacrifice which began in the Upper Room was completed on Calvary when He shed every last drop of Blood for the redemption of the world. Christ's "hour" had come—the hour of His Passion, death and resurrection which the prophet Simeon had foretold— and to which Christ referred at Cana when He told His mother that His "hour" had not yet come. His death reconciled the human race with its Creator. It is the central event of salvation history, an event which will transform and unify Christians until the end of time. "And when I am lifted up from the earth, I will draw everyone to myself" (Jn 12:32).

Sacramental Sacrifice. Jesus left His future disciples a means of sharing His hour—the Eucharist. The Mass is the same sacrifice of the Cross, commemorated sacramentally. At the Last Supper, on the night when he was betrayed, our Savior instituted the Eucharistic Sacrifice of His Body and Blood. He did this in order to perpetuate the sacrifice of the Cross throughout the centuries until His Second Coming. At Mass we unite our lives to Christ's sacrifice. "When we take the cup, give thanks and give it to one another at Mass," Father LaVerdiere writes, "we join Christ in offering our blood for others. We forgive one another, extend peace to one another and strengthen the covenant relationship that makes us one people of God."[73] Through the Mass Christ's disciples are *included* in His sacrifice. Their lives, with their joys and sorrows, victories and defeats, become part of His sacrifice of praise and atonement offered to the Father. The Eucharist unites the faithful to Christ in His dying—and in His glory.

The First Nail/James Tissot

So they took Jesus, and carrying the cross himself he went out to what is called the Place of the Skull, in Hebrew, Golgotha. There they crucified him, and with him two others, one on either side, with Jesus in the middle. Pilate also had an inscription written and put on the cross. It read, "Jesus the Nazorean, King of the Jews." (Jn 19:16-19)

Mary and John at the Foot of the Cross

ome gospel accounts portray the holy women of Galilee standing at a distance, while John the Evangelist placed those dearest to Jesus at the foot of the Cross. Overcome with grief were Jesus' mother Mary, her sister-in-law Mary, Mary Magdalene, and John, "the disciple whom Jesus loved" (Jn 19:26)—the only one of His apostles to stay with Him to the bitter end. Now Our Lord looked down from His Cross into the faces of the two most beloved creatures that He had on earth—His Blessed Mother and John.

Jesus Speaks to Mary and John. The sword foretold by Simeon forty days after Jesus' birth now pierced Mary's heart. We can imagine that His mother would have wanted to take His place. From the cross Jesus said to His mother, with John at her side, "Woman, behold, your son. . . ." (Jn 19:26). Jesus had used the title "Woman" in prior encounters—once with His mother at Cana, then with the Samaritan woman, again with Mary Magdalene, the Canaanite woman and the woman crippled with arthritis. By addressing His mother as "Woman" Jesus designated her as the Mother of all Christians, the Mother of the Church.

Then He said to John, His beloved disciple, "Behold, your mother" (Jn 19:27). He did not refer to John by name because to do that would have been to address him as the son of Zebedee and no one else. In the person of John He addressed the Church composed of all the faithful until the end of time.

The "Woman" in Scripture. According to the account of Catherine Emmerich, after Jesus spoke these words His mother was so overcome with grief that she almost fainted and was helped by the women.[74] When Jesus called the Blessed Virgin "Woman" instead of "Mother," Jesus indicated she was *that woman* spoken of in Scripture who was to crush the head of the serpent. "I will put enmity between you and the woman, /and between your offspring and hers; /He will strike at your head, /while you strike at his heel" (Gn 3:15). That promise was accomplished in the death of her Son. At the side of the Conqueror (Jesus) is "the Woman" (Mary) who, with her Son, had been the enemy of Satan and now would share her Son's triumph. In place of Eve came Mary, "the mother of all the living" (Gn 3:20), bringing new life to the world—eternal life through Jesus.

Death Came Quickly. Crucifixion in most cases was a slow death, with victims lingering as long as two days. Pilate was surprised that Jesus died in three hours. Instead of breaking his legs to hasten death through asphyxiation as was the custom, the soldier pierced His side with a lance which would have killed Him had He not already been dead, because the wound was large enough for St. Thomas later to insert his hand.[75] Thus was Scripture fulfilled: "You shall not break any of its bones" (Ex 12:46) and "They shall look on him whom they have thrust through" (Zec 12:10).

Blood and Water. According to the eyewitness account of St. John, from the side of Christ came blood and water. This phenomenon follows upon the hemorrhage caused by the rupture of the heart. The blood decomposes, the red globules fall to the bottom of the sack around the heart, and the lighter serum floats on top as a watery liquid. If the heart is pierced before the blood coagulates shortly after death, the two parts flow out separately.[76]

But the blood and water have a deeper spiritual significance. They signify the marriage of Christ and the Church, which took place on the Cross, and which is continued throughout the whole Church by Baptism and the Eucharist. Baptism perpetually regenerates Christians by plunging them into the death of Christ, and the Eucharist continually makes them grow by giving them the strength which comes from His side, that is, by communion in His Risen Body.[77]

Eucharist is New Covenant. The covenant relationship between Christ and His faithful is sealed in the Eucharist—through which the faithful are united to Christ as a bride is wedded to her husband. St. Paul compared matrimony to the union of Christ and the Church:

> So [also] husbands should love their wives as their own bodies. He who loves his wife loves himself. For no one hates his own flesh but rather nourishes and cherishes it, even as Christ does the church, because we are members of his body. "For this reason a man shall leave [his] father and [his] mother and be joined to his wife, and the two shall become one flesh." This is a great mystery, but I speak in reference to Christ and the church. (Eph 5:28-32)

St. Paul refers back to Genesis—to the marital covenant God made with Adam. When Eve came forth from Adam's side he proclaimed her "bone of my bones and flesh of my flesh" (Gn 2:23). Joined to him in marriage, she became one body with him. Similarly, from the side of Christ pierced by a lance came the Church. The Church is the new Eve united to Christ, her Bridegroom through the Eucharist. "The Eucharist is the sacrament of the consummation of the marriage between Christ and His Church," writes Scott Hahn. "In the Eucharist He renews the New Covenant, which is His marriage covenant with her. It is much more than a banquet. It is a wedding feast. We, the Bride, receive our Bridegroom's Body in the Eucharist."[78]

The Crucifixion/Carl Bloch

Standing by the cross of Jesus were his mother and his mother's sister, Mary the wife of Clopas, and Mary of Magdala. When Jesus saw his mother and the disciple there whom he loved, he said to his mother, "Woman, behold, your son." Then he said to the disciple, "Behold, your mother." And from that hour the disciple took her into his home. (Jn 19:25-27)

"It is Finished"

hen Jesus died, an eclipse of the sun darkened the earth for three hours, while an earthquake devastated Jerusalem and Palestine. Across the valley and beyond the wall from Golgotha, the crossbeam of the great entrance to the sanctuary or "Holy Place" of the Temple cracked down the middle. The huge curtain hanging from it—a carpet in white, purple, blue and red—was "torn in two from top to bottom" (Mt 27: 51). A brass gate of the inner Temple building, which normally required twenty men to move, swung open by itself. The central light of the great candelabrum went out.

Much of this information comes from Jewish, not Christian sources. The Talmud dates the strange opening of the brass gate specifically to the year 30 AD.[79] And chasms opened in the rock of Golgotha, the effect of a seismic disturbance according to those who have studied it.[80]

Jesus Fulfills Covenants. The death of Jesus Christ devastated—and saved—the world. He brought the *human* light and warmth of God's divine love into a darkened world as Isaiah had prophesied: "I will make you a light to the nations, /that my salvation may reach to the ends of the earth" (Is 49:6). His death was the low point and the high point of salvation history. It was the beginning of the end—the new way to heaven which He bridged with His life—so that we "might have life and have more abundantly" (Jn 10:10). In union with His eternal Father in the work of salvation, Jesus Christ brought to perfection all the covenants made with Adam, Noah, Abraham, Moses and David. He offered a New Covenant—His love given unconditionally to redeem and save each and every child of His Father. The Eucharist is the sign and seal of His covenant promise: "I am with you always, until the end of the age" (Mt 28:20).

Jesus Perfects all Sacrifices. God sent His Son to be our companion on the way to heaven—to strengthen and fortify us with eternal food, so that we would never hunger or thirst. Jesus is the new Manna, the true food and drink of the People of God (cf. Jn 6:55). Just as He transformed the water into wine at the wedding feast of Cana, so did He change wine into His Blood at the Passover feast which He celebrated with His disciples—the Last Supper—saying "this is my blood of the covenant, which will be shed on behalf of many for the forgiveness of sins" (Mt 26:28).

To complete the sacrifice of the New Covenant—and to perfect all sacrifices—Christ presented Himself as the new and eternal Paschal Lamb, the supreme victim foretold by Isaiah. He was "like a lamb led to the slaughter" (Is 53:7). The sacrifice of Jesus replaces the sacrifices which in all religions and all times people have offered to God. He is the priest and victim of His own sacrifice, thus fulfilling the office of priesthood. Jesus, a "high priest forever according to the order of Melchizedek" (Heb 6:20), offered bread and wine at the Last Supper, which was prefigured in the thanksgiving offered by the high priest, Melchizedek.

Jesus' Final Moments. In His life's final moments, Jesus cried out in a loud voice: "My God, my God, why have you forsaken me?" (Mt 27:46). It was a piercing prayer from His parched lips, so dry that again He cried, "I thirst" (Jn 19:28). Moments before His death, one of the soldiers lifted up a sponge soaked in wine on a sprig of hyssop. Hyssop is the same plant which was dipped in blood and sprinkled on the doorposts of the Israelite homes during Passover. And it was King David who, after his sin, said he would be purged with hyssop and be made clean. "When Jesus had taken the wine, he said, 'It is finished.' And bowing his head, he handed over the spirit" (Jn 19:30).

The Fourth Cup. According to Scott Hahn, the "it" in Jesus' statement, "It is finished," was the Passover begun in the Upper Room, but interrupted and completed on the Cross by Jesus drinking the sour wine, the "fourth cup." At the Last Supper, the fourth cup of the Passover dinner was omitted—an *obvious* omission—which Jesus noted: "I shall not drink again the fruit of the vine until the day when I drink it new in the kingdom of God" (Mk 14:25). The fourth cup was the cup of suffering and death which Jesus, sweating blood in the Garden of Olives, had asked His Father to let pass from Him.[81]

From the Cross. Jesus looked upon all those He loved until the end of time and saw that His suffering and death would make no difference in the lives of some. Jesus *experienced* the fourth cup for us and invites us to drink the cup with Him—the "cup of blessing" of the Eucharist, but also the "fourth cup" of suffering and death. We do that by conforming our lives to His, by imitating and drawing courage from Him Who anticipated death in the fullness of life.

To live the paschal mystery is to feel alone and abandoned in the midst of His disciples. It is to be the "light of the world" (Jn 8:12) but to see His people choose the darkness; to have the ability and power to free people from the bondage of disease and death, but not to free Himself; to invite everyone to share in His kingdom which "does not belong to this world" (Jn 18:36), only to be rejected and unwanted by many. Jesus came to tell us that on the other side of death is eternal life for all who believe in Him. That life, He said, begins now, with a banquet which He hosts—the Eucharist. To be His disciples is to know with certainty that Jesus Christ is there for us, even if we are never there for Him—no matter what.

"It Is Finished"/James Tissot

There was a vessel filled with common wine. So they put a sponge soaked in wine on a sprig of hyssop and put it up to his mouth. When Jesus had taken the wine, he said, "It is finished." And bowing his head, he handed over his spirit. (Jn 19:29, 30)

EMMAUS

arly Sunday morning Mary Magdalene, Joanna, and Mary the mother of James went to the tomb and were astonished to find it empty (Lk 24:10). The stone had been rolled away and Jesus was not there. Two angels reminded them of Jesus' words concerning His crucifixion and rising on the third day. The women ran to tell the apostles. Peter and John arrived first, and when John, the beloved disciple, saw the burial cloths, he "saw and believed" (Jn 20:8). While others came and went, Mary Magdalene remained at the tomb weeping. Then Jesus appeared, called her by name, and asked her not to hold on to Him but to tell the apostles that "I am going to my Father and your Father, to my God and your God" (Jn 20:17). It is easy to imagine Mary bursting in upon the apostles with great excitement saying, "I have seen the Lord" (Jn 20:18).

Two Disciples. Early that same afternoon two of Jesus' followers, Cleopas and his companion, had left Jerusalem bound for Emmaus, a town about seven miles from the city. The two disciples had already heard about the appearance of the angels to the women and of the visit of Peter and John to the empty tomb. They did not know about Jesus' appearance to Mary Magdalene. They, like the apostles when they first heard the news of Jesus' resurrection from the women, considered it "nonsense and they did not believe them" (Lk 24:11).

A Stranger Joins Them. These men were saddened and confused by the crucifixion and death of their Master. As they walked along they were discussing the events of the past few days when a stranger caught up with them and joined their conversation. It was Jesus, Whom they were unable to recognize. Father LaVerdiere conjectures that the inability of the two disciples to recognize Jesus is related to their lack of understanding after Jesus' announcement of His Passion:[82] "The Son of Man is to be handed over to men" (Lk 9:44) Jesus said, but "they did not understand this saying" (Lk 9:45). They didn't really know who Jesus was. They looked upon Him as the mighty prophet whom they had hoped would liberate Israel—not as the Son of God and Savior of the world.

"Stay with Us." Jesus rebuked them for not believing all that the prophets had taught concerning the Messiah's need to suffer before being glorified: "How slow of heart to believe all that the prophets spoke!" (Lk 24:25). Their faith was stirred when Jesus explained the Scriptures to them, showing how His coming, death and resurrection was foretold by the prophets. Had they known the Scriptures, they would be able to understand who Jesus really was (Lk 24:19); they would be able to make sense of the crucifixion (Lk 24:20), grasp the significance of "the third day" as the day of divine deliverance (Lk 24:21), and believe the announcement that Jesus was alive (Lk 24:22-24). Had they known the Scriptures, they would have believed in Calvary. They were deeply touched by this Stranger. As they neared their destination, they didn't want to part His company. "Stay with us" (Lk 24:29) they implored Him.

Recognition. During dinner when they reclined at table as was the custom, Jesus took the bread, blessed and distributed it, a role usually reserved for the master of the household. The taking of the bread, breaking it and giving it to them was not an ordinary act of courtesy. Although they were not present at the Last Supper, they had surely seen Jesus break bread many times during His public life. At this dinner His actions closely resembled those of the Last Supper when He took the bread—which was His Body—broke it and gave it to His apostles. It was a rite which He asked the apostles to repeat as a memorial of His death.

As soon as He gave them the bread, "their eyes were opened and they recognized him, but he vanished from their sight" (Lk 24:31). In the moment of the breaking of the bread, they *knew* Jesus. Their hearts and minds were opened to know the living Christ—no longer a stranger accompanying them along the road. He vanished from their sight in order to show them that from then on the disciples will know Him in the breaking of the bread. They are now able to connect His suffering and death foretold by the prophets to His resurrection, and to His sacramental presence in the meal.

Energized by His Presence. The disciples were filled with joy and aware now of the meaning behind Jesus' prophecy: "I have eagerly desired to eat this Passover with you before I suffer, for, I tell you, I shall not eat it [again] until there is fulfillment in the kingdom of God" (Lk 22:15-17). The kingdom of God was being fulfilled in their midst! They met the Messiah and were so energized by His Presence that they rushed back to Jerusalem to tell the eleven apostles about "what had taken place on the way and how he was made known to them in the breaking of the bread" (Lk 24:35).

Jesus gave a priceless gift to the disciples at Emmaus and all future disciples—the promise of His presence when the faithful gather to celebrate Eucharist. There are many ways in which Christ is present to His Church, but at the heart of it all is His substantial, real, permanent presence in the Eucharist. When our hopes and dreams are shattered we, too, can count on Him to restore us to life, just like He did to the Emmaus disciples. Jesus anticipated our need for Him to "Stay with us" (Lk 24:29) and so He left us *Himself* in the Sacrament of the Eucharist.

The Supper at Emmaus/Rembrandt

And it happened that, while he was with them at table, he took bread, said the blessing, broke it, and gave it to them. With that their eyes were opened and they recognized him, but he vanished from their sight. Then they said to each other, "Were not our hearts burning [within us] while he spoke to us on the way and opened the scriptures to us?" So they set out at once and returned to Jerusalem where they found gathered together the eleven and those with them who were saying, "The Lord has truly been raised and has appeared to Simon!" Then the two recounted what had taken place on the way and how he was made known to them in the breaking of the bread. (Lk 24:30-35)

AT THE SEA OF TIBERIAS

After the events of the Passover week in Jerusalem some of the apostles returned to their former lives and to the Sea of Tiberias (Sea of Galilee), so full of tender memories. In the Gospel of John, the Lord's Eucharistic teaching is first given and last celebrated at the Sea of Tiberias. Galilee would now be the scene of the Lord's last miracle, as it was the scene of His first, when He turned the water into wine at Cana. On the first occasion, there was no wine; on this last occasion there were no fish. In both, the Lord uttered a command: at Cana, to fill the waterpots; in Galilee, to cast the nets into the sea. Both resulted in a full supply; Cana had its six water pots of wine with the best wine served at the last; Galilee had its nets full of fish.[83] The apostles were learning to expect the unexpected from Jesus, that He always reached out with love to those around Him—filling them to overflowing.

Apostles Go Fishing. Back in their native country, the apostles didn't know when Jesus would return. He had told them He would go before them into Galilee. Peter, taking the lead as usual and inspiring the others, said he was going fishing. They were seven in all, including Peter, Thomas, the one who had doubted, Nathanael from Cana, Zebedee's sons James and John, and two others. They went fishing, and after laboring all night they caught nothing. Just as dawn was breaking, a stranger on the shore called out to them: "Children, have you caught anything to eat?" (Jn 21:5).

Jesus Calls to Them. To be called "children" did not surprise them; it was a term of familiarity and was commonly used when speaking to young people. Their boat was about a hundred yards from shore and in the glimmer of the first light of day, they did not recognize that it was Jesus. From the shore Jesus suggested that they cast their net to the right side of the boat where they would find some fish. One of them threw out a casting net and the result was immediate and astonishing. Their net filled with so many fish—153 in all—that they could hardly haul it in!

John Recognizes Jesus. When John, the disciple whom Jesus loved, realized that the stranger on the shore must be Jesus, he rejoiced, saying to Peter, "It is the Lord!" (Jn 21:7). Peter jumped out of the boat immediately and waded over to Jesus, dragging the catch of fish behind him. The others followed.

The number of fish must have reminded them of a similar happening three years prior, when Jesus first called Simon Peter and his companions to follow Him (Lk 5:1-11). At that time Jesus told them to put out into deep water and lower their nets for a catch. The circumstances were similar in that they had fished all night and caught nothing. When they did as Jesus suggested, they caught so many fish that they feared their nets would tear.

Jesus Prepares Breakfast. Now Jesus had worked a similar miracle. Then He fed them with bread and fish, an act of love which must also have reminded them of the bread and fishes Jesus multiplied when He fed the multitudes and proclaimed Himself as the Bread of Life. "I am the living bread that came down from heaven; whoever eats this bread will live forever; and the bread that I will give is my flesh for the life of the world" (Jn 6:51). In that discourse which He gave on the same shoreline where they now stood, Jesus was preparing them to partake of His flesh and blood in the Eucharist. On the shore, the apostles noticed a charcoal fire with fish cooking and some bread beside it. Bread was a figure of the Eucharist, and fish in the Early Church was a symbol of Christ. Jesus invited them to, "Come, have breakfast" (Jn 21:12).

Jesus Feeds Them. This story reveals the loving, caring, *human* side of Jesus. It was His third appearance to His apostles after His resurrection (the first two were in Jerusalem). He was, as always, solicitous of their welfare and enjoyed surprising them. Jesus had spent so much of His public life sharing meals with people which gave Him a way to be really present to their needs. Meals afforded Jesus the opportunity of nourishing people with His love, which He would give to them as Food for all time in the Eucharist. In this post-resurrection meal, Jesus prepares the food and gives it to His apostles, an action reminiscent of the Last Supper. Once again, He is sensitive to their needs, their hunger. But their hunger is not for food; it is for Jesus, for His Presence which they had grown accustomed to and now missed so much. Jesus loved being with "his own" (Jn 1:11), and we can imagine this intimate scene by the lake when they were now alone together. By sharing Himself with His apostles through a meal after His resurrection, Jesus is showing "His own" for all times where they can find Him—in the Eucharist.

Mission of the Apostles. This is a story rich in symbolism. According to ancient biologists, the sea contained one hundred and fifty three varieties of fish. Fish was a symbol of Jesus and the Christian faith and this catch, therefore, implied a universal catch. That the net was not torn suggests the unity and integrity of the Church. The apostles understood that Jesus had called them to be fishers of souls, so this great catch symbolized the faithful who would ultimately be brought to the Church—and fed with the Eucharist—through them.

Christ Appears on the Borders of the Tiberias Sea/James Tissot

When they climbed out on shore, they saw a charcoal fire with fish on it and bread. Jesus said to them, "Bring some of the fish you just caught." So Simon Peter went over and dragged the net ashore full of one hundred fifty-three large fish. Even though there were so many, the net was not torn. Jesus said to them, "Come, have breakfast." And none of the disciples dared to ask him, "Who are you?" because they realized it was the Lord. Jesus came over and took the bread and gave it to them, and in like manner the fish. This was now the third time Jesus was revealed to his disciples after being raised from the dead." (Jn 21: 9-14)

St. Peter

At the beginning of His Galilean ministry, Jesus traveled on foot "curing every disease and illness among the people" (Mt 4:23). Simon (later to be named Peter) and his brother Andrew lived in Capernaum, a town tucked along the shoreline of the Sea of Tiberias. When Jesus passed through the area, Simon invited Him to look in on his mother-in-law who had a high fever. When Jesus prayed over her, she was instantly healed. As word of these cures spread, crowds began to follow Jesus. Simon, a fisherman by trade, had a boat moored by the lake. Jesus asked to use the boat so that He might get some space from the people who were pressing on Him and teach them from the boat.

Jesus Commissions Simon. After He finished speaking, Jesus suggested to Simon that they "put out into deep water" (Lk 5:4) to catch some fish. Simon protested because they had fished all night without any success. But he did as Jesus requested. When they lowered their nets, they caught so many fish that their nets were tearing. Their partners in the other boats came to help, and they, too, caught so many fish that they were afraid they would sink. Astonished by this miracle, Simon Peter "fell at the knees of Jesus and said, 'Depart from me, Lord, for I am a sinful man'" (Lk 5:8). It was the first time Simon recognized Jesus as someone special sent by God. Jesus then commissioned Simon to be His disciple saying, "Do not be afraid; from now on you will be catching men" (Lk 5:10).

Peter's Faith in Jesus. Jesus gathered more disciples around Him and His fame spread everywhere. Great crowds followed Him wherever He went and there were constant rumors of His identity. Jesus took His Twelve to the district of Caesarea Philippi, on the northern border of Palestine, and asked them, "Who do people say that the Son of Man is?" (Mt 16:13). Some replied that He was John the Baptist, others Elijah, and still others Jeremiah. But it was only Peter who replied decisively, saying, "You are the Messiah, the Son of the living God" (Mt 16:16). His public profession of faith in the messiahship of Jesus earned His Master's trust and blessing—and the leadership of His Church.

> "Blessed are you, Simon son of Jonah. For flesh and blood has not revealed this to you, but my heavenly Father. And so I say to you, you are Peter, and upon this rock I will build my church, and the gates of the netherworld shall not prevail against it. I will give you the keys to the kingdom of heaven. Whatever you bind on earth shall be bound in heaven; and whatever you loose on earth shall be loosed in heaven" (Mt 16:17-19).

Peter's faith in Jesus was given to him by the Father, Who singled Peter out as the foundation of His Son's community. When Jesus first met Peter, He told him that he will be called Kephas (Jn 1:42), an Aramaic word which means "rock." Here Jesus clearly named Peter as the foundational authority of His Church.

Jesus, the Living Bread. Of the twelve who became Jesus' apostles, Peter was the boldest, the most outspoken. He was inquisitive, a risk-taker, even if his heart occasionally came before his head. When Jesus taught the people that He is the new Manna, the living Bread sent by His Father to feed people with His Flesh and Blood, "many [of] his disciples returned to their former way of life and no longer accompanied him" (Jn 6:66). He turned to the Twelve and asked, "'Do you also want to leave?' Simon Peter answered him, 'Master, to whom shall we go? You have the words of eternal life. We have come to believe and know that you are the Holy One of God'" (Jn 6:67-69). Just as Peter was the first to acknowledge Jesus as the divinely sent anointed-one, so was he the first to overcome the "hard teaching" and put his faith in Jesus as the Bread of Life.

Shepherd of the Church. When the Lord told Peter that he would deny Him three times before the cock crowed twice, Peter protested: "Even though all should have their faith shaken, mine will not be" (Mk 14:29). When Jesus was arrested, Peter denied knowing Him—three separate times. We presume that he never saw Jesus alive again until after the resurrection.

Now, as Jesus and Peter walked along the shore after breakfast on the Sea of Tiberias, Jesus engaged Peter in a dialogue. Peter no doubt still felt ashamed that he had betrayed His Lord. Three times Jesus asked Peter to express his love, a grace-filled reversal of his three denials. Having made love the condition of service to Him, the Risen Savior now told Peter, "Feed my lambs" (Jn 21:15). When for the third time Jesus told Peter to feed His sheep, Jesus led Peter into a reaffirmation of faith and love that confirmed His forgiveness. He reaffirmed Peter's leadership over the Christian community, confiding His whole sheepfold to Peter's care. "I will appoint over you shepherds," Jesus said through the prophet Jeremiah, "shepherds after my own heart" (Jer 3:15).

Martyrdom. Peter, in imitation of his Master, the Good Shepherd, offered his life for his sheep and was crucified in Rome. According to Early Church tradition, Peter was fleeing from certain martyrdom when he met Christ and asked Him, *Domine quo vadis*? ("Lord, where are You going?"). Jesus replied that He was going to Rome to be crucified again. Peter responded, "Lord I am going back to follow You." Peter understood the words referred to his own martyrdom, namely, how the Lord would be crucified again in him. He embraced his cross joyfully, giving glory to God.

The Crucifixion of Peter/Caravaggio

Then Peter proceeded to speak and said, "In truth, I see that God shows no partiality. Rather, in every nation whoever fears him and acts uprightly is acceptable to him. . . . We are witnesses of all that he did both in the country of the Jews and [in] Jerusalem. They put him to death by hanging him on a tree. This man God raised [on] the third day and granted that he be visible, not to all the people, but to us, the witnesses chosen by God in advance, who ate and drank with him after he rose from the dead." (Acts 10:34, 35, 39-42)

PENTECOST

efore Jesus died, He had promised the apostles He would send His Holy Spirit. The Spirit would complete the work Jesus started, lead them in all truth and help them in the building up of the Church which Christ founded. Gathering daily in the "upper room" where the Last Supper and the first Eucharist had been celebrated, the apostles waited with Mary, and with a number of other disciples that grew to 120 during the ten days between the Ascension and the Feast of Pentecost (cf. Acts 1:15).

Coming of the Holy Spirit. In ancient times, the "Feast of Weeks" (in Greek, *Pentecost*) was celebrated in thanksgiving for the first fruits of the harvest, fifty days after the Passover. Later, Pentecost was an anniversary celebrating the Sinai covenant when Israel was called to be God's own people. Fr. Bill McCarthy explains that in the Old Testament, God's Spirit usually worked externally—through oaths, sacraments, covenants, prophets and priests. Now, in the fulfillment of the New Covenant at Pentecost, God's Spirit enters *within* His people, transforming them so that they can think, love and act like Jesus. Pentecost became the celebration of God's Spirit dwelling in His people.

John the Baptist had prophesied about the coming of the Spirit, saying: "I am baptizing you with water, but one mightier than I is coming. . . . He will baptize you with the holy Spirit and fire" (Lk 3:16). The apostles and disciples of Christ were gathered together in prayer when they experienced the visible presence and power of the Holy Spirit, first by a great wind which could be heard in the city, and then by tongues of fire. The wind was a symbol of the Holy Spirit who would disperse the little community to the whole world; fire was a symbol of the power and presence of God.

Manifestation of the Spirit. The apostles were given a new spiritual language. Many Jews from distant lands came to Jerusalem for the feast of Pentecost. When the apostles came out to address them, each listener heard them perfectly in his own native language. As theologian Warren Carroll points out, all timidity, confusion, doubt and obstinate adherence to erroneous popular ideas of the Messiah were gone from the apostles now, blown away forever by the breath of the Holy Spirit, Who had conferred His precious gifts upon them—most especially, understanding and fortitude.[84]

Empowerment. The Holy Spirit empowered the disciples to boldly proclaim the gospel. Following the outpouring of the Spirit with the disciples speaking in different tongues—which looked like drunkenness—Peter delivered his first sermon (cf. Acts 2:14-36). He presented the teaching of Jesus so forcefully that on that day alone, there were three thousand conversions. After the descent of the Spirit, the apostles converted, baptized and devoted themselves "to the breaking of the bread and to the prayers" (Acts 2:42). It was as if the Holy Spirit Himself had directed them toward the Eucharist, Pope John Paul II says. "Guided by the Holy Spirit, the Church from the beginning expressed and confirmed her identity through the Eucharist."[85]

Where the Spirit Dwells. The Spirit dwells in us through Jesus who gifts us with His Real Presence in the Eucharist. And where Jesus is, so is the Father and the Holy Spirit. St. Luke clearly shows us that in all the key moments of Christ's life in the world, His death and resurrection, Jesus is seen doing the Father's will under the guidance, direction, prompting and assistance of the Holy Spirit.

"In fact," says Fr. Lawrence Hennessey, "it is the Holy Spirit who makes our prayer and worship possible at all."[86] (cf. Rom 8:26, 27). To experience God, he says, is to experience the Holy Spirit, Who is the effective power of God in the world, the effective energy of Love in our lives. He cites seven different "moments" of *epiklesis,* a technical word for calling down the Spirit, in which the Church invokes the Holy Spirit during the Eucharistic Liturgy. Regarding the "moment" of Consecration, Father Hennessey says that in the Early Church there was a profound awareness that the Holy Spirit effected the transformation of the bread and wine into the Body and Blood of the Lord. This awareness and invocation of the Spirit is explicit today in our own Eucharistic Prayers II and III:[87]

> Let your Spirit come upon these gifts to make them holy, so that they may become for us the body and blood of our Lord, Jesus Christ.
>
> And so Father, we bring you these gifts, We ask that you make them holy by the power of Your Spirit, that they may become the body and blood of your Son, our Lord Jesus Christ, at whose command we celebrate this Eucharist.

The Holy Spirit is the Sanctifier, the One who changes the bread and wine into the Body and Blood of Christ and Who changes us, consecrating us "in Spirit and truth" (Jn 4:24). When the Holy Spirit came upon Christ's apostles and His mother, Mary, at Pentecost, He filled them with divine life, transforming and uniting them as one apostolic community. The Church was born, gifted for all time with the fullness of the Spirit of God. We are now the living temples of the Holy Spirit (cf. 1 Cor 3:16) and "our churches are the upper room where not only is the Last Supper renewed but Pentecost also."[88] It is through the power of the Holy Spirit that Christ's disciples will be "witnesses in Jerusalem, throughout Judea and Samaria, and to the ends of the earth" (Acts 1:8).

The Pentecost/Louis Galloche

*When the time for Pentecost was fulfilled, they were all in one place to-
gether. And suddenly there came from the sky a noise like a strong driving
wind, and it filled the entire house in which they were. Then there appeared
to them tongues as of fire, which parted and came to rest on each one of
them. And they were all filled with the holy Spirit and began to speak in
different tongues, as the Spirit enabled them to proclaim.* **(Acts 2:1-4)**

SACRAMENT
The Eucharist Celebrated

Jesus Pierced with a Lance/James Tissot

Nay in addition to this, a wonderful mystery was then effected. "Blood and water at once flowed out of the wound." It is not by mere chance or unwittingly that these two fountains sprang up at this juncture. It is because blood and water are two constitutive elements of the church. Those already admitted to the sacred rites know this well; those, I mean, who have been regenerated in the waters of Baptism and who in the Eucharist feed on Christ's flesh and blood. It is to this one source that all the Christian mysteries trace back their origin. And so when you apply your lips to this awesome cup, do it as though you drank that precious blood from the open side of Christ Himself.

—St. John Chrysostom

THE APOSTLE PAUL

hen Peter invoked the name of Jesus Christ and healed a crippled beggar at the gate of the Temple called the Beautiful (Acts 3:2), two thousand more converts came into the Church. It was this healing that led to the first arrest of Christians.

Saul of Tarsus. The inspired and forceful preaching of a young deacon, Stephen, had scandalized the Pharisees, who ordered him to be stoned to death. Guarding the cloaks of the people stoning Stephen was a young Jew from Tarsus named Saul. A devout Pharisee and scholar, Saul hated the disciples of Christ, whom he considered traitors to the Jewish faith. He became a leader among the oppressors of the new sect, many of whose members had been imprisoned or had taken refuge in Damascus, the capital of Syria.

Saul wrote a letter to the high priest asking for an introduction to the synagogues in Damascus, saying "if he should find any men or women who belonged to the Way, he might bring them back to Jerusalem in chains" (Acts 9:2).

Saul's Conversion. While en route to Damascus under armed escort, Saul, who later would be called Paul, experienced a profound spiritual conversion. (For the Hebrews, a name was not a mere social label but represented one's divinely ordained nature, character and destiny).[1] A light from heaven suddenly flashed about him and he fell to the ground. Then he heard a voice say, "Saul, Saul, why are you persecuting me?" (Acts 9:4). When he said, "Who are you, sir?" The reply came, "I am Jesus whom you are persecuting. Now get up and go into the city and you will be told what you must do" (Acts 9:5). Paul often referred to this experience in his epistles. "I have indeed been taken possession of by Christ [Jesus]" (Phil 3:12), he later wrote to the Philippians. And to the Galatians he wrote that God "was pleased to reveal his Son to me, so that I might proclaim him to the Gentiles" (Gal 1:15, 16). His encounter with Christ changed his hatred into passionate love. It was the point of departure for his whole apostolate and the beginning of thirty years of unceasing and untiring activity for the sake of the gospel.

Breaking Bread. The apostles and the newly baptized Christians attended worship in the Temple of Jerusalem which included a liturgy of prayers, psalms and Scripture readings, and sacrificial rites. Although Paul had been a rabbi who observed the Jewish law to the letter, he now argued fearlessly that a person had to be "in the Spirit" and not simply "of the law" (Gal 3:2) to be a true Christian. "For Christ is the end of the law for the justification of everyone who has faith" (Rom 10:4). He looked upon the law like a scaffolding used for a building under construction; it was not needed once the building was completed. "Before faith [Christianity] came, we were held in custody under law, confined for the faith that was to be revealed" (Gal 3:23). ("Custodian" in Greek referred to a guardian). Paul preached that justification no longer came from the law but from faith in Jesus Christ (Gal 3:24).

The Lord's Supper. The Eucharist and the consequences of becoming a member of the Body of Christ were central to Paul's life and teaching. The first converts to the new Christian Way "devoted themselves to meeting together in the temple area and to breaking bread in their homes" (Acts 2:46). According to Fr. Johannes Emminghaus, this reference to "breaking bread" as a Jewish ritual even at ordinary meals is an important indication of the earliest form of Eucharist.[2] After their temple service, the new Christians went from "house to house" where they had meals of fellowship known as agape meals, or "love feasts," which recalled the Paschal meal of the Last Supper[3] and included the Eucharistic service. At Corinth, sometimes these supposedly modest meals turned disorderly and divisive. In some cases the rich ate luxuriously while the poor went hungry. St. Paul forcefully reproached them for these abuses of "the Lord's supper," pointing out that if they made the Lord's supper into their own individual meal, they might as well eat and drink at home and not assemble in common (1 Cor 11:20).

Commitment to the Body. Paul appealed for unity among the Corinthians, challenging them to reflect on the profound commitment of belonging to Christ's Body. "Therefore whoever eats the bread or drinks the cup of the Lord unworthily will have to answer for the body and blood of the Lord. A person should examine himself, and so eat the bread and drink the cup. For anyone who eats and drinks without discerning the body, eats and drinks judgment on himself" (1 Cor 11: 27-29). Paul considered himself to be a father to his spiritual children. He felt obligated to correct community abuses—quarrels, factions, jealousies, drunkenness—which were a serious threat to the very meaning and purpose of the Eucharist. He admonished the Corinthians to evaluate their relationship to each other in the light of the love shown by Christ before celebrating the Eucharist, because anyone who profaned the Body would be guilty of a sin against the Lord Himself.

Eucharistic Ritual. To drive home his point, Paul reminds the Corinthians that he speaks with authority, saying that the source of his information is Jesus Christ, Himself. "For I received from the Lord what I also handed on to you" (1 Cor 11:23). Paul is presenting already established liturgical rituals which he learned in Antioch, a city second in importance to Jerusalem, where "the disciples were first called Christians" (Acts 11:26).

*Ruins with the Apostle Paul Preaching/*Giovanni Paolo

Paul preached the death and resurrection of Christ—a theme at the heart of his personal life and ministry. Although Christ's sacrifice was sufficient for the reconciliation of the whole world, Christ willed to associate us with that sacrifice, a truth St. Paul strongly expresses: "Now I rejoice in what was suffered for you, and I fill up in my flesh what is still lacking in regard to Christ's afflictions, for the sake of his Body, which is the Church" (Col 1:24). Each Mass is an opportunity for us, the members of Christ's Body, to unite our lives, our joys and sufferings, with Christ's sacrifice. We stand before the Father, in Christ, with something of our own to offer—gifts which He has given us—which are added to all the good achieved by Christ.

Msgr. James T. O'Connor
The Hidden Manna

85

APOSTLE TO THE GENTILES

A story in the Acts of the Apostles gives us a rare glimpse of the celebration of the Eucharist in the Apostolic Church. It occurred during Paul's journey to Rome when he broke bread with the community at Troas (in Bithynia, now Turkey). Late one Sunday evening, Paul gathered the faithful together in an upstairs room. A young man named Eutychus, who was sitting on the window sill, fell asleep and toppled to his death. The community rushed downstairs and Paul prayed over him, restoring him to life.

When they went back upstairs they "broke the bread, and ate; [and] after a long conversation that lasted until daybreak" (Acts 20:11), Paul departed for Jerusalem. This story illustrates an actual New Testament Eucharistic celebration, notes Fr. Eugene LaVerdiere. The Eucharistic assembly, Paul's ministry of the Word, and the breaking of the bread are presented as giving life to the community.[4]

Warning About Idolatry. Paul was constantly dealing with problems in the Christian community. One difficulty concerned the Corinthians who were divided over the question of eating meat which had been sacrificed to idols. Parts of the pagan sacrificial animals were sold in the common market to raise funds for the upkeep of the temple and the salary of the priests.[5] Most of the Corinthian Christians were of Gentile background who had taken part in the worship of idols and in religious banquets associated with it. As converts to Christ they had turned away from idol worship, but still had to deal with living in a pagan environment.[6]

Paul warned them against participating in public temple banquets where meat offered to idols was served. They were now Christians who worshiped Christ and must therefore separate themselves from pagan practices. Some in the community felt that idols were harmless images whose worship meant nothing, while to others, idols represented demonic presences. Paul appealed to those who thought that their faith in Christ freed them from concern about this. "The cup of blessing that we bless, is it not a participation in the blood of Christ? The bread that we break, is it not a participation in the body of Christ? Because the loaf of bread is one, we, though many, are one body, for we all partake of the one loaf" (1 Cor 10:16-18). Like their ancestors in the Exodus who lost faith and slipped back into idolatry, Paul warned those who felt so sure of themselves to "take care not to fall" (1 Cor 10:12).

No Compromise. "What they sacrifice, [they sacrifice] to demons, not to God, and I do not want you to become participants with demons" (1 Cor 10:20), Paul preached. "The Christian sacrifice is not like the pagan or even the Jewish sacrifice," observes Jesuit liturgical scholar Fr. Joseph Jungmann, "where the quantity and value of the outward gift could influence the deity. The Christian sacrifice is different; it is spiritual."[7] Paul argued that one who eats meat that has been sacrificed to idols is guilty of *sacrificing* to the idols and thus participates in the worship of devils. "You cannot drink the cup of the Lord and also the cup of demons. You cannot partake of the table of the Lord and of the table of demons" (1 Cor 10:21).

Sacrifice. The sacrifice which Paul preached was the *sacrifice of Christ*. "He indeed died for all, so that those who live might no longer live for themselves but for him who for their sake died and was raised" (2 Cor 5:15). Jesus left a memorial of His death at the Last Supper—the Eucharist—by which He sealed His love in a covenant meal promising to bring His followers life through His death. Whenever Christians celebrate the Eucharist they commemorate the life and death of Christ. (Commemoration to Jews meant the remembered event becomes really present so that persons can actually participate in it). "Commemorating the Lord's death was not just a matter of words," writes Father LaVerdiere, "it was a matter of deeds. They were to be the body of Christ in the world, proclaiming by the gift of their own life in Christ—and Christ's life in them—the death of the Lord until His coming"[8] (1 Cor 11:26).

Priesthood of Christ. Some of the Jewish Christians were growing indifferent to their new faith. To restore their lost fervor, the author of the Epistle to the Hebrews, probably a disciple of St. Paul, focused on the sacrifice and priesthood of Jesus as a fulfillment of the Old Testament sacrifices and promises (Heb 8:1-13). He shows the meaning God ultimately intended in the sacrifices of the Old Testament (Heb 9:1-28), concluding that these sacrifices pointed to the unique sacrifice of Christ, which alone obtains forgiveness of sins (Heb 10:1-18). The epistle emphasized Jesus' once-and-for-all sacrifice on Calvary, where He established the New Covenant by the physical shedding of His own blood, and it also refers to Christ's continuing Eucharistic sacrifice: "Through him [then] let us continually offer God a sacrifice of praise. . . ." (Heb 13:15). Christ's "once for all" (Heb 7:27) sacrifice points to His perpetual intercession on their behalf represented now by the Eucharistic sacrifice on our altars.

Final Days. Deserted by everyone in Asia and abandoned in a Roman prison, in a letter to Timothy Paul wrote that he is "being poured out like a libation, and the time of my departure is at hand. I have competed well; I have finished the race; I have kept the faith. From now on the crown of righteousness awaits me. . . ." (2 Tm 4:6-8). We can imagine what courage Paul exhibited at his beheading. Paul sacrificed his life for Christ, believing that "if we have died with him /we shall also live with him" (2 Tm 2:11).

St. Paul Escapes Damascus in a Basket/Monreale Cathedral, Sicily

   Three years after his conversion Paul returned to Damascus where he confounded the Jewish Scribes and Pharisees with his masterly arguments "proving that this [Jesus] is the Messiah" (Acts 9:22). His life was in danger. One of the disciples, whose house adjoined the city wall, smuggled Paul into his home in the middle of the night and lowered him in a wicker basket through a window in the wall. St. John Chrysostom, writing in the fourth century, described the greatness of St. Paul as that of a man "whose likeness the world shall never see again."

THE *DIDACHE*

This ancient document known as the *Didache* was discovered in the Jerusalem Monastery of the Holy Sepulchre at Constantinople in 1873. The *Didache*, whose full title in Greek means "The Teaching of the Twelve Apostles," is an anonymous compilation from various sources which describes the traditions of church communities some scholars place in Antioch, Syria. Written as a manual of catechesis and sacramental instruction, it describes the *Two Ways, Life and Death.* The *Didache* was written around the same time as the four Gospels, between 70 and 100 AD. It is important because it is the oldest extra-Biblical record of the Christian Eucharist.

Eucharist. The expressions, "to break bread" and "to give thanks," words designating the Eucharist, are found grouped together in the document. They entreat the early Christians to "break bread" on Sunday, "the Lord's day of the Lord," with the understanding that they should also be reconciled and go to Communion.

> On the Lord's day of the Lord, assemble in common to break bread and offer thanks, but first confess your sins so that your sacrifice may be pure. However, no one quarreling with his brother may join your meeting until they are reconciled; your sacrifice must not be defiled. For this is that which was spoken by the Lord, 'In every place and time offer me a pure sacrifice, for I am a great king' says the Lord, 'and my name is wonderful among the heathen.'[9]

This passage recalls the words of the Acts of the Apostles as to celebrating the Eucharist on Sunday, the resurrection day of Jesus: "On the first day of the week when we gathered to break bread, Paul spoke to them because he was going to leave on the next day. . . . "(Acts 20:7). Pliny the Younger in his famous letter to the Emperor Trajan (c. 112) says that the Christians assemble on Sunday evening to "take their food, which, despite what is said, is ordinary and innocent." Echoing Paul's warning to the Corinthians of the seriousness of partaking of the Body of Christ, those who break bread "must first confess your sins, so your sacrifice may be pure." Here the Eucharist is already likened to a sacrifice, reinforced when the writer quotes the Lord from Malachi, "Everywhere they bring sacrifice to my name, /and a pure offering" (Mal 1:11).

Jewish Table Prayers. The Eucharistic prayers in Chapters 9 and 10 of the *Didache* are based on Jewish table prayers in the setting of a Christian meal. The words "after you have eaten" indicated that the agape feast and the Eucharist are still joined. Their separation would come later, around the time of St. Justin Martyr.

> After you have eaten your fill, give thanks like this: We give thee thanks, O holy Father, for thy holy name which thou has made to dwell in our hearts, for the knowledge, faith and immortality that thou hast revealed to us through Jesus, thy Child. Glory to thee forever! It is thou, almighty Master, who hast created the world, that thy name may be praised; for their enjoyment thou hast given food and drink to the children of men; but us thou hast graciously favoured with a spiritual food and with a drink that gives eternal life, through Jesus thy Child. . . . May the Lord come and may this world pass away! Amen. Hosanna to the house of David! He who is holy, let him approach. He who is not, let him do penance. Maranatha! Amen. Let the prophets indeed give thanks as they wish.[10]

Of particular interest are the instructions for administering the thanksgiving prayers over the wine and bread. Although, Passover-style, the first cup of blessing and the final *Berakah* blessing are still separated by the agape meal, the prayers have been Christianized: they thank the Father for the truth "revealed to us through Jesus thy Child." The *Didache* admonishes the early Christians to approach the holy Table in the state of grace. The Aramaic word *Maranatha*, meaning "Come Lord," is an expression of longing for their Eucharistic Lord. St. Paul used it as a Eucharistic watchword when speaking to the Corinthians (1 Cor 16:22).

There has been considerable debate among scholars whether these are mere blessings over the agape food or prayers of a sacramental rite. Internal evidence indicates that they are prayers of Eucharistic consecration. For example, the prayers transform the bread and wine into "spiritual food and drink that bestows eternal life" to be shared only by those "baptized in the name of the Lord."

Role of Clergy. Fr. James O'Connor, professor of theology at St. Joseph's Seminary in Dunwoodie, New York, writing in *The Hidden Manna,* says that the prophets who are mentioned in the *Didache* ("Let the prophets indeed give thanks as they wish") are the "high priests" of the Christian community. They are the ones who offer the Eucharist, and the task of the overseers or bishops is identical with theirs.[11]

Today, almost two thousand years later, some of the words in the Church's Eucharistic Prayer III are reminiscent of the *Didache*:[12] "From age to age you gather a people to yourself, so 'from the rising of the sun to its setting' a perfect offering may be made to the glory of your name."

Breaking of the Bread/Catacomb of St. Priscilla

This early second century fresco called the **Fractio Panis** *(Breaking of the Bread) is the oldest known representation of the Eucharist. Discovered in the Greek Chapel of the Catacomb of St. Priscilla, it shows seven people gathered around a table on which rests a two-handled cup (the chalice), a plate with two fish and another with five small round loaves of bread. At the far left is a bearded figure dressed in tunic and pallium (most likely the celebrating bishop), who extends his arms to break the bread. The third guest from the right is a woman whose head is veiled which was the custom for women at Eucharistic services. Wicker baskets of bread on either side of the people symbolize the multiplication of the loaves and fishes.*

St. Ignatius of Antioch

The seeds of sacrifice continued to germinate in the fertile soil of the Church as many of Christ's disciples spilled their blood rather than sacrifice to pagan gods. One after another, they embraced the instruments of their torture and fulfilled their baptismal commitment to lay down their lives for Christ and rise with Him to new life.

On the night of July 18, 64 AD, Rome was set on fire—a fire which raged for nine days. The Emperor Nero falsely blamed the Christians to divert attention from his own complicity in the arson. The resulting persecution of Christians continued for the next 250 years until Constantine's Edict of Milan in 313, which legalized Christianity.

Christian Warrior. One who fearlessly proclaimed his faith in Christ was Ignatius, a convert who served as the Bishop of Antioch for thirty years. Dr. Warren Carroll writes that Ignatius was the most venerated living member of the Church at the outset of the second century and probably was trained by the Apostle John. An earthquake had rocked the city of Antioch in 115 AD and the devastation, like the fire in Rome, was blamed on the Christians. Ignatius was taken prisoner as an elderly man and brought to Rome to be thrown to the lions in the arena.[13]

Authentic Letters. While enroute to Rome during a few weeks in the summer of 116, Ignatius wrote seven letters from Smyrna and Troas in Asia Minor. They give us a privileged glance into the spirituality of a man whose life and death was centered on the mystery of Our Lord's Body and Blood in the Eucharist. Father LaVerdiere writes that Ignatius' letters show his attachment to the Eucharist as the presence of Christ—human and divine—as central to the being and unity of the Church, and as the source and the goal for Christian life. Steeped in the New Testament's apostolic tradition, his teaching on the Eucharist provides a bridge from the apostolic to the post-apostolic age.[14]

Eucharistic Themes. Ignatius speaks of Christ, the historical figure, as truly human. "As for me, I know and I believe that even after the resurrection he was in the flesh," he writes to the Smyrnaeans. Being "in the flesh" had implications for the Eucharist in which Christ gives not just His body, but His flesh as nourishment. Reference to Christ's body (*soma*) or person does not of itself imply His presence in the flesh. Reference to the flesh (*sarx*) associates the Eucharist with the incarnation and refers to Christ's bodily, personal presence in the flesh.[15]

Church Unity. "Be careful to observe [only] one Eucharist; for there is only one Flesh of Our Lord Jesus Christ and one cup of union with His Blood, one altar of sacrifice, as [there is] one bishop with the presbyters and my fellow-servants, the deacons,"[16] Ignatius writes to the Philadelphians. The internal unity of the Church—one of his most basic concerns—was based on the union between the crucified and risen Body of Christ and His Eucharistic Body.[17] He also stresses the concept of the Eucharist as sacrifice referring to the "altar of Eucharistic sacrifice" as a sign of Church unity and as a symbol of his own personal sacrifice as Christ's martyr.[18]

Dr. Carroll maintains that Ignatius repeatedly emphasized the central emerging role of the bishop in the Christian community. Ignatius taught that the bishop alone may authorize the celebration of the Mass, a concept that soon became normative in the Catholic Church and has remained so ever since.[19]

Early Church Belief. In his letter to the Smyrnaeans, we find "the Catholic Church" mentioned for the first time in Christian literature. "Wherever the bishop appears, there let the people be, even as wherever Christ Jesus is, there is the Catholic Church."[20] Ignatius urges his fellow Christians to assemble in common, obeying the bishop, and "breaking one bread that is the medicine of immortality and the antidote against dying that offers life for all in Jesus Christ."[21]

To the Christians of Tralles he compares the virtues of faith and love to the Eucharistic Mystery: "Therefore, arming yourselves with gentleness, renew yourselves in faith, which is the Flesh of Our Lord, and in charity, which is the Blood of Jesus Christ. Hold nothing against your neighbor."[22]

Approaching Death. Ignatius tells the Christians in Rome not to dissuade him from martyrdom because he wants to meet Christ who has become the food and drink of Christians. His theme, as always, is the Eucharist.

> You can do me no greater kindness than to suffer me to be sacrificed to God while the place of sacrifice is still prepared. Thus forming yourselves into a chorus of love, you may sing to the Father in Jesus Christ that God gave the bishop of Syria the grace of being transferred from the rising to the setting sun. It is good to set, leaving the world for God, and so to rise in Him. . . . Beg only that I may have inward and outward strength, not only in mind but in will, that I may be a Christian not merely in name but in fact. . . . Let me be thrown to the wild beasts; through them I can reach God. I am God's wheat; I am ground by the teeth of the wild beasts that I may end as the pure bread of Christ.[23]

Ignatius' letters reveal a courageous Christian who eagerly awaits his end, praying that he "may have joy in the beasts, and find them prompt. If not, I will entice them that they may devour me promptly, not as they have done to some, refusing to touch them through fear."[24]

St. Ignatius of Antioch/Holy Transfiguration Monastery

St. Augustine said that if the martyrs had the strength to bear witness to the Lordship of Christ, even to shedding their blood, it is because they drank of the Blood of Christ; it is because they sat at the table of Christ. Seated at the table of Christ, they looked at what was served to them; then, as upright people, they said: In my turn, I will have to receive my Host and treat Him as well as He has treated me. And that is what they did: Christ gave Himself completely, as friend and as nourishment, at His banquet; they, in turn, give themselves entirely to Christ even to the shedding of their blood, and they have drawn this courage in the Eucharist.

Fr. Athanase Sage, AA
The Religious Life According to Saint Augustine

"The Christian Question"

hree quarters of a century had passed since Christ's death, and the memory of the Apostles was still fresh in the youthful Church. The persecution of Christians escalated; to be a leader in the Church virtually assured martyrdom. Despite the opposition, St. Paul boasted of the work of his fellow missionaries: "Their voice has gone forth to all the earth, /and their words to the ends of the world" (Rom 10:18). Twenty-five years later even whole provinces would become largely Christian. The Church could rightly be called "catholic," that is, universal.[25]

The Problem of Informers. One of the most valuable sources of information on the apostolic Eucharist comes from Pliny, an adopted pagan son of a Roman administrator who followed his father and entered public service. Pliny the Younger became the Roman governor of the Province of Bithynia, a largely Christian province in Asia Minor (now Turkey). He did not persecute Christians in particular, but became aware of them because they were being prosecuted by private citizens acting as informers.[26] He wrote letters about the year 112 to inform the emperor Trajan concerning the Christian assemblies, at which the Eucharist was offered. In these letters he reports on his investigation and disposition of "the Christian question."

Investigation. Pliny's first information was received from apostate Christians, but it seems to have been confirmed by the testimony of faithful Christian women who were interrogated under torture.[27] Two of Pliny's letters dealt with the policy to be adopted toward the Christians. *Letter 96* describes the Christian gatherings and makes the earliest non-Christian reference to the celebration of the Eucharist and agape meal.[28]

Pliny was looking to verify pagan stories which recounted tales of cannibalism at these "infamous" gatherings. He extracts information obtained through Christian informers who, under threat of persecution, denied their allegiance to Christ. And then Pliny writes:

> It was their practice to meet, on an appointed day, before sunrise, to sing together among themselves a hymn to Christ, as to a god, and to bind themselves by an oath, not for any criminal activity, but not to commit theft, or robbery, or adultery, and not to perjure themselves.... Upon the completion of these activities, their practice was to separate, and to assemble again to take food, but of an ordinary and harmless kind. They said they abandoned this practice after the promulgation of my edict, whereby, following your instructions, I had forbidden the existence of societies. So I considered it all the more necessary to investigate the truth of the matter by interrogating, under torture, two female servants who were called "ministrae" (deacons). I discovered nothing but perverse superstition.[29]

Trajan replies to one of Pliny's letters telling him that he acted rightly in handling the cases of the Christians by executing any who, after three chances, refused to denounce the Faith. Trajan writes, "If anyone says that he is not a Christian, and shall actually prove it by adoring our gods, he shall be pardoned as being repentant, even though he may have been suspect in the past."[30] However, Pliny was not to accept the denunciations of Christians by informers.

Sunday Services. Father Jungmann observes that "we quite probably have in the first-named gathering the celebration of the Eucharist, and in the hymn sung alternately the prayer of thanks"[31] (which refers to the Consecration). The prayer of thanks closed with the "amen" of the people and may have even included the *Sanctus* said in common. Father Jungmann conjectures that their oath not to do any wrong was equivalent to a Sunday confession of sins (our Penitential Rite), which Paul had demanded for the Eucharistic celebration and of which the *Didache* speaks. The kiss of peace took place at the start of Mass. In this early period one can see forming the outlines of the later Eucharistic liturgy, and indeed of our present day celebration.[32]

The second assembly to which Pliny refers was the evening agape, which was discontinued after he intervened, but would later be resumed.

Charges Against Christians. The communal life of the early Christians was centered around the Eucharist and agape. They were under suspicion for cannibalism in part because of sacred texts such as, "Unless you eat the flesh of the Son of Man and drink His blood. . . ." To the more sensational charge of cannibalism, the general charge of atheism or impiety (non-participation in the state religion) touched upon the Eucharist, for the Christians abstained from the common sacrifices of the civic community. They offered their own sacrifice and excluded others from participating. This inevitably led to charges that the Christians were undermining the state by refusing to participate in the sacrifices of atonement required by the polytheistic state religion. One defense by Christians brought against this charge was the explanation of what was involved in the true understanding of God and the sacrifice due Him.[33]

The great thanksgiving prayer of the first and second century Christians is in the forefront of their liturgy. The sacrificial aspect of the liturgy evolved from the prayer of thanks, whose main subject was the salvation they received through Christ. Their *Eucharistia*—which means "to give thanks with praise and favor"—possessed a certain beauty which should inspire today's Christians to equally value their thanksgiving in the Mass; to thank God "always and everywhere through Christ Our Lord" for His saving love.[34]

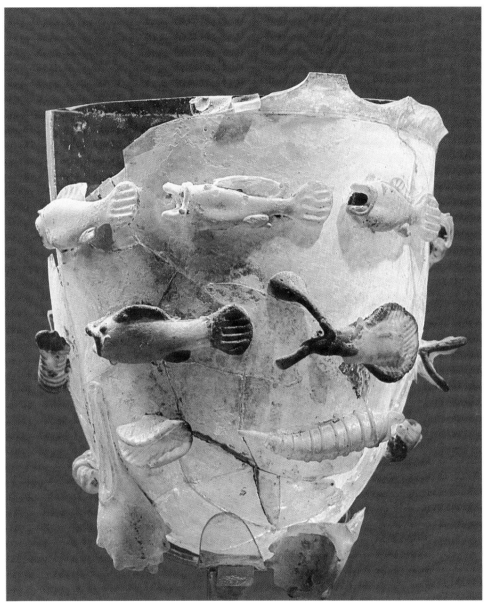

Glass chalice/Vatican Museum

Three rows of sea creatures encircle the glass goblet, made about 300 AD, when the Romans still prized glass as a precious substance. According to explanations given by St. Augustine and others, the word "fish" was used for Christ since the initial letters of the phrase, "Jesus Christ, Son of God, Redeemer," spell out the Greek word for fish. The fish, whose life element is water, symbolically represented Baptism, but it was the most favored symbol for the Eucharist. Christ as a fish was employed in a special sense for Christ as food. This chalice can be seen today in the Vatican Museum in Rome.

ST. JUSTIN MARTYR

ne of the greatest defenders of Christianity in the Early Church was Justin Martyr. Born into a gentile family from Palestine at the end of the first century, he spent many restless years searching for the truth. After studying pagan culture, he became a Christian because of a dialogue with a saintly old man whose witness of salvation through Christ led to his conversion.

Defender of the Faith. In Rome, Justin opened a Christian school of philosophy. About forty years after Pliny's letters to Trajan, around 150, Justin wrote two defenses of the faith, or *Apologies*, to two different Roman emperors. These writings have survived along with his *Dialogue with Trypho*, a vindication of Christianity in the face of Jewish objections.

Christian Worship. Justin addressed his *First Apology* to the Emperor Marcus Aurelius. He sought to dispel some of the same suspicions about Christians—tales of cannibalism—which Pliny and Trajan had related and which still persisted. In these writings, Justin explained Christian worship simply and openly. His report tells us that the basic form of the Mass, as we know it today, had already been shaped. He speaks of a "communal celebration" held on Sunday. There is a Liturgy of the Word with an Old Testament and New Testament reading presented by a lector, the presider's sermon, and what would later be called the "Prayers of the Faithful." These are followed by the Liturgy of the Eucharist in which the one presiding offers up the prayers of consecration in a free-form manner.

> And on that day which is called after the sun, all who are in the towns and in the country gather for a communal celebration. And then the memoirs of the Apostles or the writings of the Prophets are read, as long as time permits. After the reader has finished his task, the one presiding gives an address, urgently admonishing his hearers to practice these beautiful teachings in their lives. Then all stand up together and recite prayers. After the end of the prayers, the bread and wine mixed with water are brought, and the presider offers up prayers and thanksgiving, as much as in him lies. The people chime in with Amen. Then takes place the distribution, to all attending, of the things over which the thanksgiving had been spoken, and the deacons bring a portion to the absent.[35]

Justin's description tells us that at the end of this prayer, what had been bread and wine has now become the Body and Blood of Christ. He states that the consecratory thanksgiving takes place through a prayer, the author of which is Christ. The thanksgiving is pronounced free-style by the presider alone ("as much as in him lies"). There are as yet no liturgical books and no fixed texts.[36] Justin gives us the expression "eucharistized bread" in reference to the consecrated species. The name for the celebration of Mass since the beginning of the second century is *Eucharistia*. Ignatius used this name and so did the *Didache*.[37] Says Justin:

> This food we call "eucharist," and no one may share it unless he believes that our teaching is true, and has been cleansed in the bath of forgiveness for sin and rebirth, and lives as Christ taught. For we do not receive these things as if they were ordinary food and drink. But, just as Jesus Christ our Savior was made flesh through the word of God and took on flesh and blood for our salvation, so too—we have been taught—through the word of prayer that comes from Him, the food over which the eucharist has been spoken becomes the flesh and blood of the incarnate Jesus, in order to nourish and transform our flesh and blood.[38]

Temple Sacrifices Replaced. Justin's *Dialogue with Trypho* is a debate with a prominent Jew of the time. It is based on an actual dialogue which the Early Church historian Eusebius placed at Ephesus, but it is written as a literary device which allows Justin to argue his case for Christianity. It contains valuable references to the Eucharist.

Justin refers Trypho to the Old Testament sacrifices once offered by the Jews according to the prophet Malachi. The sacrifice of Christ's own Body and Blood—the Eucharist—has replaced the bloody animal sacrifices of the Temple, a replacement, Justin notes, desired by God and predicted by Malachi. He shows how the Eucharist fulfills the prophet's announcement that God's name would be great among the gentiles, who in every place would offer incense to his name, as well as a clean oblation. Malachi's prophecy is fulfilled in the Eucharistic bread and cup offered as a sacrifice of prayer and thanksgiving by people of every race and nation.

Justin's Sacrifice. In the second of his *Apologies*, Justin wrote: "I expect to be waylaid and placed upon the rack, perhaps by Crescens, that lover of empty bombast . . . who publicly condemns us for something of which he has no knowledge, namely, that we are impious and godless."[39] When Justin was brought before the pagan Roman prefect, Rusticus, he was urged to submit to the gods and obey the emperors. Even after the threat of being beaten and beheaded, he and his six companions said, "Do as you wish, for we are Christians and do not sacrifice to idols." They were scourged and beheaded.[40]

Like Ignatius of Antioch, Justin was strengthened by the Body and Blood of Christ to offer up his own body and blood for Christ. From the divine Sacrifice he drew the courage to sacrifice his life. The heroism of the Early Church saints came from the Eucharist, the same Eucharist which we receive today in the hope of becoming saints ourselves.

Tombstone of Abercius/Vatican Museum

An inscription on a tombstone from about 170 AD bears the epitaph of Abercius, a bishop who composed these verses in poetic language as a disguise to bear witness to his faith. He presents himself as a world traveler who found fellow believers and substantial uniformity in ritual wherever he went. Acquainted with Sacred Scripture, Baptism and the Eucharist, he writes that Christians everywhere partake of Christ in the observance of the Lord's Supper. The faithful receive bread as food and wine mixed with water, but faith tells them that it is really the great, pure fish, that is, Christ, born of the Virgin Mary. Implicit in his message is the importance of the Roman Church, veneration of the Virgin Mary and the communion of saints.

St. Hippolytus

As in the days of the Apostles, Rome remained the intellectual center of the Christian world, attracting teachers who varied widely in their orthodoxy. During the pontificate of Zephyrinus (200-217), a priest named Hippolytus (170-235) emerged who came into conflict with Zephyrinus. The pope was criticized by some for misjudgment in dealing with the problem of false teaching. Hippolytus was schismatic for a time, but was reconciled with the Roman Church through his martyrdom and was later proclaimed a saint.

Apostolic Tradition. Hippolytus was reputed to be the most important theological writer in the early days of the Church. He is best known for his *Apostolic Tradition*, a book of Church ordinances that codified long-standing liturgical traditions. While Justin Martyr had offered a description of the rites, Hippolytus produced actual liturgical texts. He leaves us a treasured record of the Eucharistic practices and belief of our early Christian ancestors.

Most valuable is his writing on the Eucharist, notably the Canon of the Mass—otherwise known as the Eucharistic Prayer—the Church's great thanksgiving prayer which includes the words of consecration. Father Emminghaus notes that Hippolytus gives the oldest recorded prayer for consecrating the Eucharist. It has been incorporated into our Roman Missal today as Eucharistic Prayer II. The text is extremely important since it conveys the earliest of all Eucharistic Prayers, and testifies to the continuity of such prayers over almost two millennia.[41]

Privileges of Baptism. In the Early Church, the sacraments of Baptism and the Eucharist were closely related, as they are today. Baptism is a sacrament of initiation into the kingdom through which we are freed from sin and reborn as sons and daughters of God. "Having become a child of God clothed with a white robe, the neophyte is admitted 'to the wedding feast of the Lamb' (Rev 19:9) and receives the food of new life, the body and blood of Christ" in the Eucharist.[42] The *Didache* cautioned that only the baptized could receive the Eucharist because it is the "spiritual food and drink" of the people of God. Through it they are spiritually reborn as children of God's kingdom. The early Christians appreciated Baptism and the Eucharist because these sacraments made them disciples of Jesus and helped them conform their lives to Christ in preparation for martyrdom. Hippolytus described Baptism being administered by immersion, repeated three times, and signifying not only death and purification, but also regeneration and renewal.

St. Peter encouraged the early Christians to "let yourselves be built into a spiritual house to be a holy priesthood to offer spiritual sacrifices acceptable to God through Jesus Christ" (1 Pt 2:5). Baptism established them as a priestly people whose chief privilege was to offer sacrifice. Their greatest blessing was their ability to partake of *the* sacrifice, the sacrifice of the Eucharist.

Eucharist Strengthens Martyrs. The early Christians believed that the "breaking of the bread" brought them into communion with Jesus. The Mass gave meaning to their suffering so that they wanted to imitate Christ's death and resurrection and offer their lives for the Church—their brothers and sisters in Christ. Some exhibited bravery to such a degree that pagan bystanders converted to Christianity because of their example.

Stories of the early martyrs help us to renew our appreciation of the Mass today. A certain layman by the name of Emeritus was arrested for allowing a Mass to be celebrated in his house (public assembly by Christians was forbidden under penalty of death). The magistrate asked Emeritus, "Was the meeting held in your house despite the imperial prohibition?" Emeritus replied, "Yes, it was in my house that we celebrated the Lord's feast." "Why did you let the people in?" "Because they are my brothers, and I could not close my doors to them." "But you should have." "I could not for we could not continue to exist without the Lord's feast."[43]

United to Christ. Our early Christian ancestors did not celebrate Mass out of a sense of obligation. They needed and wanted the Eucharist because it brought them into contact with the dying and rising of Christ. The Mass gave meaning to their suffering.

We know the early Christians celebrated Mass at least every Sunday, provided persecution did not prevent a Christian gathering. In some cases there were daily celebrations of Mass as we see from Hippolytus: "Every day His precious and immaculate Body and His Blood are consecrated, and are offered on the mystic and divine table, in memory of that memorable first table of the mysterious divine Banquet."[44]

Hippolytus was martyred in Sardinia. He was buried in Rome in a cemetery on the Via Tiburtina which was later named after him. Near the cemetery they erected a statue of him seated on a throne, the sides of which bear engravings of his writings. This statue, as well as pieces from the inscription on his sepulcher, may be seen today in the Lateran museum in Rome.[45]

The Martyrs in the Catacombs/ Jules Eugene Lenepveu

Situated outside the walls of Rome, the underground catacombs were used by the early Christians as hiding places to escape persecution and as burial sites. This painting shows the niches in which bodies were arranged for burial during the first centuries of the Church. Christians maintained the custom of coming to the tombs of their friends and relatives on the anniversary of their deaths to celebrate a funeral banquet. Their commemoration was part of a cult of the dead in which the Sacrament had been substituted for a simple meal. Here the bishop presides at a funeral liturgy. According to a letter of St. Cyprian, Pope Sixtus II was "put to death in a cemetery, on August 6" of 258, probably while he was presiding at the Eucharistic Liturgy. Sixtus' name is still mentioned in the Roman Canon of the Mass throughout the world.

St. Augustine

Doctor of the Church and one of her greatest intellects, Augustine was born in Tagaste in North Africa in 354. He studied the classics and rhetoric which he taught in Carthage and then in Rome. Although raised a Christian, he postponed his Baptism until he was an adult. Augustine led a dissolute life until his conversion at age thirty-two. He joined the Manichees, an heretical sect who denied the humanity of Christ and through them found his way to Rome and eventually to Milan where he was given a chair as a professor. In Milan, Augustine listened to the sermons of St. Ambrose who motivated him to read Scripture. He later broke off from Manichaeism and began studies to enter the Catholic Church.

Influence of St. Monica. It is possible that Augustine's mother, St. Monica, inspired his deep devotion to the Eucharist. We know from his *Confessions* how they loved each other and how St. Monica implored the Lord for her son's conversion at Mass "where she was present every day without fail."[46] Even before his baptism Augustine wrote of his love for the Eucharist, saying, "You drove back the weakness of my sight, shining upon me most powerfully, and I shook with love and fear. I found that I was very far from You, in the 'land of unlikeness,' as if I heard Your voice from on high: 'I am the food of grown men; grow up and you shall feed upon Me. You shall not convert Me into you, like your bodily food, but you shall be changed into Me.'"[47]

Conversion and Priesthood. After a long and emotional struggle to find God, his heart was pierced by the light of God's Word. While sitting under a fig tree he heard a child repeating the words, "Take up and read, take up and read."[48] Augustine opened Scripture to an epistle of St. Paul which inspired Him to give His heart completely to Christ. "Let us conduct ourselves properly as in the day, not in orgies and drunkenness, not in promiscuity and licentiousness, not in rivalry and jealously. But put on the Lord Jesus Christ, and make no provision for the desires of the flesh" (Rom 13:13-14).

Ambrose baptized Augustine in Milan on the eve of Easter in 387. He returned to Africa where he was ordained a priest and eventually became Bishop of Hippo, a seaport town where, for the next thirty five years, he brilliantly defended the Church against major heresies which sought to undermine the teaching of Christ.

Eucharist: A Commemoration. Augustine's conversion to Christianity was centered on the truth expressed by John that "the Word became flesh and made his dwelling among us" (Jn 1:14), a verse which he never tired of citing.[49] Christ had touched his heart and mind, calling him to a greater awareness of the gift of the Eucharist. Augustine viewed the Eucharist as a commemoration—a memorial of all the wonders and mercies of God summed up in the paschal mystery of Christ's death and resurrection. As a commemoration of the passion of Christ, the Eucharist is also a sacrifice. Christ sacrificed His life for us, said Augustine, not out of any need of His to be a sacrifice, but to show us that God wanted us *to become His sacrifice.* Through the Mass, Christ's Body and Blood are placed on the altar. As members of His body, we are also placed there by our gifts of bread and wine, making ourselves the sacrifice of God.[50]

When Christ said to His disciples, "Do this in commemoration of me," it was not so much for His benefit as for ours. Augustine urges us never to forget the mercies of God on our behalf and to renew frequently the grace of our Baptism by the celebration of the Eucharist. It is in this context of commemoration that Augustine focused his sermons on the Eucharist as a source of life, unity and sacrificial love.

Life and Unity. Augustine wants us to see the Mass as a symbol of an invisible *sacrifice* in which Christ is the High Priest who offers Himself, just as He did on Calvary, as a victim for our redemption. "This is the sacrifice of Christians," he writes, 'we, the many, are one body in Christ'" (Rom 12:5), and "this is the sacrifice which the Church continually celebrates in the Sacrament of the Altar."[51]

Augustine spoke to his neophytes one Easter morning as a pastor intent on leading his flock to understand to what extent, following Baptism, the Eucharist entered into the very heart of their new life. "You yourselves are then what you eat," he told them. "Be then what you are. Become so more and more; live as Christ. . . . Your individual egoisms, in the course of the rites of baptism, have been ground and crushed like grains of wheat and grapes to become bread and wine. In becoming the body of Christ you also have become the bread of Christ."[52] F. Van der Meer, in his renowned study *Augustine the Bishop,* wrote that Augustine preached from his personal experience of the Eucharistic mystery, namely, of people becoming one with one another and with Christ through this sacrament and, thus, becoming of one body and one blood.[53]

In the fourth and fifth centuries the Donatists tried to create a separate African Church. Augustine fiercely defended his belief in the unity of the Church which stemmed from the apostles, saying, "I will never give up *communion* with her, neither in Africa nor anywhere else, so help me God."[54]

St. Augustine/Noel Quillerier

Augustine recommended daily reception of the Eucharist at a time when it was not a universal custom. In order to bear witness to our faith, he said that we need the nourishment of the Eucharist just as the martyrs did. "Great is the table where the food is the Lord of the table Himself. No one feeds his guests with himself, but this is what Christ the Lord does. He it is who invites us, but he himself is the food and the drink. The martyrs recognized what they ate and drank, so that they paid him back in a similar way" (Sermon 329). Before his own death, Augustine asked for the penitential psalms to be written out and hung in tablets on the wall by his bed; as he lay there he read them with tears. Then Mass was celebrated by his bed. Just before he died, he laid hands on a sick man and restored him to health.

POPE ST. GREGORY THE GREAT

ope Gregory was a bridge between the ancient and the medieval worlds, building on the foundation Augustine laid to reverence the Eucharist as a source of unity and sacrificial love. He was born into a sixth century world of disaster and oppression. Wars, earthquakes and disease reduced the once glorious city of Rome to shambles, so that Gregory would later write in his *Dialogues:* "What has become of her who once appeared the mistress of the world? Ruins upon ruins everywhere! Where is the Senate? Where are the people? Deserted Rome is in flames. . . ."[55]

Gifted for God. Born into a wealthy and devout family who had given two popes to the Church, Gregory followed his father into public life and was appointed prefect of Rome at the age of thirty. His brilliant mind combined with his enormous wealth assured him a promising political career, which he soon gave up to devote his life to prayer and fasting. After his father's death, he converted his home into a Benedictine monastery. A monk at heart, Gregory's few years spent in seclusion were the happiest of his life. But severe fasting undermined his health and caused stomach trouble that remained a lifelong trial for him.

Elected Pope. Gregory was called to serve the Church in Rome, first as a deacon then as counselor to Pope Pelagius, who died during an outbreak of the plague in 590 AD. Gregory was elected pope by popular acclaim. Still drawn to the contemplative life, he wrote to the emperor and begged him not to confirm the election. Although he eventually yielded, Gregory's early letters as pope reveal the inner tension he experienced between his desire to be a monk and God's call to shepherd the whole Church.

Despite increased responsibilities, Gregory cared for his flock like a true spiritual father. He became known as the "Servant of the servants of God," a papal title still used today. His textbook was the Bible and his scriptural homilies became the talk of Rome; he is often represented in art as receiving His teachings directly from the Holy Spirit.

The Liturgy. Although the framework of the Roman Mass was essentially determined by the turn of the fifth century, Jesuit liturgical scholar Father Jungmann writes that Gregory added a few modifications. He codified the rules for selecting deacons and priests to make these offices more spiritual. (Deacons were elected not because of their holiness but because they had good voices to help sing the liturgy). Because he so loved the solemn celebration of the Eucharist, Gregory devoted himself to compiling the Antiphonary, which contained the chants of the Church used during the liturgy, today known as Gregorian Chant. He established the foundation for the Schola Cantorum, Rome's famous school for choristers. (Before this time the songs

were handed down by oral tradition). The Mass book we use today is called the Gregorian Sacramentary.

Gregory also ordered the *Kyrie Eleison* ("Lord have mercy") and the *Christe Eleison* ("Christ have mercy") to be sung alternately by the clergy and laity during Mass and positioned the Our Father near the Consecration, feeling that the Lord's own prayer should be said over the Body and Blood of the Lord. Many of the prayer texts in use today stem from Gregory, namely, the Christmas preface, the Oration for Epiphany, and the Prefaces of Easter and Ascension.[56] Gregory preserved, enhanced and stabilized the liturgical traditions of the Church, forming her worship into a thing of splendor.

Eucharist as Sacrament and Sacrifice. Gregory viewed the Eucharist as both a sacrament and a sacrifice. He believed in the real presence of Christ in the Eucharist, although he did not define the manner of the Real Presence. The Blood of the Lamb, he said, is taken both with the mouth of the heart and with the mouth of the body. "We receive the Sacrament of His Passion with the mouth for our redemption,"[57] he said in one of his homilies.

Following in the footsteps of Augustine, Gregory preached on the need to imitate the Eucharistic Sacrifice that we celebrate—through repentance, self-discipline, and above all through forgiveness of injuries. "Then it will truly be a sacrifice to God" he wrote, "when we have made ourselves a sacrifice."[58] He believed that the words of consecration effect a "cosmic transformation" which brings the Body and Blood of Christ into the mouths of the faithful. He saw the Mass as a renewal of Calvary, a mediation point between the human and divine realms. "For who of the faithful doubt that at the very moment of the sacrifice, at the voice of the priest, the heavens open and choirs of angels are present at the mystery of Jesus Christ: the highest is united with the lowest, heaven is joined to earth, and a oneness is made from the invisible and visible."[59] Gregory praised the sacrifice of the Mass for the great benefit it brings to souls both living and deceased.

"Gregorian Masses". Gregory's *Dialogues* were written stories inspired by oral tradition through which he instructed his flock. One narrative involved the monk, Justus, who broke his vow of poverty by hoarding three gold pieces before he died. Although he died repentant, the abbot ordered that Mass be offered for thirty days for the repose of his soul. We have St. Gregory's own testimony that when the last Mass was offered, the dead man's soul appeared to Copiosus, his natural brother, assuring him that he had been in torment but was now released.[60] Gregory's teaching on the value of the Mass in releasing souls from Purgatory is now a tradition in the Church known as "Gregorian Masses for the Dead."

The Mass of St. Gregory/Adriaen Isenbrandt

One day during the celebration of Mass by Pope St. Gregory the Great, one of the servers began to doubt the Real Presence of Christ in the Eucharist. Tradition recounts that St. Gregory started to pray, and Christ Himself descended from the crucifix to appear to the faithful, showing His stigmata and surrounded by the instruments of His Passion. This has been immortalized in art around the world.

THE GROWTH OF THE CHURCH

he Church grew to be *the* great spiritual power in the western world, acquiring large landholdings and spreading the Gospel to Gaul (France), Spain, Ireland, England, Germany, the East, and even to Eastern Europe and Russia. Side by side with the great cathedrals arose "cathedrals of the spirit": monks and missionaries who worked diligently to preserve the purity of the Gospel against heretical teaching and to strengthen devotion to the Eucharist. St. Patrick converted Ireland by preaching, building churches and establishing monasteries. A host of others followed.

The Church Fathers. The Fathers of the Church left a rich legacy of teaching on the Eucharist. They were mainly concerned with the Presence of Christ Himself in the Sacrament and the sacrificial aspect of the Sacrament. The Presence was the Word made Flesh born of Mary, and so the Eucharist was to be adored. They reflected upon the change that takes place in the elements of bread and wine. The Reality that the bread and wine became in the Consecration created the unity of the Church and was the motive and cause for fraternal charity. St. Thomas Aquinas wrote: "The common spiritual good of the whole Church is substantially contained in the Sacrament of the Eucharist." The teaching of Aquinas can be considered a fair summation of the writings of the Church Fathers.[61]

Roman Liturgy. During the early Middle Ages the Mass was fairly standardized for both the East and the West. Eucharistic worship was central to Christian life and the Eucharistic liturgy became the official worship of the Roman Empire. The Church had to cope with new invasions by the Vikings and Saracens but was strengthened by her alliance with the Holy Roman Emperor, Charlemagne. It was Charlemagne who made the recitation of the Nicene Creed compulsory after the Gospel reading at Mass.[62]

After Gregory, all components of the Roman liturgy were set down in writing, which made it easier to spread the Faith.[63] The Order of Mass, sacramentaries and lectionaries were written by the monks, followed in the twelfth century by missals and breviaries for the Curia. The *Agnus Dei* ("Lamb of God") which is prayed during Mass before Communion, was introduced into the Roman liturgy at the end of the seventh century by Pope Sergius as a song to accompany the Breaking of the Bread. Father Jungmann described this addition as the first indication of a more personal intercourse with Christ present in the Eucharist.[64]

Real Presence. Jesuit theologian Cardinal Henri de Lubac notes that, from the ninth century on, the faithful began to look upon the Sacrament of the Eucharist almost entirely from the viewpoint of the Real Presence. The people were learning that at Mass the Blessed Sacrament was not so much a *thing,* Christ's Body and Blood as sacrificial gift and sacrificial meal to be offered up prayerfully and devoutly, but rather a *person,* the person of the Lord, to be accompanied thoughtfully on His path of redemption.[65]

Adoration. Gothic architecture placed the sanctuary far from the laity and so it was difficult for the faithful to be involved in the Mass, which the priest said facing the altar with his back to the people. During this time the celebrant elevated the sacred Host immediately after the Consecration, so the people could share in this sacred moment. Periods of Eucharistic adoration in which the Sacrament was placed on the altar became common, and would become more common when the monstrance was introduced, enabling the faithful to view and adore the sacred Host.[66]

St. Bernard. In the middle of the eleventh century, a Benedictine monk gifted the Church with a powerful witness of Christ's real presence in the Eucharist. Bernard discerned the call of Christ as a young twenty-two year old, when he left home bound for the Benedictine abbey of Citeaux. Unable to resist his eloquent appeals and enthusiasm, four brothers, an uncle and twenty-five friends followed him to the monastery. Apparently, wives and mothers feared that their husbands and sons would be won over by his powerful appeal and go off to Citeaux with him! They would hide them whenever Bernard passed through town.

Miracles at Mass. Bernard's enthusiasm only grew stronger with time. He was to become the most eloquent and influential man of his age. He reacted to the pomp and circumstance of the monastery of Cluny—and of the Church in general—by simplifying the Eucharistic liturgy according to the reformed Cistercian tradition. During his lifetime he established sixty-eight Cistercian monasteries, preached crusades in Europe and engaged in complicated politics to preserve the peace of the Church. His reputation as a holy priest became well known, especially by the miracles wrought through his prayers. His first miracle happened while he sang Mass, when he restored the power of speech to a man in time for him to confess his sins before he died.[67]

Another time during Mass he asked the people to join him in prayer for a lady who had lost her sight, hearing and speech, and whose tongue protruded from her mouth. When he made the sign of the cross over the Host, he also made it over the sick woman. Breaking the Host he said, "May the peace of Christ be with you always." The woman was cured instantly. The people were so filled with joy they rang the Church bells, and the whole city hastened to the church to witness the miracle and to give thanks to God.[68]

Vision of St. Bernard/Fra Bartolomeo

St. Bernard suffered from poor health and recurring illnesses which weakened him, sometimes to the point of death. One time he was so sick and his pain grew so intense that he asked two of his fellow priests to go to the church and beg God for some relief. Filled with love and compassion for their abbot, they prostrated themselves before the Blessed Sacrament, imploring God for help. Bernard, meanwhile, had a vision of the Virgin Mary (to whom he was very devoted) accompanied by Sts. Lawrence and Benedict, under whose invocation he had consecrated the two side altars of his church. He recognized them as soon as they entered his room. They touched Bernard's body and he was instantly cured.

M. L'Abbe Ratisbonne
The Life of St. Bernard

St. Francis of Assisi

rancis Bernardone (1181-1226) was a wealthy young playboy who dreamed of a career of knightly chivalry. But he also had a spiritual hunger which led him to wander about the country praying and meditating. He was responding to God's call deep in his heart to shed his wealth and nobility for the sake of the Gospel. In his early twenties, Francis had a vision of Christ crucified which St. Bonaventure tells us "pierced to the marrow of his bone."[69] Francis was beginning to see Christ in all people. When he met a leper on the road he overcame his revulsion, dismounted from his horse, gave him some money and kissed his hand. Francis referred to this incident as the occasion when he "left the world."[70]

The Call of Christ. Francis knelt before a painted crucifix of Christ the King in the abandoned Church of San Damiano and prayed for faith. Christ responded from the crucifix saying "Francis, go and repair My Church, which, as you see, is in ruins." He took Christ literally and begged for money to repair the physical structure. Francis learned later that Christ wanted him to *spiritually reform* His Church. Two years later he understood his vocation when the voice of Christ spoke to him in the Gospel reading at Mass: "If you wish to be my disciple, then go and sell everything you have and give it to the poor" (cf. Mk 10:21).

Francis Responds. Francis gave away his clothes to live the life of a beggar. If poverty was his rule, obedience was his guide. He taught that "he has never perfectly renounced the world who keeps hidden in his heart the treasure of his own will." His desire to be *with* Christ and to be *like* Christ in all things led him to the Eucharist. Everything he did stemmed from his love for the humanity of Christ. One Christmas at Greccio, he set up a manger filled with straw, stationed an ox and an ass nearby and placed an altar over the manger where a priest celebrated Mass. Francis, who was a deacon, sang the Gospel and preached a sermon which touched the hearts of all who had come from the surrounding area. St. Bonaventure said that Francis spoke so tenderly of the "little Babe of Bethlehem" that "Christ was awakened in many hearts where formerly he slept."[71]

A contemporary biographer, Thomas of Celano, wrote, "Francis burned with a love that came from his whole being for the sacrament of the Lord's Body." Francis attended daily Mass and considered it an unpardonable sin not to do so. He frequently received Holy Communion, and he did so "with such devotion that he made others also devout."[72]

Priests and Eucharist. Francis' desire to be with Christ gave him a deep love for the Eucharist, which he considered a special meeting place where he came as near as it was possible to see and touch Him. Jesus had told His disciples that the bread and wine of the Eucharist were, in fact, His Body and Blood, His physical being; and Francis had taken Him literally. He urged people to show respect for priests, and especially to their hands, since it was they who made possible the physical contact with the risen Christ. He wrote to the priests of his Order: "I beg you to show the greatest possible reverence and honor for the most holy Body and Blood of our Lord Jesus Christ, through whom all things, whether on earth or in heaven, have been brought to peace and reconciled with almighty God."[73]

And to his fellow friars, Francis said, "Our whole being should be seized with fear, the whole world should tremble and heaven rejoice, when Christ the Son of the Living God is present on the altar in the hands of the priest. O sublime humility! . . .That the Lord of the whole universe, God and the Son of God, should humble Himself like this and hide under the form of a little bread for our salvation."[74]

Order of Friars Minor. Francis and his friars attracted huge crowds through their joyful singing and simple call to conversion. Even though Francis had not planned on starting an Order, the Order came to him, so to speak. The number of those wishing to join them grew to about five thousand very quickly. In 1212 Francis founded a second Order in cooperation with St. Clare, who had been so touched by the love of Christ in Francis that she gave her life to God as a "Poor Clare."

Francis' extraordinary energy was fueled by divine love which he received in the Eucharist. One day a rather worldly friend asked him: "Father, what do you do during those long hours before the Blessed Sacrament?" "My son, in return I ask you what does the poor man do at the rich man's door, the sick man in presence of his physician, the thirsty man at a limpid stream? What they do, I do before the Eucharistic God. I pray. I adore. I love."[75]

Suffering. Francis felt especially close to Christ in His suffering and prayed that he might share in it. At LaVerna, an isolated mountain retreat where he liked to pray, Francis received the *stigmata,* the wounds of Christ's passion on his hands, feet and side—visible lesions which bled and were very painful. He also had recurring eye infections and a chronic stomach complaint. Francis was slowly conforming his life to his crucified Lord. His great comfort was the Eucharist. The reception of Communion for Francis was intimately linked with the commemoration of the death of Christ. Francis became a victim with Christ the Victim—who offered Himself completely on the Cross. In his last *Testament* he urged his brothers to follow the Rule, and to follow Christ in His Passion and in the Eucharist, which for Francis was a continuation of the Incarnation.[76]

St. Francis of Assisi /J.G. Holmes

"Everyday, Jesus humbles Himself just as He did when He came from His heavenly throne into the Virgin's womb; everyday He comes to us and lets us see Him in abjection, when He descends from the bosom of the Father into the hands of the priest at the altar. He shows Himself to us in this sacred bread just as He once appeared to His apostles in real flesh. With their own eyes they saw only His flesh, but they believed that He was God, because they contemplated Him with the eyes of the spirit. We too, with our own eyes, see only bread and wine; but we must see further and firmly believe that this is His most holy Body and Blood, living and true."

—St. Francis of Assisi

St. Thomas Aquinas

St. Thomas Aquinas is an institution in the Church. A truly great philosopher and theologian, he was a man of deep contemplative and mystical prayer. French Thomist philosopher Jacques Maritain relates that twice Thomas had a vision of the soul of his sister Marotta, a Benedictine abbess, who first asked him for Masses to deliver her from purgatory. She appeared again to tell him of her deliverance and related that their brother Rainaldo, who had been unjustly put to death by Frederick II, was in heaven.[77]

Early Life. The youngest of many brothers and sisters born into the noble Aquino family (c. 1225), Thomas was sent to the Benedictine Abbey of Monte Cassino for schooling. Resisting his family's plans for him to become an ecclesiastical dignitary, Thomas was drawn to the Dominican Order of Preachers. His teacher and mentor was Albert the Great, with whom he studied in Paris and Cologne, where he was ordained to the priesthood. By the age of thirty he was reputed to be the most sought-after professor at the University of Paris.

Fruit of Prayer. Thomas lived as he wrote—simply and prayerfully. For a person of such accomplishments, he had a great deal of humility. One could say that his writing and preaching were the fruit of his prayer. He spent some years writing the *Summa Theologiae*, a system of philosophy and theology which became a theology textbook for the entire Church. Peter Kreeft notes that at the Council of Trent in the sixteenth century, St. Thomas' *Summa* was placed on the high altar in second place only to the Bible.[78]

Real Presence. The heart of St. Thomas' teaching concerns Christ's Real Presence in the Eucharist. Although he did not originate the concept, Thomas fully defined the idea of "transubstantiation," a word which describes the change of the bread and wine into the Body and Blood of Christ during the Consecration at Mass. The substance of the bread and wine *become* the substance of Christ's Body and Blood, even though the appearances of bread and wine remain. Thomas states emphatically that to receive the sacrament of the Eucharist is to receive Christ Himself. "We have under this sacrament—under the appearance of bread—not only the flesh, but the whole body of Christ, that is, the bones and nerves and all the rest."[79]

He spoke of the Eucharist in terms of "covenant," saying it is appropriate that the Body and Blood of Christ be truly present in the sacrament "because of the perfection of the New Covenant. The sacrifices of the Old Covenant contained the true sacrifice of Christ's Passion only in symbol . . . therefore it was necessary that the sacrifice of the New Covenant, instituted by Christ, have something more, namely, that it contain Christ Himself who has suffered and contain Him not only in symbol but in reality."[80]

Sacrament and Sacrifice. In the Eucharist, says Aquinas, Christ is truly present and truly received. He, like Augustine, urged daily reception of the Sacrament saying it is "our spiritual food,"[81] and while it is not necessary for salvation, it is "required that a person may be kept alive."[82]

Theologian Brian Davies writes that Thomas taught that Christ's death is re-presented in the Eucharist. So all the benefits involved in the Incarnation (His presence on earth) carry over into the Eucharist.[83] "The celebration of this sacrament is a definite image re-presenting Christ's passion, which is his true sacrifice. . . [and]. . . by this sacrament we are made sharers in the fruit of the Lord's passion."[84] Thomas often wept copiously while saying Mass, behaving as if he were present in person at Calvary. Thomas' behavior leads us to believe that he *participated* in Christ's sacrifice.

Mystical Writing. Thomas loved Gregorian chant and the beautiful hymns of the Office. When Pope Urban IV commissioned him to compose the *Liturgy of the Hours* for the newly instituted Feast of Corpus Christi—honoring the Body and Blood of Christ—he composed a masterpiece of mystical writing. Theologian Fr. John Hardon names three hymns he wrote in honor of the Blessed Sacrament as the most beautiful in the Catholic liturgy: *O Salutaris Hostia, Tantum Ergo Sacramentum* and *Panis Angelicus*. These express, he says, the unchangeable faith of the Church in the abiding Presence of her Founder on earth and also explain why the faithful adore Christ in the Blessed Sacrament.[85]

A Revelation. While celebrating Mass one day, Thomas underwent an astonishing transformation. He immediately put away his writing materials, leaving his great *Summa* unfinished. "I can do no more" he said, "all that I have written seems to me like so much straw compared to what I have seen and what has been revealed to me. Now, after the end of my work, I must await the end of my life."[86]

Thomas' Last Words. Three months later Thomas became gravely ill. While the friars prayed the *Song of Songs*, he received Our Lord in the Eucharist. When he saw the Host, he threw himself on the ground, burst into tears and adored It: "I receive Thee, price of my redemption, Viaticum (from the Latin *via or way*, it means Communion on the way to heaven) of my pilgrimage, for love of Whom I have studied and kept vigil, toiled, preached and taught. Never have I said aught against Thee; if I have done so, it was through ignorance and I do not persist in my intention, and if I have done anything ill, I leave the whole to the correction of the Roman Church. In that obedience I depart from this life." He died three days later, on March 7, 1274. He was forty-nine years old.[87]

St. Thomas Aquinas/Mary Evans Picture Library

At Paris, when the Masters sought his advice as to the proper method of teaching the mystery of the Eucharist, he went first and laid his answer on the altar, imploring the crucifix; brethren who were watching him suddenly saw Christ standing in front of him on the draft which he had written and heard these words: "Thou hast written well concerning this Sacrament of My Body and thou hast well and truthfully resolved the problem which had been put to thee, so far as it is possible to be known on earth and described in human words." And the force of the ecstasy was such that the saint rose a cubit in the air.

Jacques Maritain
St. Thomas Aquinas

ST. CATHERINE OF SIENA

atherine Benincasa was the twenty-third child (a twin) born to a prosperous merchant and his wife Lapa in Siena, Italy, on the feast of the Annunciation in 1347. Her confessor and biographer Bl. Raymond of Capua relates that at age seven, following a vision of the Savior surrounded by His saints, she consecrated her life to God.

Novitiate. Catherine had a deep devotion to St. Dominic and yearned to become a Tertiary of the order which he founded. At seventeen, following a dream in which St. Dominic held out the black and white habit of the Sisters of Penance of St. Dominic, she was accepted into the Mantellate (wearer of cloaks), the affectionate name given to its members. In the world but not of it, they moved about freely, vowing obedience to a superior, going to Mass together and living lives of abstinence and prayer. Catherine spent three years in seclusion, staying in her cell-like room, eating and sleeping little, venturing out only to attend Mass. "Such was her novitiate," wrote biographer Giordani, "the novice master was Our Lord Himself, who many times appeared to her and spoke to her heart."[88]

Nourished on Eucharist. Catherine was a vivacious and charming "mother" to a host of followers (her "children") who lovingly referred to her as the "Blessed Child of the People." The love she radiated came from the fire of Divine life within her—the Eucharist—which she was allowed to receive daily through the intercession of Pope Gregory XI. "Father, I am hungry," she would beg her confessor, "for the love of God, give me the Food of my soul!" For long periods of time she took no food other than the Eucharist.[89] All her early biographers agree that the Eucharist sustained her spiritually and materially; it can be said that her entire life was a great Eucharistic miracle.[90] During the Consecration at Mass, Catherine often saw Jesus dressed as a priest, repeating the words he spoke at the Last Supper. Sometimes she saw the baby Jesus in the Host. One day, when a priest tried to trick her by substituting an unconsecrated host at Communion, she lashed out at him in anger.[91]

The Wounds of Love. At Communion, Catherine often went into ecstacy. Once during Communion when she asked Jesus for a sign that her prayers were being heard, He asked her to hold out her hand which He pierced with a nail. It was the beginning of the stigmata, the painful wounds of Christ which He allowed her to carry.[92] Many of the saints were given the special privilege of bearing invisibly—and sometimes visibly—the wounds of Christ in their hands, feet and side.

Mystical Betrothal. Raptures, ecstacies, visions, conversations—all were expressions of her one love, Jesus Christ, to Whom she was mystically betrothed. When she was twenty years old, Jesus placed a diamond ring on her finger (visible only to her) espousing her to Him as His "bride." It was after this that Our Lord told her to begin her service to the world saying, "I desire to draw you to Myself more strongly by means of your love of neighbor."[93] Catherine *loved* the Eucharist; now she would *live* the Eucharist.

Active Apostolate. Her influence on public affairs was extraordinary—as a nurse, theologian, preacher, peacemaker and ultimately Doctor of the Church. Catherine plunged into an active nursing apostolate and tended to the victims of the Black Plague at La Scala Hospital. She had boundless energy and there was nothing that she wouldn't do for the Lord. She gave her possessions to the poor, accompanied prisoners to their executions and interceded in Church politics through a vigorous letter-writing campaign. She dictated letters involving a Crusade against the Turks and tried to mediate in the war between Florence and the papacy. Although unsuccessful in the latter, it was largely through her efforts that Pope Gregory XI decided to end the seventy year exile of the papacy in Avignon and return to Rome.

The Blood of Jesus. Catherine received an apparition in 1372 in which she was allowed to drink the Blood of Jesus from His side. She shared with Blessed Raymond that after drinking the Blood of Jesus, she couldn't eat anymore. She was neither hungry, nor could she hold anything in her stomach other than the Sacred Species, the Body and Blood of Jesus. For seven years prior to her death, she took no food other than the Eucharist. Most of her great accomplishments occurred during that period.

Dialogues with God. In her *Dialogues*, conversations she had with Christ while in ecstacy, she left her spiritual testament to the world: "Dearest daughter, contemplate the marvelous state of the soul who receives this bread of life, this food of angels, as she ought," God said to her regarding the Eucharist. "When she receives this sacrament she lives in Me and I in her. Just as the fish is in the sea and the sea in the fish, so am I in the soul and the soul in Me, the sea of peace. Grace lives in such a soul because, having received this bread of life in grace, she lives in grace. . . ."[94]

Early Death. Only thirty-three when she died, her last words were a prayer for Christ's Mystical Body, the Church, for which she offered her life. When Pope Paul VI declared her a Doctor of the Church in 1970 he said that Catherine "saw the Blood of the Savior continually flowing in the Sacrifice of the Mass and in the sacraments. . . for purification of the whole mystical body of Christ." Paul VI ranked her next to the "glorious Paul," whose bounding and impetuous style she reflected.

St. Catherine Dictating Her Dialogues to Raymond of Capua/Giovanni di Paolo

"I beg you, for the love of Christ crucified, to respond with joy and eager longing to the invitation to this glorious wedding-feast [the Eucharist], with its promise of sweetness, joy and every delight. At this feast we leave all uncleanness behind; released from sin and suffering, we dine at the table of the Lamb, where the Lamb himself is both our food and our servant. The Father, you see, is our table, bearing everything that is—except sin, which is not in him. The Word, God's Son, has made himself our food, roasted in the blazing fire of charity, while the servant at the table is that very charity, the Holy Spirit, who gave and gives us God with [the Godhead's] own hands."

—St. Catherine of Siena

THE COUNCIL OF TRENT

hen Catherine of Siena died, the Renaissance was just beginning in Italy. It was a time of rebirth for humanity due to increased commerce and technological inventions such as the printing press. It was also a period of renewed faith in the Eucharist. With the establishment of the Feast of Corpus Christi, devotion to the Real Presence of Christ in the Eucharist intensified. Processions were introduced to honor the Blessed Sacrament, and monstrances created in order to expose the large Host for adoration.[95]

The Reformation. Between the end of the fourteenth and beginning of the sixteenth centuries, the popes became patrons of the arts and literature. The Vatican Library was founded, and Michelangelo and Raphael were commissioned to immortalize the walls and ceilings of the Vatican Palace and the newly built Sistine Chapel. It was during this time that the Reformation began through the instigation of an Augustinian friar named Martin Luther, who challenged many Church doctrines including those related to the Mass and the Eucharist. Large segments of the faithful in Europe broke away from Catholicism to unite under the banner of Protestantism.[96]

The Church's Response. In response to the Reformation, the Council of Trent convened in the small town of Trent, Italy, on December 13, 1545 to clarify Catholic doctrine and to rectify errors and abuses that were infecting the bone marrow of the Church. The Council met over a period of eighteen years and held twenty-five sessions. Cardinal Pole opened the Council with a moving speech: "Before the tribunal of God's mercy we, the shepherds, should make ourselves responsible for all the evils now burdening the flock of Christ. . . . Let us come to what are called abuses. . . . It will be found that it is our ambition, our avarice, our cupidity that have wrought all the evils on the people of God."[97] (Abuses included a great variety of Mass rites—even within the same Church—prefaces with legendary content, various chants after the consecration and new Mass formularies of questionable origin, to name a few).[98]

Decrees and Canons. Ten articles involving errors related to the Eucharist were submitted for rebuttal, first by the theologians present, then by the Council Fathers. Their debates generated the formation of canons which condemned heresies, as well as accompanying chapters which contained doctrinal summaries.

The Fathers first addressed the Eucharist as a Sacrament, and then the Eucharist as a sacrifice. Regarding the Sacrament, the *Decree on the Most Holy Eucharist* dealt with the theology of Eucharistic Presence. The Church's doctrinal position was reestablished and it condemned the position of those who dissented (like Swiss reformer Zwingli), who said the bread and wine are called 'body' and 'blood' only in so far as they are *signs* of Christ's presence.[99] While Luther believed in the Real Presence, he rejected transubstantiation as a statement of how Christ becomes present in the bread and wine.[100] The Council reinstated its position on transubstantiation saying that at the Consecration of the Mass, the bread and wine are changed *substantially* into the Body and Blood of Christ. Also included in this document were chapters calling for worship and veneration to be shown to the Blessed Sacrament, the reservation of the sacrament in churches that it might be carried to the sick, and a proper preparation for receiving the sacrament, including sacramental confession in case of mortal sin.

Protests. The Protestant Reformers denied the sacrificial character of the Mass. The Eucharist, said Luther, 'is something we receive, [and it is not a sacrifice because] a sacrifice is something we offer.'[101] For the Reformers the active role in redemption is entirely God's, and was carried out on the Cross. They maintained that Christ's saving action belongs in the past, and that is why worship can only be to receive, not to give. They denied that the Mass could benefit people who did not participate in the [Eucharistic] banquet. The real issue for the Catholics was the belief that the Mass is more than a banquet. It is an offering of atonement calling down God's grace and mercy on all for whom it is offered.[102]

Eucharist as Sacrifice. In the *Decree on the Sacrifice of the Mass,* Trent clearly defined the truths regarding the Mass as a sacrifice, its intrinsic relation to the sacrifice of the Cross, its propitiatory character (its power to atone and make satisfaction for sin) and the importance of the Canon (Eucharistic Prayer which includes the Consecration).

The final document recognized Jesus Christ as a priest of the New Covenant "according to the order of Melchizedek" (Heb 7:11, cf. Ps 110:4, Gn 14:18) who "offered His Body and Blood to God the Father under the appearance of bread and wine. He did this in order to leave His beloved Bride the Church a visible sacrifice. . . . by which that bloody sacrifice to be accomplished once and for all on the Cross might be represented and its memorial remain until the end of the world, and so that its saving power might be applied to the remission of those sins that we commit daily."[103]

The Council of Trent confirmed and theologically systematized the Eucharistic belief and practice of the Church dating back to Christ Himself.

The Holy Eucharist/Antoon Wierex

The Council of Trent confirmed that not only was the Eucharist to be received, it was also to be worshiped and adored. It was in a Counter-Reformation context that Wierex's engraving of the Sacred Host and the six other sacraments was produced. This woodcarving of the seven sacraments features the Holy Eucharist as the most important—the Sacrament. The focus of the work is on the crucifixion scene imprinted on the Host to show that the sacraments are efficacious through Christ's merits and Passion. The Council decreed the Mass a sacrifice in its intrinsic relation to the sacrifice of the Cross, professed belief in the Real Presence of Christ in the Eucharist (transubstantiation), and urged the faithful to worship and adore the Blessed Sacrament.

ST. TERESA OF AVILA

he great St. Teresa (1515-1582) resembles Sts. Clare and Catherine, especially in her mysticism and her deep devotion to the Eucharist. Like Clare, she shed the material comforts and security of a good home, secretly fleeing at age twenty to a convent to give her life to God. She, too, suffered from illnesses her whole life. One day after Communion, St. Clare "in great beauty" appeared to Teresa, encouraging her resolve to strip the Carmelite convents of their material comforts.[104] And like Catherine, Teresa was mystically wedded to Christ and shared the relationship in writing, leaving the Church a rich legacy of her experience of God.

"His Majesty." Part of Teresa's appeal as a saint and a mystic is that she became holy while still being very human. She struggled with her love of "the world" and her dependence on friendships for twenty years. "On the one hand, God was calling me, on the other, I was following the world,"[105] she wrote during a time when she found it hard to pray. She began to experience frequent interior visions and voices and wrote to her brother that she was mortified that her "raptures" sometimes occurred in public. But in her autobiography Teresa said that she wouldn't exchange these visions for all the delights of the world. She calls Jesus "His Majesty," saying, "He comes with such majesty that no one can doubt it is the Lord Himself; this is especially so after Communion [when] He reveals Himself so completely as the Lord of that inn—the soul. . . ."[106]

Communion. Teresa wrote of "the good Jesus" remaining in a soul after Communion for as long as the accidents of bread and wine remain. Her practice was to welcome the Lord into her "house" where she imagined herself at His feet like Magdalene, and where she remained even if she felt no devotion. If the sick were healed by merely touching His clothes when He walked among them, Teresa reflected on the miracles Christ will work within a soul when we invite Him into our "house." "He has many ways of revealing Himself to the soul through deep inward emotions and by various other means," she encouraged her nuns in *The Way of Perfection.* "Delight to remain with Him. . . do not lose such an excellent time for talking with Him as the hour after Communion." She adds that this is a very profitable hour for a soul who yearns for the Lord because "He will bestow His treasures on those who He knows greatly desire Him, for these are His true friends."[107]

Prayer a Dialogue. Teresa taught her community that meditation is a dialogue. "Do you suppose that because we cannot hear Him, He is silent? He speaks clearly to the heart when we beg Him from our heart to do so," she wrote. Continuing with this theme, she said, "Soon after we have begun to force ourselves to remain near the Lord, He will give us indications that He heard us."[108] Teresa considers mental prayer as a heart-to-heart conversation with Christ by Whom we know ourselves to be loved.

Teresa Sees Christ. God often favored Teresa with His visible presence at Communion. "Almost invariably the Lord showed Himself to me in His resurrected body," she wrote, "and it was thus, too, that I saw Him in the Host. Only occasionally, to strengthen me when I was in tribulation, did He show me His wounds, and then He would appear sometimes as He was on the Cross and sometimes as in the Garden." When Teresa shared these revelations, she suffered many trials. Some people thought she was possessed and wanted to exorcise her.[109]

Christ Within. Teresa grew close to Christ through these experiences. One in particular, she said, profited her greatly. After Communion, she saw her soul reflecting light like a mirror in the center of which was an image of Christ. She understood that for a soul in mortal sin, the mirror is covered with a thick mist and remains darkened so that the Lord cannot be pictured or seen in it, even though He is always present. In some, the mirror is broken. This vision helped Teresa realize the great gift of Christ's indwelling presence and caused her deep regret for the many occasions when, through her fault, her soul became darkened and she was unable to see the Lord.[110] She recalls the "well put" words of the glorious St. Augustine who wrote that neither in market-places nor in pleasures nor wheresoever else he sought Christ, did he find Him as he did within himself.

Reforms. Teresa's desire to correct the abuses stemming from the Protestant Reformation and to reform the Church according to the decrees of the Council of Trent led her to establish Carmelite monasteries throughout Spain, for both women and men. Teresa would stop at nothing to reform her Order according to its original spirit, which she believed Christ wanted. She wrote hundreds of letters and even appealed in person to King Philip II to support her in an effort to form an independent branch of her Order, the Discalced Carmelites.

Doctor of the Church. Teresa gifted the Church by sharing her mystical prayer life and encouraged the faithful to realize how intimate Christ wishes to be with every soul, especially in the Eucharist. She died as she lived, opening wide her arms and her heart to the Lord saying over and over again, "A broken and contrite heart, Lord, thou wilt not despise . . . Cast me not away from Thy face."[111] Canonized on the same day in 1622 as Ignatius Loyola, Francis Xavier and Philip Neri, in 1970 Teresa was given the title Doctor of the Church.

St. Teresa of Avila/Peter Paul Rubens

"On that night a priest of that house of the Company of Jesus [Jesuits] had died; and while I was commending him to God as well as I was able, and hearing a Mass that was being said for him, I became deeply recollected and saw him ascending to heaven in great glory, and the Lord ascending with him. I understood that it was by a special favor that His Majesty bore him company."

—St. Teresa of Avila

113

ST. MARGARET MARY ALACOQUE

espite the number of saints and consecrated souls working for the Church, in seventeenth century France the love of God in people's hearts had grown cold. On one hand, there was widespread rebellion and immorality and, on the other, the destructive influence of Jansenism, a heresy which proposed rigid reforms of the Church not in keeping with her spirit or traditions.

The Sacred Heart. Into this era was born Margaret Mary Alacoque (1647-1690) who, along with John Eudes and Claude de la Colombiere, were the official messengers of devotion to the Sacred Heart of Jesus. Dr. Ronda Chervin, professor of philosophy and theology, writes in one of her many books that some Church historians regard devotion to the Sacred Heart as the Holy Spirit's remedy for the spirit of Jansenism.[112]

History of Devotion. Veneration of the Sacred Heart is an outgrowth of devotion to Christ's sacred humanity, writes Dr. Timothy O'Donnell, President of Christendom College. Its roots lie deep in Sacred Scripture and although devotion took on recognizable forms only after the first millennium, there is much evidence of the veneration of Christ's wounded humanity in the Early Church.[113] Devotion to the Sacred Heart was spread through saints like Gertrude the Great, Catherine of Siena and Teresa of Avila, whose own hearts were pierced by Christ's love. Although St. John Eudes is not the first apostle of devotion to the Sacred Heart, before Margaret Mary's revelations took place he had already established a liturgical feast to venerate to the Sacred Hearts of Jesus and Mary.[114] (The feast was observed in the seminary where he taught, then other dioceses adopted it).

Early Trials and Suffering. As a child Margaret Mary sought refuge in the chapel of her godmother's chateau where the Blessed Sacrament was reserved and where her "greatest delight was to kneel before the Tabernacle."[115] When she was eleven, she suffered a serious attack of rheumatism which kept her bedridden for four years. She made a vow to the Blessed Virgin, "promising that if she cured me I would some day be one of her daughters."[116] As soon as she made the vow she was cured. Although she wanted to enter the convent, she had to care for her sick mother and they both had to endure the cruelty of relatives who lived with them. Her suffering was so intense at times that she spent her nights crying in front of her crucifix. The Lord explained that His aim "was the undisputed mastery of my heart, and that my earthly life would be one of suffering like his. He would become my Master just for this: to make me aware of His presence, so that I'd behave as He did during His own cruel suffering, which—He showed me—He had endured for love of me."[117]

Revelations. When she did enter the Visitation Convent at Paray-le-Monial in 1671, Margaret Mary experienced a strong sense of Jesus' *presence.* Once when she was kneeling before the Blessed Sacrament she found herself surrounded by this divine Presence and heard our Lord inviting her to take the place which St. John (it was his feast) had occupied at the Last Supper. Our Lord spoke to her "in so plain and effective a manner as to leave no room for doubt [that it was He]. . . ." "My divine Heart is so inflamed with love for people," Jesus said, "and for you in particular, that it cannot keep back the pent-up flames of its burning charity any longer. They must burst out through you and reveal my Heart to the world. . . ."[118] Margaret Mary was to be the messenger of the Sacred Heart.

Jesus Appears. Author and retreat master Fr. Benedict Groeschel connects devotion to the Sacred Heart with the Eucharist, saying, "inasmuch as the revelations of St. Margaret Mary occurred in her convent chapel in close proximity to the tabernacle, the two devotions of the Holy Eucharist and the Sacred Heart have remained intimately linked ever since."[119] Jesus continued to appear to Margaret Mary in the Eucharist. "The Blessed Sacrament was exposed, and I was experiencing an unusually complete state of recollection. . . when Jesus Christ, my kind Master, appeared to me. He was a blaze of glory—His five wounds shining like five suns, flames issuing from all parts of His human form, especially from His divine breast which was like a furnace, and which He opened to disclose his utterly affectionate and lovable heart. . . . He revealed to me the indescribable wonders of His pure love for people: the extravagance to which he's been led for those who had nothing for Him but ingratitude and indifference. 'This hurts me more,' He told me, 'than everything I suffered in My passion.'"[120]

Our Lord's Requests. The Lord requested that His Heart be honored as a Heart of Flesh. He asked her to make reparation for the coldness and ingratitude of so many hearts through certain devotions: Mass and Communion of reparation on the First Fridays of each month, a Thursday night holy hour of adoration in memory of His bitter agony in Gethsemani, and the institution of the liturgical Feast of the Sacred Heart on the Friday after the octave of Corpus Christi.

As this devotion spread, priests wrote to St. Margaret Mary promising to offer Masses for her intentions. She was extremely touched by this gift which she felt was sent by the Lord Himself. In a letter to Fr. Rolin, her spiritual director, she wrote about the infinite blessings Christ bestows on priests, consecrated religious and families who practice the "pure love" of the heart of Jesus.[121] Devotion to the Eucharistic Heart of Jesus soon spread throughout the dioceses and countries of the world, and in 1856 the Feast of the Sacred Heart was extended to the universal Church.

The Crucifix, the Sacred Heart and the World/Sr. Margaret Mary Nealis, RSCJ

"Once the image [of the merciful Jesus] was being exhibited over the altar during the Corpus Christi procession [June 20, 1935]. When the priest exposed the Blessed Sacrament, and the choir began to sing, the rays from the image pierced the Sacred Host and spread out all over the world. Then I heard these words: 'These rays of mercy will pass through you, just as they have passed through this Host, and they will go out through all the world.' And at these words, profound joy invaded my soul."

Blessed Faustina Kowalska
Diary of Divine Mercy

St. Peter Julian Eymard

ruised by the French Revolution (1789) and its aftermath, the Papacy struggled to survive during the eighteenth and nineteenth centuries. The effort to destroy Christianity was overcome by a host of heroes and martyrs of the Church. Priests and bishops offered Mass in secret rather than break their loyalty to the pope. Widespread atheism, rampant immorality and the growth of rationalism (fueled by the Society of the Freemasons) sought to undermine Church teaching and devotion. Persecution by anticlerical liberals and Jansenism continued to plague the Church, which struggled to maintain its spiritual leadership in the face of its collapsing political power.

Bedrock of Faith. Like a beautiful hand-sewn tapestry, the Church's spiritual vitality and beauty were strengthened by the knots on the back side. Pope Pius IX (1792-1878) and the bishops of the world solidified the authority of the Church at Vatican Council I by declaring the doctrine of papal infallibility (the pope was infallible when speaking officially on matters of faith and morals). Pius IX defended the Church against rampant heresies in his *Syllabus of Errors,* and added the Feast of the Sacred Heart to the Church calendar. Thousands of churches, religious congregations and monasteries were founded and dedicated to the Sacred Heart of Jesus. There was a bedrock of faith and devotion to the Eucharist and Our Lady. In the nineteenth century, Our Lady was reportedly appearing throughout France—at Rue du Bac in Paris, La Salette in the Alps and Lourdes in the south of France. She came to gather her children under her mantle, to shield them from the approach of modernist liberalism by leading them closer to the heart of her Son. The Church honored Our Lady by promulgating the doctrine of the Immaculate Conception as an article of faith.

Our Lady's Guidance. The Church gained new life through missionaries and saints such as John Marie Vianney, Therese of Lisieux and Peter Julian Eymard. Known as "the priest of the Eucharist," Peter Julian (1811-1868) forged a new spiritual path for the Church in leading both faithful and clergy to a deeper awareness of the need for Eucharistic contemplation and adoration. He noted in his journal that it was Our Lady who led him to the priesthood and then to the Blessed Sacrament. Father Tesniere, his friend and biographer, wrote that one day Peter Julian's sister found him atop a ladder behind the altar in Church. When questioned, he responded "I am near Jesus, and I'm listening to him." He was four or five years old.[122]

Priesthood. Thirty years after his First Holy Communion, Peter Julian still shed tears over the graces he received that day: "When I embraced Jesus in my heart I told him: I shall be a priest, I promise you!" When he was thirty-two he entered the *Oblates of the Blessed Virgin Mary,* choosing that order because of his love for the Blessed Mother and because their community honored the Blessed Sacrament. In his final year of seminary when he was a deacon, he preached a sermon which led a classmate to recall years later: "It seemed, by his masterly presentation, that we were already hearing a missionary."[123]

New Religious Orders. While carrying the Blessed Sacrament in a Corpus Christi procession one day, Peter Julian felt an attraction towards Our Lord which inspired him to want to "bring all the world to the knowledge and love of Our Lord; to preach nothing but Jesus Christ, and Jesus Christ Eucharistic."[124] He received a special grace while on retreat—the desire to found an Order to honor Jesus in the Blessed Sacrament. Two months later he was laying the foundations for a new religious order. "The greatest grace in my life has been a lively faith in the Blessed Sacrament,"[125] he wrote in his prayer journal. He eventually founded two religious congregations for men and women whose primary purpose was to witness to the need and value of prayer and adoration before the Blessed Sacrament.

Adoration. Father Eymard had many friends with whom he kept a running correspondence. Writing to Mme. Tholin-Bost, a lady of great faith who had created an Association of Adoration of the Blessed Sacrament in the home, Father Eymard reflected on the remedy for the widespread indifference to the Faith, saying, "The Eucharist, the love of Jesus Eucharistic. The loss of faith comes from the loss of love; darkness, from the loss of light; the coldness of death, from the absence of fire." He encouraged her to light the divine fire of Jesus' love all around her.[126]

The Real Presence. Following a forty-day retreat in Rome, Father Eymard published a manifesto on the Eucharist. His words are timeless and speak to us today as if they were intended for us. "The great evil of the times is that people do not go to Jesus Christ as their Savior and their God," he wrote. "Society is dying because it has no center of truth and charity—no more the life of the family." He proposed a return not to the Jesus of history or to Jesus glorified in heaven but "to Jesus in the Eucharist." Why? Because "the Eucharist enables us Christians to pay our respects to our Lord in person. This presence is the justification of public worship as well as the life of it. If you take away the Real Presence, how will you be able to pay His most sacred humanity the respect and honor which are due it? Without this presence, divine worship becomes an abstraction. Through this presence we go straight to God and approach Him as during His mortal life."[127]

St. Peter Julian Eymard/Paul Montfollet

"There, now, I have found the whole secret of it: the unconditional gift of self to our Lord. I made this gift and took an oath on it before the Blessed Sacrament at the Consecration; my tears ratified it. At Communion, I placed my heart—in the act of giving itself—in the ciborium that it might itself become a ciborium. Jesus wants to be my Raphael, my means, my center. I shall renew my gift of self with my every breath. I now feel that I was fleeing from this divine servitude, that I wanted to choose what I should give and to hold fast to my **ego.** **Totus tuus** *(My God, You are all mine and I am all Yours); but no pilfering! This morning's meditation is fundamental: I am the servant of Jesus Christ."*

St. Peter Julian Eymard
Notes from the Great Retreat of Rome, 1865

A EUCHARISTIC RENAISSANCE

he Church continued to defend her faith against revolutionaries and all the "isms": rationalism, liberalism and a new heresy which was a synthesis of them all—Modernism. Although the Papacy suffered the loss of its considerable landholdings and political power, each pope planted seeds of reform deep in the Church's soil which bore fruit in the spiritual renewal of the late nineteenth and twentieth century. Although the Church appeared powerless in an Age of Reason which criticized religion and denied God, providence raised up shepherds who addressed religious, social and moral issues which revitalized the Church.

Leo XIII. Pope Leo XIII (1810-1903) drew the faithful to the Eucharist and to Our Lady. In 1899 he published the encyclical, *Annum Sacrum,* in which he consecrated the entire human family to the Sacred Heart of Jesus.[128] He gave his approval for the first Eucharistic Congress which was held in Lille, France, in 1881, and supported its purpose of "repairing the iniquities wreaked upon the Most Holy Sacrament and of promoting Its worship."[129] The Congress was the inspiration of a French woman, Mary Martha Tamisier, who had worked with St. Peter Julian Eymard. After witnessing the French Parliament dedicate themselves and their work to the Sacred Heart in the presence of the Blessed Sacrament, she conceived the idea of a worldwide celebration of the Eucharistic Real Presence.

Pius X and Eucharistic Reform. Leo's successor, Pius X (1835-1914), felt unqualified to assume the Chair of Peter and urged the Conclave not to elect him. Admitting that he didn't want it, he yielded when he knew it was God's will. Kneeling at the foot of the altar, he remarked to Merry del Val, his Secretary of State, that they would suffer together for the love of the Church.

His motto, "To restore all things in Christ," applied especially in the area of Eucharistic worship. He first issued a decree recommending frequent and even daily Communion for anyone free from mortal sin and in the state of grace. After centuries of dispute, this decree gave the final death-blow to Jansenism, a heresy which claimed that only the most worthy could receive communion. Fr. Joseph Jungmann writes that Pius X's decree *On Frequent and Daily Communion* marked a milestone in liturgical history. For years, the faithful had regarded Communion as an exercise complete in itself, detached from the Mass. This decree helped situate Communion in its natural liturgical relationship—as an integral part of the holy Sacrifice of the Mass.[130]

Communion for Children. Pius X also changed a deeply-rooted custom which forbade children to receive Communion until the age of twelve. He reasoned that they no longer should be kept away from the Eucharist under the pretext that they could not understand the sublime mystery, as if one needed to understand the chemical composition of bread in order to benefit by it![131]

"Pope of the Eucharist." Pius X loved children, he loved people, he loved life—and he loved our Eucharistic Lord. He was a simple, warm, saintly man who said daily Mass in his private chapel, then heard a second Mass in thanksgiving. Affectionately titled the "Pope of the Eucharist," he set about to reform the worship life of the Church. He revised the Code of Canon Law, the Breviary and the Liturgy. By restoring Plain Chant to the Liturgy, he helped promote an atmosphere of reverence towards the Eucharist. Pius X knew music, and his secretary, Merry del Val, recalls that he could read any score on sight, beating time with his hand. "Those who heard him chant the Mass in St. Peter's or intone solemn Benediction in the Sistine Chapel will recall his suave, melodious voice."[132]

On the thirteenth centenary of St. Gregory the Great's death, Pius X invited artists and musicians from all over the world to attend a Congress of Liturgical Art to honor the Pope who had been its great patron. Fifteen hundred voices filled St. Peter's with Gregorian Chant.

Modernism. Pius X denounced Modernism, a heresy which tainted everything it touched by watering down Christ's teachings to accommodate "modern" thought. Indirectly, his strictures on the errors of Modernism had an important impact on the theology of the Eucharist, notably the error about the origin of the sacraments, the origin of dogma and about the authority of the Church.[133]

Eucharistic Revival. The goal of his pontificate was to center religious devotion in the Eucharist—a plan which he pursued from the days of his early priesthood. To further devotion to the Eucharistic Heart of Jesus, he approved the decree which established the First Friday of each month as solemn.[134] His reforms inspired a greater participation by the people in the Liturgy, rekindling their devotion to the Mass and the Eucharist. Contributing notably to this revival are the Eucharistic Congresses held regularly, with participants from all over the world. Pius X is credited with inaugurating the Liturgical Movement, which culminated in the Vatican II *Constitution on the Sacred Liturgy* and in the liturgical renewal that followed.

During his last years, Pius X's sanctity was evident through the cures he effected—a man's paralyzed arm was healed, an eleven year old paralyzed child got up and walked, a nun who suffered from tuberculosis was healed. He told people not to say anything, dismissing the happenings saying "I have nothing to do with it. It is the power of the Keys, not mine."[135] Pius X's love of Jesus Eucharistic bore fruit in the gifts God gave him for healing the Body of Christ.

Pope Pius X Crowned in St. Peter's/ET Archives

Anticipating the publication of his decree on frequent, even daily, Communion (Sacra Tridentina Synodus, 1905), Pius X requested that the International Eucharistic Congress that year should be held in Rome. It was the sixteenth in sequence and the first one in the Eternal City. The Pope opened the Congress with the Mass which he celebrated and then participated in the procession with the Blessed Sacrament.

Fr. John Hardon, SJ
The History of Eucharistic Adoration

SECOND VATICAN COUNCIL

f the Council of Trent in the sixteenth century served as an anchor for the liturgical worship of the Church, then Vatican II pulled up the anchor and functioned as a rudder, steering the Church into what Pope John XXIII prayed would be a new Pentecost of spiritual renewal. The Church had grown from being a European institution into a worldwide community, which John XXIII sought to bring under the umbrella of Christ's unifying love. Less than three months after his inauguration in January 1959, Pope John XXIII convened an ecumenical council to begin a worldwide dialogue inviting the faithful to a fuller membership in the Body of Christ. In an effort to promote unity among all Christians, representatives of non-Catholic Christian communities were invited to attend the Council, a gesture which created a new climate of interfaith relations.

Constitution on the Liturgy. Over two thousand Council Fathers gathered in St. Peter's to attend the largest council in history. It was a pastoral council, meaning that it focused on the life of the Church, not on doctrine. Of the four major *Constitutions* enacted, the *Constitution on the Liturgy* was drafted first. Its goal was to make the liturgy better understood and more fully participated in by all the People of God. It dealt with such topics as changes in rites, use of modern languages, concelebration, Communion under both species, sacred music, art and architecture.

The Mass. Vatican II promulgated the centrality of the Eucharistic Sacrifice as the principal means by which the work of our redemption is carried out, and through which priests fulfill their function by acting in the person of Christ. The Eucharist, they said, is a renewal of the covenant between God and the His people. "From the liturgy, therefore, and especially from the Eucharist, grace is poured forth upon us as from a fountain and the sanctification of men in Christ and the glorification of God to which all other activities of the Church are directed, as toward their end, are achieved with maximum effectiveness."[136]

But they shifted emphasis from the focus on the Real *Presence* to a focus on the Real *Action* in the Eucharist. According to Dominican Fr. Benedict Ashley, writing in *Catholic Dossier* magazine, devotional practices had developed in the Church which seemed to treat the Eucharist primarily as a Sacred Object to be contemplated and adored, rather than to focus on the Eucharistic Christ offering Himself in the Mass through the priest and people. The participation of the laity was reduced to a passive role of "standing by" at the liturgical performance of the clergy, while engaging in their own private devotions. The pastoral motivation of the Council was to increase active participation in the liturgy by all members of the assembly.[137]

Priesthood. Jesuit theologian Fr. Avery Dulles, a professor of Theology at Fordham University, explains that, since Trent, the sacrificial aspect of the Mass had been emphasized at the expense of the communal meal, with the faithful rarely partaking of Communion. Vatican II emphasized that the sacred meal or Communion is a completion of the sacrifice, thus reestablishing the intimate connection between the Eucharistic and the Ecclesial Body of Christ so crucial in the Early Church and Pauline theology.[138]

While Vatican II revived the concept of the priesthood of the faithful, Father Dulles notes that the ordained priesthood is distinct in kind and not simply in degree from the priesthood of the baptized. The Council affirmed that Christ instituted the Apostolic College—a divinely instituted ministry which the apostles handed down in varying degrees to bishops, priests and deacons. Vatican II reaffirmed the hierarchical nature of the priesthood, clearly showing that the priesthood derives its power and authority not from the community, but from the Lord Himself. The Council stated that the priest alone, by virtue of the sacramental character received in ordination, can offer the Eucharistic sacrifice.[139]

The Reserved Sacrament. The Council Fathers urged that attention be given to the reserved Sacrament, saying that the Eucharist "is to be adored, because [Christ] is substantially present there. . . ." Fr. Dulles suggested that Vatican II accidentally kindled a reaction against the veneration traditionally accorded to the reserved Sacrament. Since the Council, the consecrated hosts are no longer regularly kept in a place of honor and benediction of the Blessed Sacrament has fallen into virtual oblivion. Fr. Dulles adds that Pope John Paul II strongly recommends prayer before the Blessed Sacrament, hours of adoration, Eucharistic benediction, Eucharistic processions, and Eucharistic congresses. Vatican II did not authorize the discontinuance of such devotions.[140]

Liturgical Changes. The Council opened a new era of liturgical renewal, invigorating the sacramental life of the Church. To encourage more lay participation in the Mass, the altar of sacrifice and the celebrant were turned to face the people. The vernacular replaced Latin, and singing was encouraged. Reception of the Eucharist under both species was introduced, the laity were invited to serve as extraordinary ministers of the Eucharist (both at Mass and to bring Communion to the sick) and the Order of Diaconate (Deacons) was initiated as a permanent ministry opened to married men. Lay persons became readers and commentators at Mass and sat on parish and pastoral councils. The Council Fathers infused new life into the Church and its members—the Body of Christ—by initiating a dialogue with other Christian denominations and by infusing the laity with the spirit of the Eucharistic celebration.

Vatican II OpeningSession/David Lees, *Life*

Over two thousand Council Fathers gathered in St. Peter's on October 11, 1962 for the opening of the Second Vatican Council, the largest in history. Over a period of three years they held four sessions and issued sixteen documents. Pope Paul VI, who succeeded John XXIII, addressed complaints and opposition even before the close of the Council with the encyclical **Mysterium Fidei.** *In it he reaffirmed the Eucharist—sacrament and sacrifice—as the core of the Church's life. He acknowledged the supremacy of the Eucharist among the sacraments, saying "it contains Christ Himself and it is "a kind of perfection of the spiritual life; in a way, it is the goal of all the sacraments."*

THE LITURGY OF THE EUCHARIST

The Eucharistic Liturgy was established on Holy Thursday and is celebrated today in imitation of the action of Christ at the Last Supper, when He took bread and wine, said thanks over them, and in *them* gave Himself to the apostles, saying, "Do this in memory of me" (Lk 22:19). "The Eucharist is a sacrifice of thanksgiving to the Father, a prayer through which the Church expresses her gratitude to God for all his benefits, for all that he has accomplished through creation, redemption and sanctification."[141]

Biblical Memorials. Nowhere does Sacred Scripture indicate that Christ asked His followers to record His words or His many acts of compassion and healing. But He did ask that His death be remembered. To that end He instituted His own memorial. Biblical memorials were significant because they *actually made present* a past event. For the Jews the Paschal meal was the memorial feast through which they dramatically relived the original Passover and the events of their deliverance from bondage in Egypt. The Exodus experiences are made present to the believers whenever Passover is celebrated so that, as one ancient Jewish commentator explained, "In every generation a man must so regard himself as if he came forth himself out of Egypt."[142]

Memorial of Christ's Death. So it is with Jesus' memorial, the Last Supper. Because it is the memorial of Christ's Passover, the Eucharist is also a sacrifice. The Second Vatican Council states that as often as the sacrifice of the Cross by which "our paschal lamb, Christ, has been sacrificed" (1 Cor 5:7) is celebrated on the altar, the work of our redemption is carried out.[143] Liturgist Fr. Johannes Emminghaus, explains how. During the meal Christ gave thanks (*eucharistia,* Hebrew *berakah*) to God for the food (bread and wine) that He expressly designated as Himself— His Body and Blood—His Body *surrendered* and His Blood *poured out,* which He actually fulfilled the next day in the sacrifice of the Cross. The Church, in obedience to Jesus' command to "Do this in memory of Me," celebrates this *memorial that makes present* Christ's Body and Blood in the holy Sacrifice of the Mass.[144] Jesus identified the bread which He blessed *with His Body,* and the wine which He offered *with His Blood.* The purpose of the Eucharistic memorial is to make Calvary present *sacramentally* so that the People of God, in all times and places, may participate in it. It commemorates the death of Jesus and renews His sacrifice in order to communicate to us the triumphant life of the Resurrection.

Sacrifice of the Church. The sacrifice of Christ and the sacrifice of the Eucharist are *one single sacrifice.* It is the ordained priest, acting in the Person of Christ, who consecrates the bread and wine and brings Christ to the altar. The faithful, who through Baptism are called to share in the royal priesthood of Christ, "offer the immaculate victim not only through the hands of the priest, but also together with him."[145] In the Eucharist the sacrifice of Christ becomes also the sacrifice of the members of His Body. Fr. Raniero Cantalamessa, a Capuchin Franciscan who serves as preacher to the papal household, suggests that we offer Christ our own body and blood. By "body" we offer all that actually constitutes our physical life: time, health, energy, ability and so forth. By "blood" we express the offering of our death; that is to say humiliations, failures, sickness that cripples us, limits due to age or health, everything that "mortifies" us.[146]

Mass: Covenant Ritual. In the Old Testament, covenant partners walked between the pieces of a slain animal signifying that they were initiating a permanent relationship with one another. They entered into a life and death bond—by "cutting a covenant" in blood—agreeing to live no longer for themselves, but for each other. In the New Testament, Jesus bound Himself to us forever and left us a ritual for responding to His love—the Sacrament of the Eucharist. Jesus "cut" the New Covenant in His Blood and bids us follow Him. The Mass allows us to enter an eternal union with Christ, our covenant partner. At Mass we walk with Him, not between the pieces of a slain animal, but to Calvary where we mingle our blood with His, promising to conform our lives to our crucified Savior."Whoever wishes to come after me must deny himself, take up his cross, and follow me. For whoever wishes to save his life will lose it, but whoever loses his life for my sake and that of the gospel will save it" (Mk 8:34-36).

Covenant Feast. We seal our covenant relationship with Christ in the sacred meal of the Eucharist in which we, like the apostles, feast on the consecrated food of His Flesh and Blood. Vatican II stated that the sacrifice and sacred meal belong to the same mystery and are linked by the closest bond.[147] Biblical scholar Fr. Ernest Lussier, sss, writes that the Eucharistic meal is sacrificial because it is the efficacious sign of the gift which Christ makes of Himself as bread of life through the sacrifice of His life and death and by His resurrection.[148] The Mass is the covenant feast of the People of God. It is the wedding feast in which Christ, the Bridegroom, consummates the marriage with His Bride, the Church, in a union of intimate belonging.

The *Catechism of the Catholic Church* refers to the Eucharist as the "Most Blessed Sacrament," describing it as "the Sacrament of sacraments," echoing Trent which said that while all the sacraments have the power of sanctifying, in the Eucharist is the Author of sanctity Himself.[149]

The Liturgy of the Eucharist/Marytown Adoration Chapel, Libertyville, IL

In the Mass the great mystery of the life, death and resurrection of the Lord Jesus Christ is celebrated in a sacramental way so that we might partake of His life. Through the Mass we can experience the curses in our lives being changed into blessings (Deut 23:5). The blessing goes deeper into the layers of pain in our lives the more we place ourselves in the presence of the One who blesses. Lord, You called us to Mass to heal us, to liberate us, to set us free. Let our healing be so deep that we walk out of Mass new creations, new people, healed in body, mind and spirit. Thank you, heavenly Father, for loving us so much. Thank you, Jesus, for not bearing to leave us, and thus sending Your Holy Spirit. Thank you, Holy Spirit, for guiding us into the freedom of children of God.

Fr. Robert DeGrandis, SSJ
Healing Through the Mass

123

ADORATION OF THE BLESSED SACRAMENT

cripture tells us that when the Wise Men saw the Child, "they prostrated themselves and did him homage" (Mt 2:11). St. John Chrysostom, a Church Father writing in the fourth century, elaborates: ". . . You see that same Body, not in a manger, but upon the altar; not carried in His Mother's arms, but elevated in the priest's hands. Let us, therefore, be roused, and tremble, and bring with us more devotion to the altar than those Eastern kings did to the manger, where they adored their newborn Savior."[150] The faithful have been adoring our Savior for two thousand years.

The Real Presence. Belief in the real presence of Christ in the Eucharist grew out of the teaching of St. Paul and the evangelists, writes Fr. John Hardon in *The History of Eucharistic Adoration.* They made it plain to the apostolic Church that the Eucharistic elements were literally Jesus Christ continuing His saving mission among people. "Once the Real Presence is properly recognized," Fr. Hardon continues, "it is only logical to conclude that we should worship the Savior in the Blessed Sacrament." He writes that after the elements of bread and wine have been consecrated in the Mass and transubstantiation has taken place, "the living Christ remains as long as the Eucharistic species remain. Then, because Christ is present, His humanity remains a source of life-giving grace."[151]

Importance of Adoration. Three months before the close of the Second Vatican Council Pope Paul VI issued the encyclical *Mystery of Faith.* "It stands as an authoritative expression of the genuine 'Spirit of Vatican II' as it applies to the Church's understanding of the Eucharist," writes Fr. Benedict Groeschel. It was written, he says, in order to "refute a number of gravely erroneous opinions regarding the Eucharist" that emerged during that time— and "to reemphasize the continued importance of adoring the Blessed Sacrament outside of Mass."[152]

The *Catechism* underscores Pope Paul's words regarding adoration, saying that the Catholic Church has always offered the practice of adoration not only during Mass but also outside of it. In 1981 Pope John Paul II inaugurated perpetual adoration of the Blessed Sacrament in the Vatican and urged every parish in the world to adopt the practice, saying, "The Church and the world have a great need of Eucharistic worship. Jesus waits for us in this Sacrament of Love. Let us be generous with our time in going to meet him in adoration and in contemplation that is full of faith and ready to make reparation for the great faults and crimes of the world. May our adoration never cease."[153]

Eucharist is Jesus. Writing in his archdiocesan newspaper, Francis Cardinal George of Chicago echoed Pope Paul VI's teaching on the different ways Christ is present in His Church. He focused on "the presence of Jesus during and after the celebration of the Eucharist which is real in an altogether unique manner—Christ's presence in the bread and wine consecrated by the priest." The Cardinal continues: "This is a real presence which includes every dimension of who Jesus is: body and blood, human soul and divine person. The consecrated Eucharistic species are the Lord and therefore command our adoration. We do not adore ourselves, nor the ordained priest, nor the Bible, even though these are vehicles for Christ's spiritual presence; we do adore the Eucharist, this blessed sacrifice made really present sacramentally."[154]

Cardinal George notes that some people today are impatient with objective explanations of the Sacrament and want to focus instead on the spiritual effects of participating in the Eucharistic celebration. This, he says, eventually erodes belief in how Christ acts to transform bread and wine into His Body and Blood. Jesus gave us the gift of the Eucharist to draw us into self-forgetfulness in Him. If we only focus on what spiritual gifts we get out of the Eucharist, we soon forget that we are receiving Christ, Body and Blood in the Eucharist. As Christians we are called to offer our lives in imitation of Christ's self-sacrifice and focus on Him Who is made truly present through the Mass.[155]

Pope John Paul II. To those who say that spending time adoring our Eucharistic Lord is selfish, Pope John Paul II responds: "Closeness to the Eucharistic Christ in silence and contemplation does not distance us from our contemporaries but, on the contrary, makes us open to human joy and distress, broadening our hearts on a global scale. Through adoration the Christian mysteriously contributes to the radical transformation of the world and to the sowing of the gospel. Anyone who prays to the Eucharistic Savior draws the whole world with him and raises it to God."[156]

Being *With* Jesus. When Jesus met the Samaritan woman at the well, He said "the hour is coming, and is now here, when true worshippers will worship the Father in Spirit and truth" (Jn 4:23). Like the Samaritan woman whose life was transformed by her dialogue with Jesus, like the blind man who received his sight, and the woman who was instantly healed by touching the hem of His garment, so will Christ touch His disciples of today who reach out to Him in faith in the Blessed Sacrament. Conventual Franciscan Fr. John Grigus, writing in *Immaculata*, explains discipleship as a call which involves "being with Jesus" and "being sent." The disciples spent three years *with* Jesus before they were sent out to evangelize the world. There can be no effective "being sent" without "being with" Jesus, Father Grigus says. Adoration is an invitation to be with Jesus to prepare for discipleship, a call which Christ extends to the faithful today no less than He did to His original Twelve.[157]

Marytown Adoration Chapel, Libertyville, Illinois

"To be able to live this life of vows, we need our life to be woven with the Eucharist. That's why we begin our day with Jesus in the Holy Eucharist. With Him, we go forward. And when we come back in the evening we have one hour of adoration before Jesus in the Blessed Sacrament, and [at] this you will be surprised that we have not had to cut down our work for the poor. The one hour of adoration is the greatest gift God could give a congregation because it has brought us so close to each other. We love each other better, but I think we love the poor with greater and deeper faith and love."

—Mother Teresa of Calcutta

ONE BODY IN CHRIST

hen St. Paul experienced his conversion on the road to Damascus, in one transforming moment he knew that nothing else mattered but belonging to Christ. Writing from his prison cell years later, he urged his flock to heed Christ's call to live as one body in one Spirit, in "one Lord, one faith, one baptism; one God and Father of all, who is over all and through all and in all" (Eph 4:5, 6). Paul awakened to the love of a personal God who was deeply interested in His creation, whose Spirit was at work in the world calling people to worship Him in Christ, who is "head of the body, the church" (Col 1:18).

The Body of Christ. Fr. Ernest Lussier, SSS, writes on St. Paul's powerful image of unity in the Body of Christ. He says St. Paul argues that we are *bodily* united with Christ's risen body by Baptism (Rm 6:4) and especially by the Eucharist (1 Cor 10:16, 17). This makes us members of Christ's body, united in such a way that together we form the Body of Christ. Father Lussier then refers to St. Augustine's image of the interdependence of the parts of a body: "The ear sees in the eye: the eye hears in the ear. The eye can say, the ear hears for me." Just as all the parts of the body conspire for the good of the body, so it should be with us Christians who form Christ's Body. United by faith, Baptism and especially the Eucharist, Christians are called to build up the Body of Christ, the Church.[158]

Eucharist Creates Union. St. Paul teaches his Corinthian converts that their unity results from sharing the Eucharistic bread and cup: "The cup of blessing that we bless, is it not a participation in the blood of Christ? The bread that we break, is it not a participation in the body of Christ? Because the loaf of bread is one, we, though many, are one body, for we all partake of the one loaf" (1 Cor 10:16, 17). Christians are united to Christ in a bond of intimate belonging through the Eucharist—which is the Body and Blood of Christ. From this Eucharistic relationship with Christ follows the real union of all the faithful with one another in one body. Baptism incorporates the Christian into the body of the risen Lord; the Eucharist in which each communicant receives the Body of Christ strengthens and cements this union.

St. Augustine often spoke of this unity.

> "Mark what you have received," he said in a sermon to his neophytes. "You will see what you have become—one body. Well, then, be what you are, loving one another, keeping the same faith, the same hope, an undivided charity. . . .This bread expresses unity. So does the wine, formed of many grapes. It is one, one in

sweetness of the cup but after pressing by the vinegrower. . . .You and I together are this mystery. Together we receive it, together we drink it, together we live it.[159]

After His triumphal entry into Jerusalem just before Passover, Jesus reflected on His upcoming death saying, "when I am lifted up from the earth, I will draw everyone to myself" (Jn 12:32). Fr. Frank Pavone, national director of Priests for Life, says that it is through the Sacrament of the Eucharist that Christ fulfills this promise. Christ, now gloriously enthroned in heaven, is drawing all people to Himself. If He is drawing us to Himself, Father Pavone says, then He is drawing us to one another. "The result of the Eucharist is that we become one, and this obliges us to be as concerned for each other as we are for our own bodies."[160]

Jesus' Prayer. The prayer from John 17:20-24 (next page) comes from the heart of Jesus. Just before His arrest, Jesus interceded with His Father in words which the disciples overheard. Often called the "high priestly prayer," Jesus petitioned His Father for His flock, asking that they be united with Him in union with His Father.

One Body in Christ. We are made one with Christ in the Eucharist. We gather in Church to receive Jesus: Body, Blood, Soul and Divinity. When we leave Church, we bring Christ with us because as St. Paul says, "I live, no longer I, but Christ lives in me" (Gal 2:20). We are part of a community of believers who receive their identity from the living Christ, Who lives and works in the world through us. This challenges us to see Christ in all people.

Pope Pius XII urges us to imitate "the breadth of Christ's love," saying,

> The Church, the Bride of Christ, is one; and yet so vast is the love of the divine Spouse that it embraces in His Bride the whole human race without exception. Our Savior shed His Blood precisely in order that He might reconcile people to God through the Cross, and might constrain them to unite in one Body, however widely they may differ in nationality and race. . . . Let us follow our peaceful King who taught us to love not only those who are of a different nation or race, but even our enemies.[161]

The Eucharist is the everyday bond of our unity. If we truly believe in the real presence of Jesus Christ in the Eucharist, we are prompted to the ever-deepening awareness that, after the Eucharist itself, the most sacred reality is the neighbor within the reach of my hand.

In His Image/William Zdinak

"I pray not only for them, but also for those who will believe in me through their word, so that they may all be one, as you, Father, are in me and I in you, that they also may be in us, that the world may believe that you sent me. And I have given them the glory you gave me, so that they may be one, as we are one, I in them and you in me, that they may be brought to perfection as one, that the world may know that you sent me, and that you loved them even as you loved me. Father, they are your gift to me." (Jn 17:20-24)

LIVING THE *EUCHARIST*

The Eucharist is God's visible, eternal covenant with His children; a bond of love which sums up the whole plan of salvation—union with His beloved. God sent His Son into the world to fulfill His covenant pledge of eternal love. Jesus' death sealed our union with God. "By dying He destroycd our death, by rising He restored our life," we pray in the Mass.

The sacrifice of Christ was initiated at the Last Supper when He gave Himself to His disciples as their Food. He did this in order to unite them in a community of His own Mystical Body. Formed by the Eucharist, Christ gifted His disciples for all time and in all places with the ability to have a deeply personal experience of Him. It is Christ who presides at His Supper as Host and gives Himself to His faithful who are His guests.

Father Lussier offers a liturgical perspective: "Christ is the sacrament of our encounter with God; the Church is the sacrament of Christ; and we Christians should be the sacrament both of Christ and of His Church."[162]

Consecration. Before Jesus took leave of His disciples, He gave them His final wishes: "I give you a new commandment: love one another. As I have loved you, so you also should love one another. This is how all will know that you are my disciples, if you have love for one another" (Jn 13:34). Jesus modeled a life of self-giving love—all the way to the Cross. He invites His disciples to walk the same walk. During the Consecration at Mass, when we unite ourselves with Christ's sacrifice, what does this mean if not consecrating our lives to His service? Any enduring relationship requires the spiritual sacrifice of self for the beloved. So does our covenant relationship with Christ require us to die to self—to empty ourselves—and follow Him for the rest of our lives. This is what St. Paul meant when he instructed the Romans to "offer your bodies as a living sacrifice, holy and pleasing to God, your spiritual worship" (Rom 12:1).

Eucharistic Community. Fr. Michael Gaudoin-Parker, noted British author, draws practical implications from this theology. He writes that a Eucharistic community is essentially an environment of grace where the least of Christ's brethren can feel at home and wanted—the housebound, the old-age pensioner, the disabled, and all those "marginalized" by a society which only recognizes those who are useful or successful. Such a community is *Eucharist-hearted,* he believes, because they receive their life and vitality from Jesus, the Bread of Life, who unites them in worship and love. "Receiving into their bodies this Sacrament, which they all adore, this community nourishes in itself a life that cannot be overcome by death—a life that preserves it from falling prey to the surrounding environment of a culture of death."[163]

Learning to Serve Christ. We love and honor the saints—and pray to them—not because of their heroic moral achievements, but because they show us Christ. "Inspired by their example, encouraged by their friendship, strengthened by their constant prayer and protection,"[164] we pray in the Mass of All Saints. They are like close friends who inspire us to find new ways of loving and serving others. They teach us to find Christ in all people.

An example from the life of St. Catherine of Siena is particularly inspiring. One afternoon when she was saying her Divine Office she glanced from her window to see a half-clothed beggar sleeping huddled against a wall. At first she closed the curtains in order to continue her prayers, but she couldn't get the beggar out of her mind. Catherine took a loaf of bread from the kitchen and laid it next to the sleeping beggar. He awakened and thanked her, asking if she had some clothing to give him. Her family forbade her to give away anything else from the house. So she took off the mantle she was wearing and gave it to him. That night, Our Lord came to thank her and to reward her for caring for Him in the disguise of the beggar. He invested her with a special grace which enabled her to go out without her mantle, even in the depth of winter, without feeling any cold.[165]

Living the Love. The Eucharist unites us to Christ and to one another in His Mystical Body. The spiritual conversion we undergo through our relationship with Christ turns our life into an offering so that our lives can be bread for others. The Eucharist is something we *do.* Christ's presence in the poor and needy is not the same kind of presence as in the bread and wine on the altar; it is, however, a personal presence. Jesus said that when we love with His love, others will see the love of God in us. They will feel His love. They will know it is Jesus.

A Eucharistic life, of its nature, is one of concrete, everyday service. Our Lord had no sooner given us the gift of his Body and Blood than his disciples began disputing about who is the greatest. Jesus immediately caught them up short, saying, "I am among you as the one who serves" (Lk 22:27). He clearly showed them what this means by washing their feet. This gesture, He then said, is to be the pattern of a Eucharistic life: "I have given you a model to follow, so that as I have done for you, you should also do" (Jn 13:15).

Christ sends us in His place to serve people, to bring His love and healing presence to a hurting and hungry world. The Passion of Jesus will last until the end of time and, by the Eucharist, we participate in His suffering. He gives us a share in His redemptive plan, calling us to rejoice in our sufferings for His sake, "filling up what is lacking in the afflictions of Christ on behalf of his body, which is the church. . ." (Col 1:24). Communion gives us the Lord as food, so that our charity may become our neighbor's food.

Pope John Paul II and Mother Teresa/*L'Osservatore Romano*

As disciples of Jesus we are called to become neighbors to everyone (cf. Lk 10:29-37), and to show special favor to those who are poorest, most alone and most in need. In helping the hungry, the thirsty, the foreigner, the naked, the sick, the imprisoned— as well as the child in the womb and the old person who is suffering and near death—we have the opportunity to serve Jesus. It is precisely in the flesh of every person that Christ continues to reveal Himself and to enter into fellowship with us, so that rejection of human life in whatever form that rejection takes, is really a rejection of Christ. He Himself said, "As you did it to one of the least of my brethren, you did it to Me" (Mt 25:40).

Pope John Paul II
The Gospel of Life

THE PAROUSIA

In classical Greek, the word *parousia* means "presence" or "arrival." It is also referred to in the New Testament as "the day of our Lord" (1 Cor 1:8), signifying an event of God's final judgment upon all people. St. Paul wrote about the presence of Christ as the concluding event of salvation history within their own lifetimes. "We, who are alive, who are left, will be caught up together with them in the clouds to meet the Lord in the air" (1 Thes 4:17). Peter urged the faithful to prepare and wait because God who called the world into being and destroyed it by the waters of the flood, will destroy it again by fire on the day of judgment (2 Pt 3:5-7).

"That Day". Jesus spoke of the Parousia during His trial before the Sanhedrin: "'You will see the Son of Man seated at the right hand of the Power and coming with the clouds of heaven'" (Mk 14:62). Biblical scholars are not in accord on the meaning Jesus intended to convey. He did say that even He did not know the "day nor the hour" (Mt 25:13), referring to "that day" and, in the Gospels of Matthew, Mark and Luke, Jesus urges vigilance in preparation for it. "But of that day and hour no one knows, neither the angels of heaven, nor the Son, but the Father alone" (Mt 24:36).

Book of Revelation. In the Book of Revelation, also known as the Apocalypse, the last book of the Bible, St. John offered a message of hope and consolation to seven church communities in Asia Minor (in modern Turkey) who were suffering ruthless persecution under the reign of Domitian at the end of the first century. The Book of Revelation is an account of visions—in symbolic and allegorical language—through which the author urged Christians in the face of insufferable evil to trust in Jesus' promise, "Behold, I am with you always, until the end of the age" (Mt 28:20). Those who remain steadfast in their faith need not fear, he said, because no matter what suffering or sacrifice Christians may endure, they will triumph over Satan and his forces because of their fidelity to Christ.

Hope in Suffering. John urged the leaders of the Church-communities to read these prophetic messages out loud at their liturgical gatherings because "the appointed time is near" (Rev 1:3). John hoped to awaken in his listeners a sense of confidence despite all terrible appearances, a sense of the spiritual kingdom to which they belonged as a priestly people who served not the emperors of Rome, but Jesus, the "ruler of the kings of the earth" (Rev 1:5). He summoned his flock to faith in the resurrection of Jesus saying, "he is coming amid the clouds, and every eye will see him, even those who pierced him" (Rev 1:7). "In his glory he will bear the marks of the passion at Calvary," writes Fr. Alfred McBride in *The Second Coming of Jesus*. The marks of His passion are at the same time "the wounds of his Mystical Body suffering persecution for their witness to love and salvation." He goes on to say that in its broadest terms, the Book of Revelation is a theology of suffering, a gift from God to give those first Christians—and the Church today—a method for making sense out of our pain.[166]

Eucharist: Pledge of Heaven. Theologian and author Fr. Paul Hinnebusch, OP, writing on the Parousia, is of the opinion that if we deeply appreciate Christ's love in giving Himself for us on the Cross and in the Eucharist, then we will look forward with eager joy to His final total gift of Himself to us in glory. Without His giving of Himself to us in glory, he writes, His sacrifice on the Cross is incomplete. And so is the Eucharist in vain if it is not completed in the gift of Himself to us in the bridal union of heaven.[167]

Father Hinnebusch adds that our union with the risen Lord will be the final effect of the Paschal Mystery of Calvary and of the Eucharist. The effect of the Eucharist, says Jesus, is eternal life and resurrection of the body. The Parousia will be the full manifestation of Christ's living presence which we now experience as a hidden but real presence in the Eucharist, veiled under the appearances of bread and wine. What Christ begins in the Eucharist, He intends to complete at His final coming.[168] "When we eat this bread and drink this cup, we proclaim your death, Lord Jesus, until you come in glory!" we pray at Mass. The Eucharist is a pledge of our future glory, a union which Jesus is preparing for His Bride, the Church.

Our Blessed Hope. At the Last Supper, the Lord Himself directed His disciples' attention toward the fulfillment of the Passover in the kingdom of God: "I tell you, from now on I shall not drink this fruit of the vine until the day when I drink it with you new in the kingdom of my Father" (Mt 26:29). The Parousia is not just the manifest presence of the glorious Lord Jesus, Father Hinnebusch says, "it is the shining forth of the glory of the whole Christ, His whole Body the Church, the glory of the whole communion of saints."[169] The Parousia will be the "coming of our Lord Jesus with all his holy ones" (1 Thes 3:13).

When the faithful open their hearts to Christ in the Eucharistic Liturgy, they are already participating in the Messianic Banquet, the eternal celebration of the union between God and the soul of His beloved, feasting on a love that is more intimate than that between a husband and wife. They are, in the words of Father McBride, participating in practice sessions for eternal life. They are beginning their sharing in the liturgy of heaven, while "awaiting our blessed hope, the appearing of the glory of our great God and Savior Christ Jesus." The "Spirit and the bride say, 'Come'" (Rev 22:17). It is the Church's most fervent prayer. "Come, Lord Jesus" (Rev 22:20).

Adoration of the Mystic Lamb/Jan van Eyck

Worshipers come from the four corners of the earth to celebrate the mystical wedding of the Lamb and the Church. The sacrificial Lamb on the high altar is alive—bearing the marks of His Passion in the glory of His resurrection. He is surrounded by angels who carry reminders of the crucifixion. We, a pilgrim people, make our way towards the new Jerusalem where "there shall be no more death or mourning, wailing or pain, [for] the old order has passed away" (Rev 21:4). We, who are redeemed by the Blood of the Lamb, will experience a "new heaven and a new earth" (Rev 21:1) and the fulfillment of God's promise to espouse us to Him forever (Hos 2:21).

Old Testament Endnotes

1 Scott Hahn, *A Father Who Keeps His Promises* (Servant Publications, Ann Arbor, MI, 1998), p. 36.

2 *Ibid* ., 58.

3 St. Augustine, *On Psalm 195*, n. 15 (PL 37, 1236).

4 Dianne Bergant, *The Collegeville Bible Commentary* (The Liturgical Press, Collegeville, MN, 1992), p. 42.

5 *Catechism of the Catholic Church* (Liguori Publications, Liguori, MO, 1994), no. 371.

6 Hahn, *op. cit* ., 49, 54.

7 Steven L. Kellmeyer, *Scriptural Catholicism, Biblical Foundations of the Faith*, (Greyden Press, Columbus, OH, 1998), p. 179.

8 Hahn, *op. cit.,* 165.

9 William McCarthy, *Jesus Lives in Our Hearts* (My Father's House, Moodus, CT, 1996), p. 1.

10 St. Thomas Aquinas, *Summa Theologiae III*, q. 65, a. 3.

11 Xavier Leon-Dufour, *Dictionary of Biblical Theology* (St. Paul Books & Media, Boston, MA, 1995), pp. 459-460.

12 Scott Hahn & Leon J. Suprenant, Jr., eds. "The Priest as Spiritual Father" by Fr. Pablo Gadenz, in *Catholic for a Reason* (Emmaus Road, Steubenville, OH, 1994), pp. 214-216.

13 St. Thomas Aquinas, *Summa Theologiae* Ia-IIae, q. 103, a. 1, ad 3 in the Blackfriars Edition, vol. 29 (McGraw-Hill Book Company, New York, 1969). See also IIa-IIae, q.87. a.1. ad 3.

14 Fr. Michael Muller, *The Holy Sacrifice of the Mass* (Tan Books and Publishers, Inc., Rockford, IL, 1992), p. 119.

15 Michele T. Gallagher, *Honey From the Rock* (Alba House, New York, 1991), p. 23. George Every in *The Mass* (Our Sunday Visitor, p. 31) says that St. Thomas Aquinas regards the sacrifices of the Old Testament as figures of our own sacrifice of ourselves, our souls and bodies to God, and at the same time as figures of the sacrifice of Christ. "We offer a calf, when we overcome the pride of the flesh; a lamb, when we curb our irrational impulses; a goat when we conquer lust; a turtle dove, when we preserve chastity." St. Thomas continues: "Christ is offered in the calf to signify the power of the cross; in the lamb to signify innocence; in the ram his dominion; in the goat, the likeness of sinful flesh."

16 Angelo Di Berardino, ed., *Encyclopedia of the Early Church* (Oxford University Press, NY, 1992).

17 Jean Danielou, *The Bible and the Liturgy* (University of Notre Dame Press, Notre Dame IN, 1956), pp. 55-56.

18 Aquinas, *op. cit.*, Ia-IIae. 85, I.

19 John Power, *History of Salvation* (Alba House, New York, 1989), pp. 67, 68.

20 *A Catholic Commentary on Holy Scripture* (Thomas Nelson & Sons, NY 1953), p. 231. Bloodless offerings were brought as an accompaniment to animal sacrifce. A portion of the offering and all the incense was burnt on the altar. This portion was called 'the memorial' because with its sweet odour it reminded God of the offerer. The rest which, after having been presented to God, had become most sacred, fell to the officiating priest. The sacredness of these offerings made it unlawful for lay persons to partake of them. It is not without significance that bread was the commonest material of the bloodless offerings in the Hebrew ritual. The typical relation of the sacrificial meal in the Old Testament to the Eucharistic meal of the New Law is obvious.

21 Hahn, *op. cit.*, p. 165. J. McKenzie, SJ. in the *Dictionary of the Bible,* writes that Aaron was associated with the golden calf but was not punished; the tradition represented him as yielding to popular pressure.

22 Nicholas Gihr, *The Holy Sacrifice of the Mass*, (B. Herder Book Company, London, 1939), p. 36. The transformation of the gift offered (through change or destruction) must take place for a sacrifice to be a proper offering. Thus, the animals were slain and their blood spilled on the altar, incense was consumed by fire, wine was poured out, bread was blessed, broken and eaten—all demonstrating that humanity is dependent upon God and ready to dedicate themselves completely to Him. An oblation is like a sacrifice in that something is offered to God, but nothing is done to it (i.e., like money).

23 Dufour, *op. cit.,* 463.

24 *Ibid.,* 392.

25 Bergant, *op. cit.,* 49.

26 *Ibid.,* 49.

27 Warren H. Carroll, *The Founding Of Christendom* (Christendom Press, Front Royal, VA, 1985), vol 1, p. 23.

28 Isidore's *Etymologies.* Translated from vol. 2 of W.M. Lindsay's critical edition of the Latin text of Isidore's *Etymologies* (1911); the passage, in the section "On Mountains," is designated XIV, 8.5, and a collateral reference to the landing of the Ark in the mountains of Armenia occurs at XIV, 3.35.

29 Dave Balsiger & Charles E. Sellier, Jr., *In Search of Noah's Ark* (Sun Classic Books, Los Angeles, CA, 1976), p. 96.

30 Power, *op. cit.,* 31-32. Smoke and fire were the common "signs" of God's presence in the Old Testament (as in: *Exod.* 3—Burning bush; *Exod.* 13—Pillar of cloud and pillar of fire in the desert; *Exod.* 19—Smoke and fire on Mount Sinai).

31 Ernest Lussier, *The Eucharist: the Bread of Life* (Alba House, New York, 1977), p. 169.

32 Hahn & Suprenant, *op. cit.,* 217.

33 *Ibid.,* 217-218. Chapter entitled, "The Priest as Spiritual Father," by Fr. Pablo Gadenz, pp. 209-228.

34 See Jerome's "Epistle 73 to the Presbyter Evangelum" on the identification of Melchizedek as Shem (*Patrologia Latina,* vol. 22, 676-81).

35 Fr. William McCarthy, unpublished notes. Also see Michael O'Carroll, *Corpus Christi* (The Liturgical Press, Collegeville, MN, 1988), p. 136. Father O'Carroll notes that if perfection had been attainable through the Levitical priesthood (for under it the people received the law), what further need would there be for another priest to arise after the order of Melchizidek, rather than one named after the order of Aaron?

36 *New Catholic Encyclopedia* (McGraw Hill Book Company, New York, 1967), vol. 9, p. 627.

37 *The Sacramentary* (Catholic Book Publishing Co, New York, 1985), p. 546.

38 Pope John Paul II, *The Mystery and Worship of the Eucharist* (Pauline Books and Media, Boston, MA), p. 4.

39 *The Rites of the Catholic Church,* vol 2 (A Pueblo Book, The Liturgical Press, Collegeville MN, 1991), pp. 45-46.

40 Power, *op. cit.,* 34. The sacrifice of a human being, so repugnant to us, would not have appeared too strange to Abraham. Human sacrifices were practiced among the pagan inhabitants of Palestine, where he lived. Among the archeological discoveries in Ur, the city where he lived, was an unbroken tomb of a king, complete with his retinue of wives, soldiers, and even dancing girls. Apparently, all were buried alive at the death of the king, so that they could continue to serve him in his afterlife.

41 Hahn *op. cit.,* 110.

42 Fr. Paul Cioffi, "Closing Mass of Forty Hours Devotion" (Institute for Pastoral Renewal, Inc., Georgetown University, Washington, D.C., 1998).

43 *Ibid.*

44 Raniero Cantalamessa, *The Eucharist, Our Sanctification* (The Liturgical Press, Collegeville, MN, 1993), p. 7. St. John Chrysostom's sermon, "A Christian's Battle," is from Catecheses III, 8-15.

45 Dufour, *op. cit.,* 409.

46 Power, *op. cit.,* 79.

47 John P. Schanz, *The Sacraments of Life and Worship* (The Bruce Publishing Company, Milwaukee, WI, 1966), p. 145.

48 John L. McKenzie, SJ. *Dictionary of the Bible* (Macmillan Publishing Company, NY, 1965), p. 541.

49 Power, *op. cit.,* 51.

50 Fr. Benedict Groeschel & James Monti, *In the Presence of Our Lord: The History, Theology, and Psychology of Eucharistic Devotion* (Our Sunday Visitor, Huntington, IN, 1997), p. 219.

51 Dufour, *op. cit.,* 94.

52 McKenzie, *op. cit.,* 23.

53 Schanz, *op. cit.,* 151.

54 Etienne Charpentier, *How to Read the Old Testament* (SCM Press, Ltd., London, 1982), p. 51.

55 Schanz, *op. cit.,* 151.

56 Eugene LaVerdiere, *Dining in the Kingdom of God* (Liturgy Training Publications, Chicago, IL, 1994), p. 140.

57 Schanz, *op. cit.,* 151.

58 Charpentier, *op. cit.,* 71.

59 Courtenay Bartholomew, *A Scientist Researches Mary, The Ark of the Covenant* (The 101 Foundation, Asbury, NJ, 1995), pp. 63-64.

60 *New Catholic Encyclopedia,* vol. 1, p. 817.

61 William McCarthy, *Twelve Keys to the Anointing* (My Father's House, Moodus, CT), p. 9.

62 *Ibid.,* 9-10.

63 Richard Foley, *Mary and the Eucharist* (Hope of St. Monica, Newtonsville, OH, 1997), p. 133.

64 Jerome Murphy O'Connor, *The Holy Land* (Oxford University Press, NY, 1992), p. 159. This church is built on the ruins of a fifth century church, sections of whose mosaic floor are still visible.

65 Cynthia Pearl Maus, *The Old Testament and the Fine Arts* (Harper & Brothers Publishers, New York, 1954), p. 203.

66 Bartholomew, *op. cit.,* 66. The veil was so thick and heavy that it took three hundred priests to hang it. The veil was woven with colored strands—white, violet, red and green. Significantly, these are now the liturgical colors of the Church. This is the same veil which stood in the Temple in Jerusalem which was rent in two when Jesus died on the cross.

67 McCarthy, *op. cit.,* 2.

68 Hahn, *op. cit.,* 257. When Pharaoh pursued the Israelites with his army and chariots, the pillar of cloud moved from in front of them and took its place behind them. It came between the army of Egypt and the Israelites and protected them. "The angel of God, who had been leading Israel's camp, now moved and went around behind them. The column of cloud also, leaving the front, took up its place behind them, so that it came between the camp of the Egyptians and that of Israel" (Ex 14: 19-20).

69 Power, *op. cit.,* 99.

70 Dufour, *op. cit.,* 109.

71 Peter Kreeft, *You Can Understand the Old Testament* (Servant Publications, Ann Arbor, MI, 1990), p. 65.

72 Power, *op. cit.,* 102-103.

73 *Ibid.,* 103.

74 Bartholomew, *op. cit.,* 59.

75 James T. O'Connor, *The Hidden Manna, A Theology of the Eucharist* (Ignatius Press, San Francisco, CA, 1988), p. 297.

76 *Ibid.,* 298.

77 Aquinas, *op. cit.,* Pt. 111. Q 79 Art 4. (See Groeschel, p. 102.)

78 O'Connor, *op. cit.,* 297-299.

79 Power *op. cit.,* 153.

80 *New Catholic Encyclopedia,* vol. 9, p. 99.

81 O' Carroll, *op. cit.,* 132.

82 McKenzie, *op. cit.,* 537.

83 Kreeft *op. cit.,* 175.

84 *Ibid.,* 83-84.

85 *Ibid.,* 78.

86 Bergant, *op. cit.,* 368-369.

87 Kreeft *op. cit.,* 85.

88 Power *op. cit.,* 155.

89 William McCarthy, *Salvation History* (My Father's House, Moodus, CT, 1999), p. 5.

90 Power *op. cit.,* 126.

91 *The Oxford Companion to the Bible* (Oxford University Press, NY, 1993), p. 329.

92 *Ibid.,* 329.

New Testament Endnotes

1 *The New Catholic Encyclopedia*, vol. 9, p. 339.

2 Pope John Paul II, Lourdes homily in August 1983 (reported in *L'Osservatore Romano*, September 5, 1983).

3 Ferdinand Prat, SJ., *Jesus Christ,* vol. 1 (The Bruce Publishing Company, Milwaukee, WI, 1950), p. 48.

4 St. Augustine, *De Virginitate*, iv; ML, XL, 898.

5 Raniero Cantalamessa, *Mary, Mirror of the Church* (The Liturgical Press, Collegeville, MN, 1992), p. 126.

6 *Ibid.,* 57.

7 St. Irenaeus, *Against the Heresies*, III, 22, 4 (Sch 211, p. 442).

8 James T. O'Connor, *The Hidden Manna* (Ignatius Press, San Francisco, CA, 1988), pp. 342, 348.

9 St. Thomas Aquinas, *Summa Theologiae,* Leonine ed. (Rome, 1888-1906), III, q.75, a. 4A, 4c.

10 Warren Carroll, *The Founding of Christendom* (Christendom Press, Front Royal, VA, 1985), p. 299.

11 Robert J. Karris, *Invitation to Luke* (Image Books, Garden City, NY, 1977), p. 48.

12 Eugene LaVerdiere, *The Eucharist in the New Testament and the Early Church* (The Liturgical Press, Collegeville, MN, 1996), p. 98.

13 Josephus, *Antiquities of the Jews,* XVIII, 63f., trans. H. St. John Thackeray in *Josephus, the Man and the Historian* (New York, 1929), pp.136-137. Warren Carroll points out that the authenticity of this passage—formerly almost universally denied—has been accepted in the twentieth century by such renowned scholars as von Harnack and Burkitt.

14 Aime Georges Martimort, *The Church at Prayer* (The Liturgical Press, Collegeville, MN, 1992), p. 82.

15 Hans Urs von Balthasar, *Light of the Word* (Ignatius Press, San Francisco, CA, 1993), pp. 265-266.

16 Prat, *op. cit.,* 94.

17 John Paul II, *The Gospel of Life* (Libreria Editrice Vaticana, Vatican City), p. 185.

18 Austin Flannery, ed., "Lumen Gentium," *Vatican Council II* (Costello Publishing Company, Northport, NY, 1996), p. 417.

19 Jean Danielou, *The Work of John the Baptist* (Baltimore, MD, 1966).

20 Lawrence Hennessey, "The Baptism of the Lord," homily given at St. Patrick's Church, Lake Forest, IL, January 10, 1998.

21 Ignace de la Potterie, *Mary in the Mystery of the Covenant* (Alba House, New York, 1992), p. xxiv.

22 Fulton J. Sheen, *The Life of Christ* (Doubleday, New York, 1977), p. 77.

23 De la Potterie, *op. cit.,* 202.

24 LaVerdiere, *op. cit.,* 115.

25 Robert J. Karris, *Luke: Artist and Theologian* (Paulist Press, Mahweh, NJ, 1985), p. 58.

26 Robert Fabing, SJ, *Real Food* (Paulist Press, New York, 1993), p. 31.

27 Eugene Laverdiere, *Dining in the Kingdom of God* (Liturgy Training Publications, Chicago, IL, 1994), p. 41.

28 *Ibid.,* 104.

29 John Paul II, ". . . in the banquet of life, to which all are equally invited by God, we should make 'the other' a sharer on a par with ourselves," *Sollicitudo rei socialis,* no. 39: AAS 80 (1988), p. 567.

30 Fabing, *op. cit.,* 38.

31 LaVerdiere, *op. cit.,* 66. Given Luke's sensitivity to include women throughout the gospel, Fr. LaVerdiere says "we may safely assume that the crowd of 5,000 included women."

32 LaVerdiere, *op. cit., Early Church,* 87.

33 Laverdiere, *op. cit., Dining,* 69.

34 Xavier-Leon Dufour, trans. Matthew J. O'Connell. *Sharing the Eucharistic Bread* (Paulist Press, New York, 1982).

35 LaVerdiere, *op. cit., Dining,* 70.

36 Fabing, *op. cit.,* 39.

37 *Ibid.,* 40.

38 Raymond E. Brown, *An Introduction to the New Testament* (Doubleday, New York, 1997), p. 346.

39 Johannes H. Emminghaus, *The Eucharist: Essence, Form, Celebration* (The Liturgical Press, Collegeville, MN, 1997), p. 21

40 Sheen, *op. cit.,* 141.

41 John O'Brien, *The Faith of Millions* (Our Sunday Visitor, Huntington, IN, 1938), pp. 217-218.

42 *Ibid.,* 217-218.

43 Sheen, *op. cit.,* 142-143.

44 O'Brien, *op. cit.,* 227-228.

45 Steven L. Kellmeyer, *Scriptural Catholicism* (Greyden Press, Columbus, OH, 1998), p. 93. Biblical citation translated literally from the Greek.

46 *Ibid.,* 94.

47 Carroll, *op. cit.,* 337.

48 Power, *op. cit.,* 73. Warren Carroll in *The Founding of Christendom* notes that the roots of the pasch can be traced to ancient pagan rites such as that of the nomads sacrificing the first-born of their flocks, p. 76.

49 LaVerdiere, *op. cit., Dining,* 130.

50 J. James Tissot, *The Life of Our Lord Jesus Christ* (The McLure-Tissot Company, New York, 1849), vol. 3.

51 Laverdiere, *op. cit., Dining,* 130.

52 Power, *op. cit.,* 67.

53 LaVerdiere, *op. cit., Dining* 137.

54 *Ibid.,* 5.

55 Aidan Nichols, *The Holy Eucharist* (Veritas, Dublin, 1991), Oscott Series, No. 6., p. 17. It is interesting to note that the references to the Apostle John in the Gospels all suggest a very young man, but not a boy. We may therefore reasonably estimate his age at the time of Jesus' Passion and Resurrection in 30 AD as 18 to 20, which would put his birth year at 10 to 12 AD. Warren Carroll (*The Founding of Christendom*) concludes that in the year 90 or 91, when John was writing his gospel, he would have been 79 or 80 years old.

56 Fabing, *op. cit.,* 76.

57 Sheen, *op. cit.,* 285.

58 George Martin, "Servants of God," *New Covenant,* April 1999. (200 Noll Plaza, Huntington, IN), p. 34.

59 John Paul II, *L'Osservatore Romano,* April 1998.

60 Scott Hahn, *A Father Who Keeps His Promises* (Servant Publications, Ann Arbor, MI, 1998), p. 234.

61 Guy Oury, *The Mass* (Catholic Book Publishing Company, NY, 1988), p. 32.

62 Vatican II, *Presbyterorum ordinis,* nos. 2, 6, 12; *Lumen Gentium,* no. 28.

63 Vatican II, *Presbyterorum ordinis,* no. 5.

64 John Paul II, *Dominicae Cenae,* no. 8, AAS 72 (1980), pp. 128-129.

65 Hahn, *op. cit.,* 237.

66 Raniero Cantalamessa, *The Eucharist, Our Sanctification* (The Liturgical Press, Collegeville, MN, 1993), p. 30.

67 *Ibid.,* 28.

68 *Ibid.,* 37-38.

69 Sheen, *op. cit.,* 365.

70 Carroll, *op. cit.,* 372.

71 Sheen, *op. cit.,* 372.

72 Anne Catherine Emmerich, *The Dolorous Passion of Our Lord Jesus Christ* (Tan Books and Publishers, Inc. Rockford, IL, 1983), pp. 270-271.

73 LaVerdiere, *op. cit., Dining,* 140.

74 Emmerich, *op. cit.,* 284.

75 Prat, *op. cit.,* vol. 2, 395.

76 *Ibid.,* 395.

77 Danielou, *op. cit.,* 206.

78 Hahn, *op. cit.,* 255.

79 Carroll, *op. cit.,* 374.

80 Prat, *op. cit.,* 398. According to the research of artist James Tissot, an extraordinary fissure in the rock of Golgotha can still be seen in the Church of the Holy Sepulchre; it is alluded to by St. Cyril of Alexandria. The fissure does not run in the same direction as the strata of the rock; it is a perpendicular rent at right angles with the layers of the rock of Golgotha. Competent authorities have declared this strange fissure to be the result of a miracle and when their testimony is compared with that of the Gospel narrative, the same conclusion is forced on us.

81 Hahn, *op. cit.,* 233. Additional comments about the "fourth cup" may be found in Raymond Brown, *Death of the Messiah,* p. 1077, and William Lane, *The Gospel According to Mark,* p. 508.

82 LaVerdiere, *op. cit., Dining,* 166.

83 Sheen, *op. cit.,* 425.

84 Carroll, *op. cit.,* 395.

85 John Paul II, *The Spirit, Giver of Life and Love* (Pauline Books & Media, Boston MA, 1996), p. 92.

86 Lawrence Hennessey, "The Holy Spirit in the Liturgy," unpublished meditation paper, (University of St. Mary of the Lake Seminary, Mundelein, IL.), June 1997.

87 *Ibid.*

88 Henri De Lubac, *Catholicism* (Ignatius Press, San Francisco, CA, 1988), p. 111.

Sacrament Endnotes

1 Peter Kreeft, *You Can Understand the Old Testament* (Servant Publications, Ann Arbor, MI, 1990), p. 33.

2 Johannes Emminghaus, *The Eucharist: Essence, Form, Celebration* (The Liturgical Press, Collegeville, MN, 1997), p. 23.

3 Joseph Husslein, SJ., *The Mass of the Apostles* (P.J. Kenedy & Sons, New York, 1929), p. 153. The *Agape* was never an integral part of the Mass as said by the apostles. It could readily enough be omitted, as is obvious from the remarks made by St. Paul, and in fact, disappeared, as a liturgical feature, after the first century.

4 Eugene LaVerdiere, *The Eucharist in the Early Church* (The Liturgical Press, Collegeville, MN, 1996), p. 109. Like Elijah (1 Kgs 17:21) and Elisha (2 Kgs 4:34) in the Old Testament, Paul threw himself on the boy and raised him to life.

5 Jerome Kodell, *The Eucharist in the New Testament* (Michael Glazier, Wilmington, DE, 1988), p. 73.

6 LaVerdiere, *op. cit.,* 32.

7 Josef A. Jungmann, *The Early Liturgy* (University of Notre Dame Press, Notre Dame, IN, 1959), p. 47.

8 LaVerdiere, *op. cit.,* 41.

9 Charles Bigg, *The Doctrine of the Twelve Apostles* (The Macmillan Company, New York, 1922), p. 40.

10 Bigg, *op. cit.,* 29-33. Fr. Josef Jungmann in a heavily footnoted chapter ("Mass of the Roman Rite," p. 12) argues that it is unlikely that the meal included a sacramental rite.

11 James T. O'Connor, *The Hidden Manna* (Ignatius Press, San Francisco, CA, 1988), p. 6.

12 George Every, *The Mass* (Our Sunday Visitor, Huntington, IN, 1978), p.186

13 Warren Carroll, *The Founding of Christendom* (Christendom Press, Front Royal, VA, 1985), p. 456.

14 LaVerdiere, *op. cit.,* 149.

15 *Ibid.,* 162.

Sacrament Endnotes cont'd

16 O'Connor, *op. cit.,* 17, taken from *Philadelphia,* 4. Idem. pp. 142-143.

17 O'Connor, *op. cit.,* 17.

18 LaVerdiere, *op. cit.,* 152.

19 Carroll, *op. cit.,* 455.

20 Herbert J. Thurston & Donald Attwater, *Butler's Lives of the Saints* (Christian Classics, Westminster, MD, 1981), vol. 1, p. 223.

21 O'Connor, *op. cit.,* p. 17. Ref. *To Ephesians,* 20.

22 *Ibid.,* 13. Father O'Connor quotes this from Ignatius' *Letter to the Christians of Tralles,* 8.

23 *Ibid.,* 13-14 Father O'Connor quotes this from Ignatius' *Epistle to the Romans,* 4 and 7.

24 Ignatius of Antioch, *Epistle to the Romans,* 5.

25 Joseph Husslein, SJ., *op. cit.,* 210. The Christians of the first three centuries had to contend with the reality that the emperor was the "supreme pontiff." The state, in the person of its head, the emperor, took over the right to regulate the religioius life of it's citizens. In addition, there was the "cult of the emperor," the adoration of the head of the state as the savior of his subjects. Christians often expressed loyalty to the Roman state, but refused to adore the emperor as a god and to swear by his "genius" (from *Introduction to the Fathers of the Church,* by Pier Franco Beatrice, Instituto San Gaetano, Vicenza, Italy, p. 61).

26 Daniel J. Sheerin, *The Eucharist* (Michael Glazier, Wilmington, DE,, 1985), p. 31.

27 *Ibid.,* 31.

28 *New Catholic Encyclopedia* (McGraw Hill Book Company, New York, 1967), vol. 11, p. 443.

29 Sheerin, *op. cit.,* 32.

30 Ludwig Hertling & Englebert Kirschbaum, *The Roman Catacombs and their Martyrs* (The Bruce Publishing Company, Milwaukee, WI, 1956), p. 89.

31 Jungmann, *op. cit.,* 18. In a footnote, Father Jungmann notes that St. Cyprian would later witness to the Eucharist as a morning sacrifice, even though it was instituted in the evening, because "we commemorate therewith the Resurrection of the Lord."

32 *Ibid.,* 18.

33 Sheerin, *op. cit.,* 24.

34 Jungmann, *op. cit.,* 47-48.

35 Sheerin, *op. cit.,* 35.

36 Jungmann, *op. cit.,* 43.

37 *Ibid.,* 39.

38 *Ibid.,* 34.

39 Hertling & Kirschbaum, *op. cit.,* 93.

40 Thurston & Attwater, *op. cit.,* p. 90, vol. 2.

41 Emminghaus, *op. cit.,* 44.

42 *Catechism of the Catholic Church,* (Libreria Editrice Vaticana), no. 1244.

43 Hertling & Kirschbaum, *op. cit.,* 126. The deacons carried the Blessed Sacrament to the homes of those who were absent. Interesting to us today is the fact that the faithful could reserve the consecrated hosts in their homes, and on days when no Mass was offered, they gave Communion to themselves. Grievous sinners were excluded from Communion, in certain circumstances, for years.

44 Husslein, *op. cit.,* 262.

45 Hertling & Kirschbaum, *op. cit.,* 41. The pieces from the inscription on his sepulcher were found between 1912 and 1939. Originally they were laid by St. Hippolytus' grave by Pope Damasus in 384 AD.

46 St. Augustine, *The Confessions of St. Augustine* (Catholic Book Publishing Company, NJ, 1997), Bk. 9, ch. 13, p. 261.

47 *Ibid.,* Bk 7, ch. 10. p. 185

48 *Ibid.,* Bk. 8, ch. 12, p. 227.

49 Michael L. Gaudoin-Parker, *The Real Presence through the Ages* (Alba House, New York, 1993), pp. 49-50.

50 Athanase Sage, *The Religious Life According to Saint Augustine* (New City Press, New York, 1990), pp. 199-200.

51 St. Augustine, *City of God,* 10, 6.

52 Sage, *op. cit.,* 200.

53 F. Van der Meer, *Augustine the Bishop* (Sheed and Ward, New York, 1961), p. 284.

54 *Contra Cresconium,* 3, 35, 39; PL 43, 517.

55 Thurston & Attwater, *op. cit.,* 566.

56 Joseph A. Jungmann, *The Mass of the Roman Rite,* (Christian Classics, Inc, Westminster, MD, 1986), p. 63.

57 F. Homes Dudden, *Gregory the Great* (Longmans, Green and Co., New York, 1905), p. 415.

58 *Dialogues,* iv. 59.

59 *Dialogues* 4.60.3. (SC 265, 202).

60 Thurston & Attwater, *op. cit.,* 568.

61 O'Connor, *op. cit.,* 80-81.

62 Philippe Beguerie & Claude Duchesneau, *How to Understand the Sacraments* (Crossroad, New York, 1994), p. 89.

63 Jungmann, *op. cit.* 67.

64 *Ibid.,* 84.

65 *Ibid.,* 118.

66 O'Connor, *op. cit.,* 186.

67 Geoffrey Webb & Adrian Walker, *St. Bernard of Clairvaux* (The Newman Press, Westminster, MD, 1960), pp. 68-69.

68 Michael Muller, *The Blessed Eucharist* (Tan Books and Publishers, Rockford, IL, 1994), p. 242. This was taken from "The Life of St. Bernard."

69 Nesta De Robeck, *Saint Francis* (Casa Editrice Francescana, Italy), p. 20.

70 Peter Doyle, *Butler's Lives of the Saints* (Liturgical Press, Collegeville, MN, 1997) p. 17.

71 De Robeck, *op. cit.,* 96.

72 Marion A. Habig, ed., *St. Francis of Assisi, Writings and Early Biographies* (Franciscan Herald Press, Chicago, IL, 1973), no. 201, p. 523.

73 *Ibid.,* 104, "Letter to the General Chapter."

74 *Ibid.,* 105-106, "Letter to the General Chapter."

75 De Robeck, *op. cit.,* 59.

76 The Testament of St. Francis, p. 67-70.

77 Jacques Maritain, *St. Thomas Aquinas* (Sheed and Ward, London, 1946), p. 22.

78 Peter Kreeft, *A Summa of the Summa* (Ignatius Press, San Francisco, CA, 1990), p. 12. Another biographer, Matthew Bunson (*The Angelic Doctor*, Our Sunday Visitor) tells an interesting story. When Karol Wojtyla, the future Pope John Paul II, was studying in Rome as a young seminarian, he wrote to a friend: "Thomas' entire philosophy is so marvelously beautiful, so delightful, and, at the same time, so uncomplicated. It seems that depth of thought does not require a profusion of words; the fewer words there are the deeper the meaning."

79 *Summa* 3a. 76. 1 ad. 2.

80 *Ibid.,* III, q. 75, a. I.

81 *Ibid.,* 3a. 73. 1 curpus ad. 1; also 3a. 79. 1.

82 *Ibid.,* 3a. 73. 1.

83 Brian Davies, *The Thought of Thomas Aquinas* (Oxford: Clarendon, 1992), p. 362.

84 *Summa,* 3a. 83. 1. St. Thomas writes that the Eucharist is a sacrifice inasmuch as it is offered and a sacrament inasmuch as it is received. Theologian Dom Anscar Vonier, OSB., in a study of the Eucharistic theology of Thomas, argued very strongly that for the Angelic Doctor sacrament and sacrifice are one: "The sacrament, for St. Thomas, is essentially in the consecration; which, again, is essentially the representation of Christ's passion and therefore sacrifice, as Body and Blood are consecrated separately" (Michael O'Carroll, *Corpus Christi*, p. 194).

85 John Hardon, *The History of Eucharistic Adoration* (CMJ Associates, Inc., Oak Lawn, IL, 1997), p. 6.

86 Maritain, *op. cit.,* 62. St. Thomas often prayed by prostrating himself in his cell or in church, where he was favored with mystical graces. Once Our Lady came to reassure him with regard to his life and doctrine and that he would always remain a simple friar. (He did not want to be elevated to a high office). Another time when he had fasted and prayed over a difficult passage from Isaiah, the apostles Peter and Paul personally came to instruct him. He ordered Reginald, who had wrung this confession from him, to promise never to tell anyone about this.

87 *Ibid.,* 64.

88 Igino Giordani, *Saint Catherine of Siena* (The Daughters of St. Paul, Boston, MA, 1980).

89 *Ibid.,* 72.

90 Lodovico Ferretti, *Saint Catherine of Siena* (Edizioni Cantagalli, Siena, 1996), p. 109.

91 *Ibid.,* 110.

92 Giordani, *op. cit.,* 75.

93 *Ibid.,* 43, 50.

94 Suzanne Noffke, *Catherine of Siena, The Dialogue* (Paulist Press, Mahwah, NJ, 1980), p. 211.

95 Jungmann, *op. cit.,* 128. Father Jungmann notes that so much reverence was paid to the Eucharist that the laity were not allowed to handle the Sacred Host, even if it meant depriving a dying person of Viaticum.

96 Lawrence G. Lovasik, *Saint Joseph Church History* (Catholic Book Publishing, NY, 1990), p. 117.

97 Council of Trent, tome IV, part I, pp. 549-550, as cited by P. Hughes, *The Church in Crisis: A History of the Twenty Great Councils* (Burns & Oates, London, 1961), p. 281.

98 Jungmann, *op. cit.,* 133. In additon to those listed, Fr. Johannes Emminghaus cites defective or inadequate education of the clergy, buying and selling of offices, and the overall neglect of morals, *The Eucharist,* p. 83.

99 Raymond Moloney, *The Eucharist* (Liturgical Press, Collegeville, MN, 1995), p. 156.

100 John P. Schanz, *The Sacraments of Life and Worship* (The Bruce Publishing Company, Milwaukee, WI, 1966), p. 243.

101 J. Dillenberger, ed., *Martin Luther: Selections from His Writings* (New York: Doubleday, 1961), p. 287.

102 Moloney, *op. cit.,* 167.

103 O'Connor, *op. cit.,* 232. This quote is from Trent's *Decree on the Eucharist as Sacrifice* issued in September 1562.

104 E. Allison Peers, trans., *The Autobiography of St. Teresa of Avila* (Image Books, Garden City NY, 1960), p. 317.

105 Peter Doyle, *Butler's Lives of the Saints* (The Liturgical Press, Collegeville, MN) New Edition, October 1995.

106 Peers, *op. cit.,* 262.

107 E. Allison Peers, *The Way of Perfection* (Image Books, NY, 1964), pp. 228-229, 231.

108 *Ibid.,* chapters 26 and 29.

109 E. Allison Peers, *op. cit., Autobiography,* 269.

110 *Ibid.,* 269.

111 Doyle, *op. cit.,* 99.

112 Ronda De Sola Chervin, *Prayers of the Women Mystics* (Servant Publications, Ann Arbor, MI, 1992), p. 164.

113 Timothy T. O'Donnell, *Heart of the Redeemer* (Ignatius Press, San Francisco, CA, 1989), p. 77.

114 Thurston & Attwater, *op. cit.,* 354. The most famous saying of St. John Eudes is that to celebrate the holy Sacrifice of the Mass properly three eternities would be required: the first to prepare for it, the second to celebrate it, and the third to give thanks for it. St. John sums up the principle of his own life, saying, "Our wish, our object, our chief preoccupation must be to form Jesus in ourselves, to make His spirit, His devotion, His affections, His desires and His disposition live and reign there."

115 Leon Cristiani, *Saint Margaret Mary* (Daughters of St. Paul, Boston, MA 1984), p. 15.

116 *Ibid.,* 17.

117 Vincent Kerns, ed. & trans., *The Autobiography of St. Margaret Mary* (London: Darton, Longman & Todd, 1976), p. 7.

118 *Ibid.,* 44-45.

119 Benedict J. Groeschel & James Monti, *"In the Presence of Our Lord: The History, Theology and Psychology of Eucharistic Devotion* (Our Sunday Visitor, Huntington, IN, 1996), p. 131.

120 Cristiani, *op. cit.,* 88-89.

121 *Ibid.,* 134 ff.

122 Andre Guitton, Conrad Goulet, trans., *Peter Julian Eymard* (Centro Eucaristico, Ponterinica, 1996), p. 17. This story was taken from the French biography by A. Tesniere.

123 *Ibid.,* 29.

124 *Ibid.,* 66.

Sacrament Endnotes cont'd

125 *Ibid.,* 87.

126 *Ibid.,* 80.

127 Gaudoin-Parker, *op. cit.,* 148. This was taken from *The Real Presence* (The Eymard League, NY).

128 O'Donnell, *op. cit.,* 158.

129 Hardon, *op. cit.,* 21.

130 Jungmann, *op. cit.,* 160.

131 Igino Giordani, Thomas Tobin, trans., *Pius X* (The Bruce Publishing Company, Milwaukee, WI, 1954), p. 94.

132 *Ibid.,* 172.

133 Michael O'Carroll, *Corpus Christi, An Encyclopedia of the Eucharist* (The Liturgical Press, Collegeville, MN, 1988), p. 162.

134 *Acta Apostolicae Sedis,* III (1911), pp. 322-323.

135 Thurston & Attwater, *op. cit.,* vol. 3, p. 477.

136 Austin Flannery, ed., "The Constitution on the Sacred Liturgy," *Vatican Council II* (Costello Publishing Company, Northport, NY, 1996), p. 6.

137 Benedict Ashley, OP, "The Eucharist," *Catholic Dossier*, vol. 2, no. 5 (P.O. Box 591120, San Francisco, CA), pp. 13, 15.

138 Fr. Avery Dulles, SJ, "The Eucharist: The Role of the Priest in the Sacrifice of the Mass" (Alba House Cassettes, Staten Island, NY, 1995). This is a cassette tape.

139 *Ibid.*

140 *Ibid.* In some sectors of post-conciliar theology, Father Dulles says there is a tendency to minimize the sacrificial character of the Eucharist and to insist almost exclusively in its character as a meal. Pope John Paul II states that: "The Eucharist is above all else a sacrifice, one that restores humanity to its right relationship with God." He warns against the false opinion that the Mass is only a banquet in which one shares by receiving the Body of Christ in order to manifest above all else fraternal communion. In some post-conciliar treatments, Father Dulles notes a tendency to emphasize the congregation to the detriment of the consecrated elements as the locus of the real presence.

141 *Catechism of the Catholic Church*, no. 1360, p. 343.

142 From the *Mishnah* (Pesahim, X, 5), trans. Herbert Danby (Oxford University Press, Oxford, 1933), p. 151.

143 Flannery, *op. cit.,* "Lumen Gentium," ch. 1, p. 351.

144 Emminghaus, *op. cit.,* 156.

145 Flannery, *op. cit.,* 111.

146 Raniero Cantalamessa, *The Eucharist, Our Sanctification* (Liturgical Press, Collegeville, MN, 1993), p. 22.

147 Flannery, *op. cit.,* "Instruction on the Worship of the Eucharistic Mystery," vol. 2, ch. 9, p. 102.

148 Ernest Lussier, *Living the Eucharistic Mystery* (Alba House, New York, 1975), p. 44.

149 *Catechism of the Catholic Church,* no. 1330, p. 336.

150 Michael Muller, *The Holy Sacrifice of the Mass* (Tan Books & Publishers, Rockford, IL, 1992), p. 513. St. John Chrysostom is saying that the Wise Men made the long journey and saw only a stable and a manger; they didn't have the benefit of all the great things we have witnessed, yet they adored Him with great reverence—the point being that we should adore Him that much more!

151 Hardon, *op. cit.,* 1, 28.

152 Groeschel & Monti, *op. cit.,* 268.

153 Pope John Paul II, *Dominicae Cenae,* no. 3, in *Vatican Council II: More Postconciliar Documents* (Vatican Collection, vol. II, 1982), ed. Austin Flannery, p. 67.

154 Francis Cardinal George, "Listening to Christ in San Antonio, in Chicago and in our Hearts" in *The New World* (Archdiocese of Chicago), March 7, 1999, p. 3.

155 *Ibid.,* p. 3.

156 Pope John Paul II, "Letter to the Bishop of Liege" in *L'Osservatore Romano*, no. 26, June 1996.

157 John Grigus, "Being With Jesus to be Sent by Jesus," *Immaculata* (Marytown, Libertyville, IL) Sept/Oct 1999.

158 Lussier, *op. cit.,* 33-35.

159 *Patrologia Latina,* 46:834.

160 Fr. Frank Pavone, "The Pro Life Commitment is Eucharistic," *Religious Life* (Institute on Religious Life, Chicago, IL) December 1997.

161 Pope Pius XII, *On the Mystical Body of Christ and our Union in It with Christ* (St. Paul Books and Media, Boston, MA) p. 45, 57-58.

162 Lussier, *op. cit.,* 47.

163 Michael L. Gaudoin-Parker, *Heart in Pilgrimage* (Alba House, New York, 1994), p. 232.

164 Prefaces 69-71, "Holy Men and Women" and of "All Saints," *The Sacramentary* (Catholic Book Publishing, New York, 1985), pp. 511-514.

165 Giordani, *op. cit., Saint Catherine of Siena,* 57.

166 Alfred McBride, *The Second Coming of Jesus* (Our Sunday Visitor, Huntington, IN, 1993), pp. 16, 21.

167 Paul Hinnebusch, "The Eucharist and the Parousia," *Homiletic and Pastoral Review,* November 1994, pp. 17-19.

168 *Ibid.*

169 *Ibid.*

Works Cited

Aquinas, St. Thomas. *Summa Theologiae.* Leonine ed. Rome, 1888-1906.

Ashely, Benedict. "The Eucharist." *Catholic Dossier,* P.O. Box 591120, San Francisco, CA, Sept/Oct 1996.

Augustine, St. *The City of God.* Vernon J. Bourke Ed. Garden City, NY: Doubleday, 1958.

_____. *On Psalm 195.*

_____. *The Confessions of St. Augustine.* New Jersey: Catholic Book Publishing Company, 1997.

Balsiger, Dave. *In Search of Noah's Ark.* Los Angeles, CA: Sun Classic Books, 1976.

Bartholomew, Courtenay. *A Scientist Researches Mary, The Ark of the Covenant.* Asbury, NJ: 101 Foundation, 1995.

Beguerie, Philippe. *How to Understand the Sacraments.* New York: Crossroad, 1994.

Bergant, Dianne, ed. *The Collegeville Bible Commentary.* Collegeville, MN: The Liturgical Press, 1992.

Bigg, Charles. *The Doctrine of the Twelve Apostles.* New York: The Macmillan Company, 1922.

Brown, Raymond. *An Introduction to the New Testament.* New York: Doubleday, 1997.

_____. *The Birth of the Messiah.* Garden City, New York: Doubleday, 1977.

_____. *The Death of the Messiah,* Vol 2. New York: Doubleday, 1994.

Cantalamessa, Raniero. *The Eucharist Our Sanctification.* Collegeville, MN: The Liturgical Press, 1993.

_____. *Mary, Mirror of the Church.* Collegeville, MN: The Liturgical Press, 1992.

Carroll, Warren H. *The Founding of Christendom.* Front Royal, VA: Christendom Press, 1985. Vol. 1.

Catechism of the Catholic Church. Liguori, MO: Liguori Publications, 1994.

Charpentier, Etienne. *How to Read the Old Testament.* London: SCM Press Ltd, 1982.

Chervin, Ronda De Sola. *Prayers of the Women Mystics.* Ann Arbor, MI: Servant Publications, 1989.

Cioffi, Paul. "Closing Mass of the Forty Hours Devotion." St. Patrick's Church, Georgetown University, October 22, 1998.

Cristiani, Leon. *Saint Margaret Mary.* Boston, MA: Daughters of St. Paul, 1984.

Danielou, Jean. *The Bible and the Liturgy.* Notre Dame, IN: University of Notre Dame Press, 1956.

_____. *The Work of John the Baptist.* Baltimore: 1966.

Davies, Brian. *The Thought of Thomas Aquinas.* Oxford: Clarendon, 1992.

De La Potterie, Ignace. *Mary in the Mystery of the Covenant.* New York: Alba House, 1992.

Di Berardino, Angelo, ed. *Encyclopedia of the Early Church.* New York: Oxford University Press, 1992.

DeGrandis, Robert. *Healing through the Mass.* Mineola, NY: Resurrection Press, 1992.

De Lubac, Henri. *Catholicism.* San Francisco, CA: Ignatius Press, 1988.

De Robeck, Nesta. *Saint Francis.* Italy: Casa Editrice Francescana.

Dillenberger, J., ed. *Martin Luther: Selections from His Writings.* New York: Doubleday, 1961.

Doyle, Peter. *Butlers Lives of the Saints.* Collegeville, MN: The Liturgical Press, 1997.

Dudden, Homes F. *Gregory the Great.* New York: Longmans, Green & Co, 1905.

Dulles, Avery. "The Eucharist: The Role of the Priest in the Sacrifice of the Mass." Cassette tape. Staten Island, NY: Alba House, 1995.

Emmerich, Anne Catherine. *The Dolorous Passion of Our Lord Jesus Christ.* Rockford, IL: Tan Books and Publishers, Inc., 1983.

Emminghaus, Johannes. *The Eucharist, Essence, Form, Celebration.* Collegeville, MN: The Liturgical Press, 1997.

Every, George. *The Mass.* Huntington, IN: Our Sunday Visitor, 1978.

Fabing, Robert. *Real Food.* New York: Paulist Press, 1993.

Ferretti, Lodovico. *Saint Catherine of Siena.* Siena: Edizioni Cantagalli, 1996.

Flannery, Austin. *Vatican Council II.* Northport, NY: Costello Publishing Company, 1996.

Foley, Richard. *Mary and the Eucharist.* Newtonsville, OH: Hope of St. Monica, 1997.

Gallagher, Michele T. *Honey From the Rock.* New York: Alba House, 1991.

Gaudoin, Michael L. *The Real Presence through the Ages.* New York: Alba House, 1993.

_____. *Heart in Pilgrimage.* New York: Alba House, 1994.

George, Francis Cardinal. "Listening to Christ in San Antonio, in Chicago and in our Hearts." *The New World*, Chicago, IL, March 7, 1999.

Gihr, Nicholas. *The Holy Sacrifice of the Mass.* London: B. Herder Book Company, 1939.

Giordani, Igino. *Saint Catherine of Siena.* Boston, MA: The Daughters of St. Paul, 1980.

_____, trans. Thomas Tobin. *Pius X.* Milwaukee, WI: The Bruce Publishing Company, 1954.

Grigus, John. "Being With Jesus to be Sent by Jesus." *Immaculata,* Marytown, Libertyville, IL. Sept/Oct 1999.

Groeschel, Benedict. *In the Presence of Our Lord, The History, Theology, and Psychology of Eucharistic Devotion.* Huntington, IN: Our Sunday Visitor, 1997.

Guardini, Romano. *Meditations Before Mass.* Manchester, NH: Sophia Institute Press, 1993.

Guitton, Andre, trans. Conrad Goulet. *Peter Julian Eymard.* Ponterinica: Centro Eucaristico, 1996.

Habig, Marion A, ed. *St. Francis of Assisi, Writings and Early Biographies.* Chicago, IL: Franciscan University Press, 1973.

Hahn, Scott. *A Father Who Keeps His Promises.* Ann Arbor, MI: Servant Publications, 1998.

Hahn, Scott & Leon J. Suprenant, Jr, eds. *Catholic For a Reason.* Steubenville, OH: Emmaus Road, 1994.

Hardon, John. *The History of Eucharistic Adoration.* Oak Lawn, IL: CMJ Associates, Inc, 1997.

Hennessey, Lawrence. "The Baptism of the Lord." Homily given at St. Patrick's Church, Lake Forest, IL. January 10, 1998.

Hertling, Ludwig & Englebert Kirschbaum. *The Roman Catacombs and Their Martyrs.* Milwaukee, WI: The Bruce Publishing Company, 1956.

Hinnebusch, Paul. "The Eucharist and the Parousia." *Homiletic and Pastoral Review*. November, 1994.

Husslein, Joseph. *The Mass of the Apostles.* New York: P.J. Kennedy & Sons, 1929.

John Paul II, Pope. *The Mystery and Worship of the Eucharist.* Boston: Pauline Books and Media, 1980.

_____. Homily given at Lourdes, August, 1983. *L'Osservatore Romano*, September 5, 1983.

_____. *The Gospel of Life.* Vatican City: Libreria Editrice Vaticana, 1995.

_____. *The Spirit, Giver of Life and Love.* Boston, MA: Pauline Books & Media, 1996.

Jungmann, Joseph A. *The Early Liturgy.* Notre Dame, IN: University of Notre Dame Press, 1959.

_____. *The Mass of the Roman Rite.* Westminster, MD: Christian Classics, Inc., 1992.

Karris, Robert J. *Invitation to Luke.* Garden City, NY: Image Books, 1977.

_____. *Luke: Artist and Theologian.* Mahweh, NJ: Paulist Press, 1985

Kellmeyer, Steven L. *Scriptural Catholicism, Biblical Foundations of the Faith.* Columbus, OH: Greyden Press, 1998.

Kerns, Vincent, ed. & trans. *The Autobiography of St. Margaret Mary.* London: Darton, Longman & Todd, 1976.

Kodell, James. *The Eucharist in the New Testament.* Wilmington, DE: Michael Glazier, 1988.

Kreeft, Peter. *A Summa on the Summa.* San Francisco, CA: Ignatius Press, 1990.

_____. *You Can Understand the Old Testament.* Ann Arbor: MI: Servant Publications, 1990.

Lane, William L. *The Gospel According to Mark.* Grand Rapids, MI: William B. Eerdmans Publishing Company, 1974.

LaVerdiere, Eugene. *The Eucharist in the New Testament and the Early Church.* Collegeville, MN: The Liturgical Press, 1996.

_____. *Dining in the Kingdom of God.* Chicago, IL: Liturgy Training Publications, 1994.

Leon-Dufour, Xavier. *Dictionary of Biblical Theology.* Boston, MA: St. Paul Books and Media, 1995.

_____. *Sharing the Eucharistic Bread,* trans. Matthew J. O'Connell. New York: Paulist Press, 1982.

Lovasik, Lawrence G. *Saint Joseph Church History.* New York: Catholic Book Publishing, 1990.

Lussier, Ernest. *Living the Eucharistic Mystery.* New York: Alba House, 1975.

_____. *The Eucharist: the Bread of Life.* New York: Alba House, 1977.

Maritain, Jacques. *St. Thomas Aquinas.* London: Sheed & Ward, 1946.

Martimort, Aime Georges. *The Church at Prayer.* Collegeville, MN: The Liturgical Press, 1992.

Maus, Cynthia Pearl. *The Old Testament and the Fine Arts.* New York: Harper & Brothers Publishers, 1954.

McBride, Alfred. *The Second Coming of Jesus.* Huntington, IN: Our Sunday Visitor, 1993.

McKenzie, John L. *Dictionary of the Bible.* New York: MacMillan Publishing Company, 1965.

McCarthy, William. *Jesus Lives in Our Hearts.* Moodus, CT: My Father's House, 1996.

_____. *Salvation History.* Moodus, CT: My Father's House, 1999.

Moloney, Raymond. *The Eucharist.* Collegeville, MN: The Liturgical Press, 1995.

Muller, Michael. *The Holy Sacrifice of the Mass.* Rockford, IL: Tan Books and Publishers, Inc., 1992.

_____. *The Blessed Eucharist.* Rockford, IL: Tan Books and Publishers, Inc., 1994.

New Catholic Encyclopedia. New York: McGraw Hill Book Company, 1967.

Martin, George. "Jesus Washes His Disciples Feet." *New Covenant,* April, 1999. Our Sunday Visitor, 200 Noll Plaza, Huntington, IN.

Nichols, Aidan. *The Holy Eucharist.* Oscott Series, No. 6. Dublin: Veritas, 1991.

Noffke, Suzanne. *Catherine of Siena, The Dialogue.* Mahweh, NJ: Paulist Press, 1980.

O'Brien, John. *The Faith of Millions.* Huntington, IN: Our Sunday Visitor, 1938.

O'Carroll, Michael. *Corpus Christi, A Theological Encyclopedia of the Eucharist.* Collegevile, MN: The Liturgical Press, 1988.

O'Connor, James. T. *The Hidden Manna, A Theology of the Eucharist.* San Francisco, CA: Ignatius Press, 1988.

O'Connor, Jerome Murphy. *The Holy Land.* New York: Oxford University Press, 1992.

O'Donnell, Timothy T. *Heart of the Redeemer.* San Francisco, CA: Ignatius Press, 1989.

Oury, Guy. *The Mass.* New York: Catholic Book Publishing, 1988.

Oxford Companion to the Bible. New York: Oxford University Press, 1993.

Pavone, Frank. "The Pro Life Commitment is Eucharistic." *Religious Life.* The Institute on Religious Life, Chicago, IL. December, 1997.

Peers, E. Allison, trans. *The Autobiography of St. Teresa of Avila.* Garden City, NY: Image Books, 1960.

Pius XII. Pope. *On the Mystical Body of Christ and our Union in It with Christ.* Boston, MA: St. Paul Books and Media.

Power, John. *History of Salvation.* New York: Alba House, 1989.

Prat, Ferdinand. *Jesus Christ,* Vol. 1 and 2. Milwaukee, WI: The Bruce Publishing Company, 1950.

Sage, Athanase. *The Religious Life According to Saint Augustine.* New York: New City Press, 1990.

Schanz, John P. *The Sacraments of Life and Worship.* Milwaukee, WI: The Bruce Publishing Company, 1966.

Sheen, Fulton J. *The Life of Christ.* New York: Doubleday, 1977.

Sheerin, Daniel J. *The Eucharist.* Wilmington, DE: Michael Glazier, 1985.

The Rites of the Catholic Church, Collegeville MN: The Liturgical Press, 1991, Vol 2.

The Sacramentary. New York: Catholic Book Publishing Company, 1985.

Thurston, Herbert J. & Donald Attwater. *Butler's Lives of the Saints.* Westminster, MD: Christian Classics, 1981.

Van der Meer, F. *Augustine the Bishop.* New York: Sheed and Ward, 1961.

Von Balthasar, Hans Urs. *Light of the Word.* San Francisco, CA: Ignatius Press, 1993.

Vonier, Dom Anscar. *A Key to the Doctrine of the Eucharist.* London: Burns, Oates,& Washbourne, Ltd., 1925.

Webb, Geoffrey & Adrian Walker. *St. Bernard of Clairvaux.* Westminster, MD: The Newman Press, 1960.

Picture Credits

The Voice of Padre Pio

*"The world could even subsist without the sun,
but it could not subsist without Mass."*

**—Blessed Padre Pio
1887-1968**